Shakespeare,
the King's Playwright,
Theater in the Stuart Court
1603—1613

ALVIN B. KERNAN

Yale University Press   New Haven and London

Published with assistance from the Kingsley Trust Association
Publication Fund established by the Scroll and Key Society of
Yale College.

Designed by Sonia L. Scanlon.
Set in Fournier type by Marathon Typography Service, Inc.,
Durham, North Carolina.
Printed in the United States of America by Edwards Brothers, Inc.,
Ann Arbor, Michigan.

Library of Congress Cataloguing-in-Publication Data
Kernan, Alvin B.
Shakespeare, the king's playwright: theater in the Stuart court,
1603—1613 / Alvin Kernan.
p. cm.
Includes bibliographical references and index.
ISBN 0-300-06181-1
1. Shakespeare, William, 1564—1616—Stage history—To 1625. 2.
Shakespeare, William, 1564—1616—Stage history—England. 3. Great
Britain—Court and courtiers—History—17th century. 4. Authors and
patrons—England—History—17th century. 5. Great Britain—His-
tory—James I, 1603—1625. 6. Theater—England—History—17th
century. 7. James I, King of England, 1566—1625. 8. Stuart, House of.
I. Title.
PR3095.K47 1995
822.3'3—dc20 94-43845
CIP

A catalogue record for this book is available from the British Library.
The paper in this book meets the guidelines for permanence and
durability of the Committee on Production Guidelines for Book
Longevity of the Council on Library Resources.
10 9 8 7 6 5 4 3 2 1

I was train'd up in the English court,
Where being but young I framed to the harp
Many an English ditty lovely well,
And gave the tongue a helpful ornament.
— *1 Henry IV*, 3.1.120

CONTENTS

CONTENTS

ILLUSTRATIONS

PREFACE

This book rounds out a four-volume social history of mainly English and American literature. Far from trying to narrate a continuous history of this vast subject, I have focused on writers who were working in times when the literary system was changing radically. *Printing Technology, Letters, and Samuel Johnson* (1987) centers on the life of the Great Cham of Literature and describes the revolutionary effects of print on letters and the writing life in the eighteenth century. *The Imaginary Library* (1982) explores the disintegration of the primary values of "Literature," the print-based literary aesthetic that developed during the nineteenth century (the author as genius of the creative imagination, the pure and perfect work of art, the superiority of art to science as a way of knowing, and the positive effects of literature on its readers and its world) in the work of four leading novelists: Norman Mailer, Bernard Malamud, Vladimir Nabokov, and Saul Bellow. *The Death of Literature* (1990) treats the end of romantic and modernist "Literature" as one event in the more general breakup of all print-culture institutions—newspapers, education, libraries, publishing, the law—in the new electronic age.

This social history would be incomplete without a study of at least some aspects of the art of writing in the courtly, patronage setting from which modern literature emerged, first in Italy in the time of Dante and Petrarch and then during the age of kings. *Shakespeare, the King's Playwright* is designed to fill this gap.

At least since 1923 and the publication of Edmund Chambers' *Elizabethan Stage* (especially volumes 1 and 4), it has been known that in Shakespeare's time an English court theater existed that, while employing public players and using their plays, was not merely an extension of the public theater but was a theater with its own interests and audience, its own conventions of production, and its own aesthetics. Far from remaining exclusively in their "wooden O" on the south bank of the Thames, isolated from the palace and the court, the players frequently performed in the court and in other aristocratic venues, where they not only wore the costumes of gentlemen and spoke with the accents of great statesmen and powerful nobles but participated in the political life of the nation. Shakespeare's Stuart plays were performed in—and at least in part were written for—this court theater; and the primary purpose of this book is to locate these plays in the social setting and the politics of the court of James I.

Chambers' picture of theater in the court has been enlarged and filled out by a number of modern scholars, most notably Glynne Wickham, Roy Strong, Stephen Orgel, and a younger group known collectively as New Historicists. These and a number of social historians like Laurence Stone, Francis Haskell, Norbert Elias, and Linda Levy Peck have given us a greatly expanded context of aristocratic social and political life in which to understand theater in the court. At the same time, particularly in the work of Roy Strong, English court theater has been placed in a wider European court scene, where art, including theater, developed richly by the sixteenth century in the service of the new strong, centralizing states. By now it is possible to see Shakespeare's Stuart plays in the context not only of the English court and its sociopolitical interests but of these European developments of the arts as official propaganda for the great kings and their houses.

No very elaborate theory is employed in the social history of literature I have been constructing. Like many in my generation, I have been slowly converted from a formalist view of literature to a view of the arts as secondary but still important to the ongoing social process of making culture. The theory that seems to fit and instrument best this by-now fairly standard conception is some variety of what is commonly called "the social construction of reality," "construction theory," or "constructivism." I have found this theory elaborated most usefully in the writings of the humanistic sociologist Peter Berger, where it offers no complex Parsonian paradigm of social organization but rather an arsenal of the devices—roles, rituals, philosophies, legal systems, cosmologies, and arts—by which men and women in society take the given world and make it witness to their own sense of order and meaning. It is this understanding of human activity as the making of meaning that informs my description of literature as a social institution that changes over time in response to political and technological circumstances, and in turn participates in the great social game of which it is a part by helping to remake the world in ways that seem plausible and useful.

I have used *The Riverside Shakespeare* for quotations from Shakespeare's plays and poems. For other quotations, authors and titles given parenthetically in the text refer to items listed in the bibliography. Short and very familiar quotations have not been cited. In the interests of space, only the first line or page number of a quotation is supplied, both in the text and in the bibliography.

Scholarly accuracy is assumed to be the appropriate norm of this kind of literary history, but I have attempted to maintain a narrative flow by eliminating footnotes and keeping bibliography and controversy over scholarly issues to a minimum. The point of view, insofar as is possible, is that of the historical events as they are taking place, not that of a scholar reporting on the inconclusive arguments various authorities have had with one another about what may have happened. Literary criticism and scholarship will only flourish again, if ever, the author believes, when they cease to focus on what one critic or another says or what objections have been made to this or that theory. The best subject for literary study is not, as too often it seems to be, scholarly controversy or a catalogue of every objection that can possibly be made to any interpretation of the evidence, but the literary work functioning in its place and times—in this case, Shakespeare's plays in the court of James Stuart, as that scene can best be reconstructed.

Oddities in older documents such as use of the staff "s," or "v" for "u," are silently corrected. January 1 is used here as the beginning of the calendar year rather than March 25, as was the actual practice in England until 1751 and Lord Chesterfield's Act. Thus, the events at the court during the Christmas season, which extended in James Stuart's time from December until somewhere near the beginning of Lent, by contemporary reckoning would all have occurred in the year in which they began. I have silently adjusted the year to accord with the modern calendar, making, for example, the Christmas season when the King's Men first performed before their royal patron at Hampton Court that of 1603—04. The ten-day lag in England of the Julian behind the Gregorian calendar, already in use on the continent in Shakespeare's time, is ignored, although it was noticed in his day. The Venetian ambassador, Nicolò Molin, thought it worth remarking in his dispatch to the Doge and Venetian Senate on the day that was designated in the continental calendar January 8, 1603, that "the English keep their Christmas according to the old style on the 4th of January, a Sunday" (*Calendar of State Papers* [Venetian], X, 128).

INTRODUCTION

SHAKESPEARE AT THE STUART COURT

The following pages offer a picture of Shakespeare as a patronage dramatist putting on his plays before King James I and his court after James came to the English throne in 1603, and of the company of players with which Shakespeare was associated as a playwright, actor, and shareholder. Scholars have long recognized that from time to time the playwright and his company, like other groups of actors, performed in the universities, in great houses, and in the court, but these plays have been thought of as designed in the first instance for performance in the public theater and modified only slightly, if at all, for aristocratic performance. "Even the masques and quasi-dramatic ceremonies of the court," says Robert Weimann, a leading Marxist historian of Renaissance English theater, in a representative statement, "reflected popular modes and conventions. The Queen herself deferred to the tastes of the London *plebs;* the best of the city's drama was always good enough for the court. Apparently the art of the common players had something special to offer not only to the people of London, but to the nation as a whole" (xviii).

In this context, the received image of Shakespeare is still largely that of a romantic artist writing, primarily out of his own creatively free imagination, plays designed for the public theater and a popular audience. So fixed is this romantic view that I need to take a moment to explain here just how and in what sense he was a patronage artist.

Shakespeare was indeed a popular commercial dramatist in the years 1603–13, but his simultaneous involvement with the court was an extensive and important aspect of his career. From the time his company became the King's Men to his retirement from the stage, it performed his plays and those of other dramatists from ten to twenty times a year at court. We know the names of many of the plays, as well as their dates, the payments made to the company, whether the king was present, the venue, and even how the Great Halls were set up for performance. Soon after James arrived from Edinburgh, someone took care, despite the press of business, to see that the Lord Chamberlain's Men (as they were then known) were issued a warrant making the king their royal patron and the company the premier acting company of the realm, the King's

Men, in terms that acknowledged their dual functions but treated both as in the gift of the prince: "aswell for the recreation of our lovinge subjectes, as for our Solace and pleasure when wee shall thincke good to see them, duringe our pleasure" (Chambers, 1923, II, 208). With this warrant, the resident playwright of the King's Men, William Shakespeare, also became official playwright to the prince. Court performance, far from being an occasional way of making a little extra money, as it had been in Elizabeth Tudor's time, with the arrival of the Stuarts began to give more dignity to what had been considered a base profession. The players continued to work in the public theaters of the city, of course—indeed, they probably still made most of their money there—but the social status of Shakespeare's acting company escalated greatly when its members became grooms of the chamber and servants to his majesty, King James I.

The King's Men played in one of the royal palaces for various occasions, especially during the Christmas season, when they regularly performed a number of plays as part of the festivities of the twelve nights of Christmas. In the old queen's time the feasting had ended on Twelfth Night, but the playing season gradually lengthened during the Stuart reign, eventually extending to the beginning of Lent, although there were not performances every night. (Appendix A provides a theatrical calendar of the court performances of the King's Men during these years.) That the king and his players were intimate is unlikely (Barroll, 1991), but the actors provided many useful services, such as taking the speaking parts for court masques, marching as the king's servants in various ceremonies, attending visiting foreign nobility, and offering entertainment on special occasions, like the plays that were given at Greenwich and Hampton Court in the summer of 1606 to mark the visit of the royal brother-in-law, King Christian of Denmark. In Shakespeare's last season at court with the King's Men, the winter of 1612–13, the company put on nearly twenty plays, many of them his, as part of the extended entertainments to celebrate the betrothal and wedding of James's only daughter, Princess Elizabeth, and Frederick, the Elector Palatine of Heidelberg.

Between 1603 and 1613, the King's Men played before the court 138 times all told, an average of nearly 14 performances a year, far more often than any of the companies patronized by the lesser members of the royal family. This same acting company had played, under various names, only 32 times in the last ten years of Elizabeth's reign. The comparative annual figures—13.8 versus 3.2—give some idea of both the increased amount of theatrical activity in the Stuart court and the increased presence of Shakespeare and his company in the palace. As the monarch's servants, the King's Men were the star company at the Jacobean court, providing 177 of the 299 plays performed there between 1603 and 1616. And whenever his company played at court, Shakespeare's plays were those most often "preferred," although the plays of a number of other playwrights who wrote on commission for the King's Men—particularly Ben Jonson and Beaumont and Fletcher—were also performed. After Shakespeare's departure from the company, his plays, all considered "old" by this point, were no longer as popular and were performed at court on only sixteen known occasions by the King's Men between 1616 and 1642, a period during which fifty Beaumont and Fletcher plays were offered by the troupe. The players, these numbers unmistakably tell us, featured in court performance the plays of their most prominent and popular playwright.

Even though not all the pieces are in place, the existing records outline the standard working patterns of Shakespeare and the King's Men at the Jacobean court. On the average, Shakespeare wrote one or two plays a year. These were produced downtown at the Globe, and then, after the production had been polished, they were taken upriver to Whitehall or Hampton Court for performance at the Christmas entertainments, at which plays were put on each night by one of several royal companies of players. Sometimes there were performances during the day as well for special audiences, as when the King's Men gave a matinee performance of *A Midsummer Night's Dream* for the royal heir, the nine-year-old Prince Henry, on New Year's Day 1604.

As the players of the king, the King's Men took pride of place, usually opening the festivities on December 26, most often with one of the new Shakespeare plays. Since the company would have, at most, only two new Shakespearean plays to show each year, the rest of its court performances in a given season would be of new plays by other playwrights and older plays by Shakespeare and others, often modified, that were still in repertory and could be considered suitable for the occasion. The company avoided putting on the same play twice in a season and made an effort to supply something that, if not new, had at least not been recently performed. Given the number of times the King's Men played at court, it is highly probable that all, or almost all, of the Shakespeare plays, and certainly all his plays written after 1602, were performed at court at least once, and many several times, during the years 1603–13.

Locating Shakespeare's plays in the palace immediately brings a world into being around them. In contrast to our sparse knowledge of the public theater, information about the court abounds. The gossip John Chamberlain, the diplomat Dudley Carleton, the courtier Arbella Stuart, and the French and Venetian envoys, among others, wrote lively letters describing festival times and sometimes actual performances, though, alas, of the spectacular masques, not Shakespeare. The offices responsible for entertainment at the court, Tents and Revels chiefly, left official records about preparations for performances. Warrants were issued for payments to the players, drawings (some of which are schematized on the illustration pages) were made of halls arranged for performance, costumes and sets for the masques were sketched, and the reactions of the king were noted by those who watched him watch the play. Ambassadors wrote home to their masters about the politics of theatrical occasions. Two court theaters, the Great Hall at Hampton Court (see figures 11 and 23) and Inigo Jones's Banqueting House at Whitehall, still stand, in good repair. The dates on which plays were performed at court, sometimes accompanied by the titles of the plays, were recorded. The palace—even, occasionally, the hall—in which performances took place was frequently stipulated.

The historical materials gathered here to set the occasions of Shakespearean performance are not, for the most part, new discoveries. You will hear once more that James was interested in witchcraft, that he disliked crowds, and that the *Hamlet* revenge plot resembles the Stuart revenge story. Rather than striving for novelty, I have assembled in one place for the first time the bits and pieces of information that have accumulated over time about what was happening when Shakespeare played at the Jacobean court. In this way, aided by the work of recent historians, I hope to give some sense of what these occasions were like, so that we can make an informed attempt to grasp what it meant to be a patronage artist in the Jacobean court. I have concentrated on what James's contemporaries thought was happening, admitting even gossip to my narrative in an effort to recover a sense of what people felt and talked about. Modern historians argue, for example, that the king was a much more effective monarch than his subjects made him out to be, but in an attempt to get close to the original scenes of performance I have purposely set Shakespeare's plays in front of the vulgar, divine-right, pedantic, self-important king whom his contemporaries saw and (behind his back) laughed at.

To see the Shakespearean plays in their court setting inevitably raises the question of their function in that place and time. Shakespeare may have originally produced his plays on the public stage, but he would have to have been remarkably dull—which he surely was not—not to have remembered after 1603 that his new plays would at Christmastime be acted before the king and his court, and that in those circumstances the courtiers and the royal patron would inevitably regard them not only as entertainments but as comments on the political and social concerns of the moment. Even had he wished to avoid politics, Shakespeare was forced to become a political playwright willy-nilly, by virtue of court performance.

But quite obviously he did not shrink from social application of his work, for most of his Stuart plays, far from being mere romps like *The Merry Wives of Windsor* (written, it is said, at Elizabeth's command), took up some of the most sensitive issues of the day. The court warrants for payment to the players do not always list the names of the plays performed, but almost half, seventeen in all, some old, some new, of the total Shakespearean oeuvre of thirty-seven or thirty-eight, are named in the warrants or identified on their published title pages as having been performed at the Stuart court while Shakespeare was still active there. The titles of the plays so named speak clearly of the kind of theater that was thought most suitable for court performance: *A Midsummer Night's Dream, Othello, The Merry Wives of Windsor, Measure for Measure, The Comedy of Errors, Love's Labour's Lost, Henry V, The Merchant of Venice, The Tempest, The Winter's Tale, 1 Henry IV, Much Ado about Nothing, Julius Caesar,* and *Macbeth. As You Like It* may well have been performed before the king at Wilton in November 1603, and we know from its title page that *King Lear* was performed at court at Christmas 1606. The Jacobean court clearly was shown plays that have continued to hold the stage because they play well—no *Henry VI,* it appears—but many of these plays also took up the most serious issues of the Jacobean political scene.

Sometimes Shakespeare wrote specifically for court occasions and addressed the particular interests of the king. In 1604 *Measure for Measure* put the question of the king's justice, which had backfired badly the year before in the Raleigh trial, onstage. *Macbeth* enacted the Stuart family lineage (which James boasted was older than that of any of the reigning European families), along with the putative central event in its history, the establishment of primogeniture in Duncan's Scotland. *Henry VIII,* written with John Fletcher and designed for the spring of 1613 and the celebrations of the marriage of James's daughter, Princess Elizabeth (though perhaps not performed then), compliments her by identifying her with Elizabeth Tudor, after whom she was originally named and whose birth, celebrated with fireworks and canon fire, climaxes the play.

Most of the time the Stuart plays were not so openly serviceable. Still, when put in a court setting, they light up in a way that shows that Shakespeare had the court and its interests very much in mind when he wrote. *As You Like It,* with its duke, exiled to the country, who loves to hunt the stag, and his fool Touchstone, was performed for James, who was obsessed with hunting, and his fool Archie Armstrong while the Stuart court was at Wilton, forced to remain in the country in late 1603 by the plague that raged in London. *King Lear,* by way of a more deliberate example, put onstage the central political issue of the Stuart reign, the divine right of kings, not long after the Gunpowder Plot and the consequent treason trials. The luxurious court of Egypt in *Antony and Cleopatra* was portrayed in a period when the Stuart court was increasingly being charged with financial and sexual corruption and compared invidiously with the stricter, more "Roman" court of Elizabeth. That odd play *Timon of Athens* would have set Whitehall abuzz with its almost undisguised reflection of the king's profligate generosity to his favorites, so unrestrained that by 1607 or 1608 it seemed to many to threaten the welfare of the kingdom, and so long remembered that a generation later it was still reputed to be the cause of the financial troubles that led to the downfall and death of Charles I.

Knowing the date, or even (in some cases) the approximate date, of the court performance puts each of Shakespeare's Stuart plays among such immediate court concerns as the marriage of a princess, the state trial of a great courtier, the king's open fondness for young men, royal improvidence, and the visit of a foreign monarch. Then too, such urgent and persistent Stuart themes as divine right, prerogative, the king's relation to the law, and the pressures of the ongoing transformation of an independent military aristocracy into a court nobility are always present, sometimes in the foreground, certainly in the background, of the royal playwright's Stuart plays.

Once it is seen that these plays take up hot political and social issues, it is impossible not to be curious about just how they relate to the court on these matters. Or, to put the matter more directly, just what kind of service did the playwright render his royal patron? Was he merely a royal apologist? It appears not. Was he a crypto-subversive covertly attacking divine-right ideology, as some recent social critics have argued? Not likely. The court would have smelled him out immediately. Did he foresee but lament the inevitable death of

kingship? Possibly. Shakespeare took his politics, like his religion and his philosophy, to his grave with him, but his plays could not have offended king or
court, otherwise he would not have remained in favor. But this once said, our
sense of how he pleased his patron and what he said about contemporary issues
depends on our interpretation of what the plays actually say, or said, to his
courtly audiences, and this is shaky ground.

Making some kind of reasonable judgment about how these plays functioned
in their court contexts requires reading them in a way that suits their original
time and place. The more elaborate interpretations of the plays in recent times
obviously do not fit that bill, and I have tried instead for fairly straightforward,
and minimal, readings of the plays, looking not for something new, sensational,
or idiosyncratic but rather for interpretations that have a chance of coming fairly
close to what ordinary attendants at court would have heard and seen in the
Great Hall of the palace. Plain interpretations of this sort have a chance of per-
mitting us to see, so I believe, just how the Shakespearean theater interacted
with court interests at the time of the plays' presentation.

My aim, then, is not to interpret the plays in some novel way—something
of an impossibility by now—but to interpret them, with a light hand, in an
aggregated performance scene that comes as close as possible to the historical conditions of production. The hope is to recover something of what it
was like when James I sat in his State in the palace of Whitehall, looking at
a play, say *Measure for Measure*, performed by his troupe of players on St.
Stephen's Night 1604, the beginning of the celebration of the twelve days of
Christmas.

The Great Hall would have been ablaze with candles and overheated from the
mass of people crammed into the temporary theater. Around the king, and
observing him carefully, were the ambassadors from Venice and Polonia, France
and Spain, fearfully jealous of one another and of their seating in relation to the
king. In boxes and on crowded "degrees" (the trestle seats constructed for the
occasion around the hall), seated hierarchically, were the members of the court,
brilliant in jewels and silk, bosoms often exposed, looking at one another and at
the king. They would key every detail of the play to the cynosure of court life,
the king and his peculiarities: his distaste—even fear—of crowds, his divine-
right political theory, his dislike of Puritans, his pride in "kingcraft," and his
delight in casuistical argument and in playing the role of Solomon. In front of
this audience the players unfolded a story of the law confounded and justice

achieved by the clever practices of a ruler in disguise working behind the scenes, as James had done in the Raleigh trial the year before.

The Shakespeare who takes shape in this patronage setting, a "bending author" (to use his own words), a helpful royal servant, a propagandist for the monarchy, a radical conservative, will no doubt seem unattractive to many who still think of him, even in this postmodernist era, as not of an age but for all time, an imperious romantic artist-genius towering above the world of words. Even more difficult to accept will be the middle-class Shakespeare who emerges from a consideration of his patronage activities: upwardly mobile, acquisitive, patrician in his interests and aspirations. The social ambition of this fashionable playwright appears nakedly in the coat of arms he bought, with its spear and falcon, and the status of gentleman that went with it. The father had applied for, but abandoned when things began to go badly, this venture into gentility, but the son successfully reopened and paid for the coat of arms in his father's name in 1596. The motto, *Non Sanz Droict*—which that agile social scrambler, Ben Jonson, making clear what the theatrical world thought of this kind of class mobility, parodied as "Not without Mustard"—does not specify the "right" invoked, but proclaims without apology a sense of self-worth and a deserved gentility. That Shakespeare was more, much more, than a social opportunist, all who have read his plays will attest. But that he was also in part at least what his class and economic circumstances made him, his involvement with patronage establishes with a substantiality that may explain why his service at court has been so long muted or ignored altogether.

Superintending the performance of his plays in court, wearing the king's livery, Shakespeare sheds the Bohemian associations of his early days in the rough-and-tumble world of the public theater where he was a companion of that "sporting Kyd" who under torture betrayed his atheistical friend Kit Marlowe—who was himself stabbed to death in a drunken tavern brawl over paying the bill. "A great reckoning in a little room," Shakespeare called it in *As You Like It* (3.3.15).

Our democratic age will resist even a partial transformation of Shakespeare into a courtly servant and a recipient of patronage. But in the palace Shakespeare, whose roots still lay in the public theater, like those of many another European court playwright in the Renaissance, takes a place among the age's great patronage playwrights: Tasso in the service of the d'Estes, Molière writing for Louis XIV in the 1660s and 1670s, Calderón de la Barca at the Spanish court of Philip IV, and Goethe, much later, at Weimar. English court theater may not have been quite as serviceable as Continental theater, but the Continent provides the background needed to understand the dynamics of English court theater, and I have not hesitated to use it in this way.

In the court setting, Shakespeare's great succession of Stuart plays—*Measure for Measure, Lear, Othello, Macbeth, Coriolanus, Antony,* and *The Tempest,* along with several others not dealt with here for reasons of space—becomes one of the master oeuvres of European patronage art, comparable to such other patronage masterpieces as, for example, Michelangelo's Medici tomb and Sistine Chapel, Titian's paintings for the emperor Charles V, Palladio's country villas for the aristocracy in the Veneto, Monteverdi's operas in Venice, Velázquez's court paintings for Philip IV of Spain, and Mozart's music for his bishop and emperor. The world of patronage, our democratic and romantic times tend to forget, produced art of towering greatness.

Once Shakespeare and his art take their place in this august company and tradition, it is immediately apparent that they are at home here, and not only by reason of their quality. He never was, even in early plays like the Senecan horror show *Titus Andronicus,* a "rim-ram-ruf" type of native writer, or a city playwright like Thomas Dekker, but always a dramatic poet with the most elevated style and subject matter. More often than not his action takes place in a court, Navarre or Elsinore, where upper-class dramatis personae are involved in aristocratic matters of state, love, manners, wit, war, and personal honor (Holderness, Potter, and Turner). Shakespeare's style, like his elaborately formalized dramatic structure, was high baroque, at times near mannerist, decorated and elegant. It was never a folk art "in King Cambyses' vein," or the crude blood-and-thunder rhetoric that was parodied in *Hamlet*—"Come, the croaking raven doth bellow for revenge." Not for him, except in mockery, were Ancient Pistol's overwrought mouthings, jumbled together from memories of drunken, swaggering afternoons at the public theaters—"A foutre for the world and worldlings base! I speak of Africa and golden joys."

Shakespeare,

the King's Playwright

1

ART AND THEATER IN THE

SERVICE OF THE LEVIATHAN STATE

In the transition from the European Middle Ages to the Renaissance and the modern world, the modern Leviathan state took shape, first in model form in the Italian city-states and then in Spain, France, and England, where it preempted the law, monopolized the legitimate use of force, and made itself the primary source of its citizens' identity and allegiance (Skinner). There had been kings before the Renaissance, but they had been in fact feudal lords, who with difficulty maintained limited authority over groups of nearly independent barons, each ruling a duchy or march in his own right. Now divine-right monarchs appeared who claimed authority directly from God over all the areas of the civil and much of the personal life of all ranks of subjects. Codes of civil law that had a Roman basis favoring imperial power were introduced to compete with ancient legal arrangements developed in local circumstances to meet such community needs as the common law. Religion was reorganized along national lines, with the king as head of church and state. Modern systems of finance involving heavy taxation emerged to provide for the fiscal needs of a nation that was always engaged in war and other expensive projects. Standing professional armies under central control replaced bands of feudal retainers maintained and mustered by the old aristocracy in times of war.

People unaccustomed to the heavy weight of this centralized authority resisted strongly and stubbornly both these intrusions into their old ways of doing things and the imposition of new burdens. In the sixteenth and seventeenth centuries, a long series of rebellions across Europe testified to subjects' disputes of the claims of overmighty kings. Many of the distinguishing features of the new monarchies originated in attempts to overcome this resistance and to make real and viable the novel powers claimed by divine-right kings. The king's personal household, down to the royal rat catcher and mole taker, was transformed into the executive branch of an expanding government bureaucracy that increasingly tried to control all the major aspects of civil life. Finance, religion, justice, warfare, education, and trade were managed centrally, to the degree possible, to subject them to royal authority. Personality cults, like those of the red-haired, bejewelled Eliza, the virgin queen (who wore a wedding ring to represent her marriage to England), or of Louis XIV of France, *le roi soleil,* deified the new rulers.

Courts developed around the persons of the divine-right kings that dictated the tone of the national culture. Manners, pleasure, style, and *bienséance* in general were to be found only in the court, as if right ways of acting, dressing, and thinking emerged only in the potent presences of kings. Writings like Castiglione's *Courtier* (1528) organized and made memorable the ethos of a court to which increasing numbers of people were drawn to supply

a great and expanding bureaucracy, a huge system of administrative centralisation, staffed by an ever-growing multitude of "courtiers" or "officers." The "officers" are familiar enough to us as a social type. We think of the great Tudor ministers in England, Cardinal Wolsey, Thomas Cromwell, the two Cecils; or of the *letrados* of Spain, Cardinal Ximénez, the two Granvelles, Francisco de los Cobos, Antonio Pérez; and we see their common character: they are formidable administrators, machiavellian diplomats, cultivated patrons of art and letters, magnificent builders of palaces and colleges, greedy collectors of statues and pictures, books and bindings. . . . But what is significant about the sixteenth century is not merely the magnificence of these great "officers," it is the number—the ever growing number—of lesser officers who also, on their lesser scale, accepted the standards and copied the tastes of their masters. . . . Princes needed them, more and more, to staff their councils and courts, their new special or permanent tribunals which were the means of governing new territories and centralising the government of the old. (Trevor-Roper, 1959, 42)

It was in these courts that the concept of Art as a general aesthetic category appeared and that the individual arts flourished. The modern concept and practice of art originated in these courts as another way of glorifying the wealth and grandeur of the absolute state, metaphysicalizing the person of the ruler and realizing his power. Painters and sculptors transcendentalized the king and his force in heroic portraits and equestrian statues; architects built great palaces like the Louvre, the Escorial, and Hampton Court; writers historicized the legendary origins of the nation and the mythical deeds of the reigning family; political philosophers like the Florentine Niccolò Machiavelli in *The Prince* (1513), Jean Bodin in France, and Thomas Hobbes in England constructed political theories to justify the absolute power of king and state; poets like Joachim du Bellay and Edmund Spenser wrote epics in their native languages that rivaled the achievements of Greece and Rome; Ben Jonson wrote and Inigo Jones (see figure 24) designed the production of masques in the Stuart court, while Shakespeare, Calderón, Molière, and Racine provided theater for performance before kings and their courtiers.

In the crudest sense, the court paid artists to produce monarchical propaganda, and the artists were understandably anxious to identify their art with the critical workings of the state. The English epic poet Edmund Spenser, for example, claimed—preposterously—that poetry had first appeared as a sacred language in the palace and church:

> Whilom in ages past none might professe,
> But Princes and high priests, that secret skill;
> The sacred lawes therein they wont expresse,
> And with deepe Oracles their verses fill;
> Then was shee held in soveraigne dignitie,
> And made the noursling of Nobilitie.
> (*Teares of the Muses*, l. 559)

New functions for the arts required new aesthetic theories, and in letters, more systematically than in painting or architecture, the old familiar ways of doing things—the sprawling medieval romances, Gothicism, and "monkish tales"—were rejected, while the complex forms and short meters of native poetry were scorned as mere "tinkerly verse." Rhyme became suspect because of its association with native writing. In place of native ways of "enditing," a neoclassical aesthetic appeared that claimed the same kind of hierarchical literary authority for the writings of Greece and Rome as the king claimed in the political realm (Hathaway).

The Italian critic Antonio Minturno declared that the poet's duty is to repre-

sent down to the last button the hierarchical differences or people in an aristocratic society, and neoclassical poetics in general coded the aristocratic social
values of the court in the guise of aesthetics. The ideals of both court conduct
and the neoclassical style were a cool precision, a calculated control of emotion,
and a careful management of detail to maximize effect and prestige (Elias). The
hierarchy of genres was as rigid as the hierarchy of rank. Tragedy and epic,
which took matters of state and other leading social concerns of the aristocracy
as their subject, were the most honored types of poetry. The epic or heroic poem
concerned itself with the foundation of kingdoms, martial life, and the adven-
tures of soldiers. The class basis of tragedy shines through a contemporary
definition of that genre: "The persons of tragedy are kings, princes, emperors,
captains, lords and ladies, queens, princesses and young women of fashion, and
rarely people of low estate, and only if the argument necessitates it. The things
or the matter of tragedy are king's commands, battles, deaths, violation of
daughters or wives, treasons, exiles, complaints, tears, cries, falseness and other
similar matters" (Laudun, 158).

Comedy fell distinctly lower in the artistic hierarchy than tragedy because its
subject matter and characters were commonplace. The plots of comedy were
fictitious, where tragedy derived from serious historical fact, and it was set in the
country and town, while tragedy took place in the palace and the capital city.
Comedy's persons were people in the everyday walks of life: servants, citizens,
merchants, and burgesses. Its purpose was not that of tragedy — to show royal
virtues to kings — but rather to instruct citizens in correct behavior.

The hierarchy of genres, paralleling the social hierarchy, was reinforced by an
equally class-conscious concept of style that determined the appropriate language for every artistic situation. Obscurity was sometimes valued because it
protected elevated matters from the understanding of the vulgar (Javitch).
Decorum, however, was the key term in art, as it was in the court, and the high
style, considered appropriate to the most noble and heroic characters, was the
most elaborate style, employing extended figures, schemes, tropes, metaphors,
circumlocutions. The long alexandrine line, with its classical associations, was
preferred to shorter meters for tragedy and the heroic poem. Even some letters
in the alphabet were considered more noble than others: *a, o, u, m, b, ss, rr* were
the "heroic letters." The French court poet Pierre de Ronsard fused literary style
and courtly fashion in a striking image of the decorations of the true epic style as
being "commes les pierres précieuses bien enchassez sur les doigts de quelque

grand Seigneur" (like jewels displayed to advantage on the fingers of some great noble; 271).

Among the arts, none, not even architecture or music, was more useful to rulers struggling to legitimate their claims of absolute authority than theater. Not only plays and masques but triumphal entries into cities, parades, mock battles, celebratory arches with performers, tableaux, and such exercises of arms as chivalric tournaments or "barriers" used acting, poetry, singing, spectacle, music, and dance in the service of the prince (Strong, 1973). New types of theatrical art, ballet, masque, and opera (in Monteverdi's Venice the latter was thought to reproduce the choric and musical effects of ancient Greek tragedy) were developed in the Renaissance courts to portray the ruler as the source of all benefits and the wielder of all powers. To mount the productions of this court theater, what Gary Schmidgall rightly calls a "courtly aesthetic" developed, featuring elaborate scenery, indoor lighting, music, dance, and complex stage effects.

Scorning native farces and the morality and biblical plays that were believed to have usurped the dignity of the theater of the ancients, a neoclassically correct *comoedia eruditus* appeared in court performance in the sixteenth century. In Italy "correct" writers like Ariosto, Machiavelli, and Giambattista Marino provided modern plays in what was believed to be the Greek and Latin mode at various ducal courts. In France courtly playwrights like Etienne Jodelle and Robert Garnier combined classical literary with contemporary political standards to celebrate, as Jodelle put it in the prologue of *Cléopatre captive*, which was addressed to Henri II, who was in the audience, not a king merely but "a god whose place is already designated in the skies."

But while this classical theater established itself as one line of court theater, the future of theater in the court was to a large degree shaped by professional playwrights and actors, like Shakespeare and his company, working in public theaters, who were pressed into service to provide plays for performance at court on various state and festival occasions. The commedia dell'arte (the improvisational street theater of Italy), Spanish *comedia* from the corrales, strolling players and the resident Parisian *confrèries* in France, and the public companies in London established professional theater in a number of major European cities in the later sixteenth century, at about the same time that the learned comedy was appearing at the court. The pattern was the same across Europe, as these talented groups found themselves regularly brought up to court to perform. It was, after all, so much cheaper to let them support themselves for the most part from public performance than to maintain them exclusively, and the bill for bringing them to the palace for an evening or two was much less than that of mounting big individual productions like the court masques. Besides, the street players were so much more lively and amusing than courtiers with their humanistic educations who tried to sound like Seneca or Plautus. Court theater at its high point in the seventeenth century was created and shaped by an interaction of the exuberant energy of public theater with the restraint of classical theory. Harlequin and *Macbeth's* witches appeared on a stage influenced by the unities of time, place, and action.

Performance at the court required enormous new theaters like the Palladian Teatro Olimpico in Vicenza, the Great Hall of the Hôtel du Petit Bourbon at the Louvre, and Inigo Jones's Banqueting House at Whitehall. Elaborate illusionistic scenery and machinery for spectacles and brilliant lightning—descending clouds and storms, for example—were developed for these theaters by designers like Donato Bramante, Sebastiano Serlio, and Jones as settings for courtly dramas by writers like Machiavelli, Tasso, Shakespeare, Jonson, Calderón, Molière, and Racine, and composers like Monteverdi, Purcell, and Handel.

This theater focused on kings, and their ideology structured its themes. The masters of the new states realized early along that theater gave rulers an opportunity to stage an idealized image of themselves in ways that created an aura around the royal person while protecting them from criticism. By the 1630s Cardinal Richlieu had thoroughly organized the French theater for political purposes. In Spain it was not until the time of Calderón and the count-duke Olivares, the chief minister of the court of Philip IV, in the mid-seventeenth century, that the potentialities of theater as an instrument of state were fully utilized. But in England the use of the theater for state purposes was well advanced by the beginning of the seventeenth century.

The paintings of Hans Holbein, the miniatures of Nicholas Hilliard, the so-called prodigy houses like Theobalds and Audley End, such palaces as Nonesuch and Hampton Court, Raphael Holinshed's *Chronicles,* the music of William Byrd, the plays of John Lyly, and Spenser's *Faerie Queene* thickened the mystique of the Tudor state. The arrival of the Stuarts in England from Scotland in 1603, however, saw the beginning of a much more vigorous art policy, with over £30,000 spent annually on cultural patronage out of a total budget of £250,000 (Smuts, 131). In time the distinguished architects Inigo Jones and

6

John Webb became the surveyor and assistant surveyor of the royal works, with a budget that increased from £4,000 to £20,000 pounds a year. Jones was commissioned to draw plans for a new London palace, which was never built except for the Banqueting House, in the latest classical style, to rival the Louvre and the Escorial. Daniel Mytens, Anthony Van Dyck, and Peter Paul Rubens were imported from the Low Countries to paint royal portraits and decorate public buildings. The king's advisers drew up schedules of sermons to be delivered in the Chapels Royal, with care for the occasion and the preacher. William Maxey, Lancelot Andrewes, and John Donne, the favored preachers of King James, developed distinct styles and methods of biblical exegesis designed to please the king and win his patronage. Antiquaries like Sir Robert Cotton collected ancient manuscripts in extensive libraries that provided precedents for modern political arguments, and William Camden described the king's realm. The King's Music, headed by John Dowland and consisting of eighty-odd musicians in various ensembles and orchestras, operated on a budget of £1,600 a year. William Byrd, John Bull, Thomas Tomkins, Giles Farnaby, and Orlando Gibbons, great musicians all, worked at one time or another for the dean of the Chapel Royal (Caldwell).

Nor were the other arts neglected. Maximilien Colt designed the statues and tombs of the great. Simon Basil (James's first Surveyor of Works), Sir Thomas Smith, Richard Kirby, and Robert Liming were the architects of the great, new prodigy (causing wonder and surprise) houses. Rowland Buckett gilded their interior decorations and used his skilled brush to turn wood to marble. Richard Butler painted the glass for window designs. John Tradescant toured Europe buying plants for formal gardens to be laid out by "Mountain" Jennings, with hydraulics by the Frenchman Salomon DeCaux (Haynes). A tapestry factory of Flemish weavers was established in the London suburb of Mortlake. City planning appeared in a commission headed by the earl of Arundel that included Jones, which had a mandate to beautify London and Westminster. Among other works, it sponsored the design and construction of Covent Garden. In a wide variety of ways, great and small, the Stuart court used art quite self-consciously to proclaim its wealth, taste, and power and to instrument its social and political aims.

The Stuart use of the arts as a branch of politics appears in concentrated form in the household of Prince Henry, which was set up soon after his arrival in England and became at once the center of opposition to the policies of the king

(Strong, 1986). A young man of only nine when he came to England, his life and its setting were nonetheless carefully crafted by his court to create, in contrast to James's shabbiness and desire for peace, a heroic martial image for the future Henry IX. The immediate models for this personality cult were those great patrons of the arts, the Medici grand dukes of Tuscany and, closer to home, that swaggering soldier, lover, and patron of artists, Henri IV of France, the Bourbon prince who had insouciantly found Paris worth a mass (he converted to Catholicism to become king).

Particularly after Henry's investiture as prince of Wales in 1610, buildings, gardens, waterworks and fountains, paintings, engravings, adulatory books, masques and shows, and collections of jewels and ingenious instruments were designed and executed for the prince by imported artists like the engineer-architect Constantino de' Servi, the painter Isaac Oliver, and the engraver Cornelius Bole. Inigo Jones, *Vitruvius Britannicus,* was the prince's surveyor, as well as the queen's, and Henry was patron to a company of actors led by Edward Alleyn, the Prince's Men. George Chapman, the translator of Homer, was that troupe's premier playwright, and he wrote for them a series of plays on life at the sixteenth-century French court, of which *Bussy D'Ambois* was the most famous. These plays at once suited Alleyn's melodramatic acting style and satisfied both the prince's Francophilia and the taste of a warlike adolescent for life lived in high heroic terms. Michael Drayton, the poet of *Polyolbion,* was also a member of the prince's entourage, and his interest in England's topography and its martial history—"Fair stood the wind for France"—advertised that a prince born in Scotland had now identified entirely with his adopted land. The cost of all this shows up clearly in the "virtually unregulated growth in the costs of Prince Henry's Household from £2,743 to £35,765 after his creation as prince of Wales. Over £33,000 went to diet, wages and stable. There were 120 officers above stairs and 113 below" (Peck, 1990, 34).

If it borrowed in the other arts, in its use of theater for political purposes, the Stuart court was in some crucial ways in advance of the Continent. Partly this was the result of the development of a system for making use of public theater in the court in Elizabeth's time, and partly it was good fortune: theater flourished in England in the early 1600s as nowhere else in the world, before or since. The English actors were famous for their skills throughout Europe, where they often toured, and their playwrights included Webster, Chapman, Tourneur, Marston, Middleton, Beaumont, and Fletcher, to name only a few of the best known. Ben Jonson was available and anxious to write the Twelfth Night court masques, which Jones designed and staged. Edward Alleyn led Prince Henry's Men, and the great actors Richard Burbage and Robert Armin wore the king's livery, as did William Shakespeare, James's official playwright.

Soon after James arrived in London the Crown issued a warrant to the company of players for which William Shakespeare was the resident playwright and part owner. The business went through the red tape of the court bureaucracy in the extraordinarily short time of two days, and was completed by May 17 (Barroll, 1991, 32). The King's Men obviously had some good friend near the throne, perhaps the earl of Southampton, perhaps the earl of Pembroke, probably both. The old Admiral's Company of Alleyn and Philip Henslowe became Prince Henry's Men, while the former Worcester's Company became Queen Anne's Company, although the formal warrants of these other royal companies were not issued until some time later, after they had performed successfully at Hampton Court at the Christmas festivities of 1603–04. Afterward, the other surviving Stuart children became the patrons of additional companies: the Lady Elizabeth's Men and Prince Charles' Men. From 1603–04 on, all playing companies licensed to perform in London and play at the court were the servants of one of the members of the ruling family. The state was thus in full control of the theater.

Each of these troupes of players had earlier been the household servants of some magnate, a survival from an age when a baron's power was measured by the size of his band of retainers. This older arrangement had had certain advantages for the players, providing them with an occasional fee and protecting them to some degree from hostile magistrates and aldermen. In return, the actors performed interludes at festivities in their patron's great house or marched in their lord's party on state occasions. But mostly it was a matter of status to patronize a company of actors, who testified to the learning, culture, and wealth of the noble whose name they carried abroad (Stone, 1967). In the struggle of the great peers for preeminence and favor in the ceaseless court competition, the size of a courtier's entourage—including the players wearing his livery—translated directly into power, and power converted readily to money (Neale). Reducing the size of these retinues was as much the concern of a strong monarch who, like James Stuart, was intent on weakening the barons and establishing his own absolute power, as it was of Lear's daughters cutting down the old king's hundred knights. ("What need one?") In this grim business of stripping the old aristocracy of its authority, the Stuart monopolization of theater was a characteristic move, putting a powerful propaganda medium in James's hands, while at the same time reducing the power of some of his grandees.

Politics was directly, as well as indirectly, at work in the transformation of Lord Hunsdon's Men, the Lord Chamberlain's Company, to the King's Men. Shakespeare's company may have been given the royal nod because they were the theatrical best, but they also had at least a modest personal claim on the king and his government. James I had come to the English throne peacefully but deviously. There was in England toward the end of Elizabeth's reign a Stuart party led by the earl of Essex that was pushing James as the successor the queen stubbornly refused to name. In 1601, desperate at the loss of favor and income, Essex launched an abortive rebellion. His chief lieutenant was the earl of Southampton, who was also Shakespeare's patron (perhaps the model for the young aristocrat of Shakespeare's sonnets, certainly the person to whom Shakespeare's two erotic poems, *The Rape of Lucrece* and *Venus and Adonis,* were humbly dedicated). On the eve of the Essex rebellion, at the request of several members of the conspiracy, Shakespeare's company performed his *Richard II* with its famous deposition scene, showing that despite Richard's stage protestations, "all the water in the rough rude sea" *could* "wash the balm off from an anointed king" (3.2.54). The censor had removed the deposition scene from the contemporary printed version, and its performance was clearly a treasonous act. Queen Elizabeth raged—"Know you not that I am Richard the Second?"—and those involved were examined sharply:

> Examination of Sir Gelly Merrick before Lord Chief Justice Popham and Edw. Fenner. On Saturday last was sevennight, dined at Gunter's in company with Lord Monteagle, Sir Christ. Blount, Sir Chas. Percy, Ellis Jones, Edw. Bushell, and others. On the motion of Sir Chas. Percy, they went all together to the Globe over the water, where the Lord Chamberlain's men used to play, and were there somewhat before the play began, Sir Charles telling them that the play would be of Harry the Fourth. Cannot say whether Sir John Danvers was there or not, but he said he would be if he could; thinks it was Sir Chas. Percy who procured that play to be played at that time. The play was of King Henry the Fourth, and of the killing of Richard the Second, and played by the Lord Chamberlain's players. (*Calendar of State Papers* [Domestic], 1598—1601, 575)

There seems to have been some confusion between *Richard II* and *Henry IV*. The actor Augustine Phillips explained to the Lord Chief Justice the next day that the company had originally intended on that Saturday afternoon, February 7, 1601, to put on some newer play that would draw a larger audience but that the offer of forty shillings changed their minds:

> Examination of Augustine Phillipps, servant to the Lord Chamberlain and one of his players, before Lord Chief Justice Popham and Edward Fenner. On Thursday or Friday sevennight, Sir Chas. Percy, Sir Josceline Percy, Lord Monteagle, and several others spoke to some of the players to play the deposing and killing of King Richard II, and promised to give them 40s. more than their ordinary, to do so. Examinate and his fellows had determined to play some other play, holding that of King Richard as being so old and so long out of use that they should have a small company at it, but at this request they were content to play it. (*Calendar of State Papers* [Domestic], 1598—1601, 578)

In the end the players were lucky to escape imprisonment, nor were their ears cropped or their nostrils slit, frequent punishments for displeasing the monarch.

Essex went to the block, but Southampton and some of the other noble conspirators were confined in the Tower. With the agreement of his chief secretary, the Machiavellian Robert Cecil, who had in 1601 urged Essex's execution, James released Southampton and the other conspirators soon after he crossed the border, although Southampton's property was not restored until later. In general the new king was most solicitous of those who had supported him and Essex during the critical transition period, and most vengeful toward those like Walter Raleigh who had pursued Essex's death. Shakespeare and his company appear to have shared in the royal gratitude for support in a critical time. It may have been that William Herbert, 3rd earl of Pembroke and the son of Sir Philip Sidney's sister, the countess of Pembroke, who was a patron of the theater—the Shakespeare first folio was dedicated to him and to his brother—also recommended the company to the new king. Pembroke, a handsome young man, caught James's eye at once. By the time of the coronation in July he was familiar enough with the king to be able to get away with kissing him on the lips rather than the hand at the ceremony, and he had great influence with the king from the earliest days of the reign.

The new king's players were appointed "grooms extraordinary without fee":

said fee for that rank, if they had received it, being set at one shilling, eightpence per day. They were "extraordinary" only in the sense of serving in the Outer Chamber, as opposed to the Privy Chamber or Wardrobe. In the royal household—still at least nominally divided into three parts: the Courtyard, the Hall and the Chamber—grooms ranked above pages and boys but below sergeants and yeomen. Playing was a part of ordinary working life in the palace, and payments to the players appear alongside those to the man who took care of King James's silkworms, the royal barber, acrobats, lutenists and other musicians, even the humble watermen and keepers of the royal hounds, and one of the king's fools, Thomas Derry, who was still being paid two shillings a day in 1634.

The Tudors constructed a considerable theatrical bureaucracy, which the Stuarts proceeded to enlarge. Everything having to do with plays in court came under the authority of the office of the Master of the Revels, which had been established in 1545 as a part of the king's household. Edmond Tilney held the mastership from 1578 to 1610, but during the early period of James's reign there was confusion in the Revels. Tilney remained officially the Master, but Sir George Buc was doing much of the work, and the two relatives, both creatures of the powerful Howard faction, were at law with one another.

Master of the Revels was an important official in the palace hierarchy. He was one of the king's footmen of the household, similar in rank to his fellows, the officers of the Leash or the Surveyor of Gates and Buildings, the Keeper of the Bears, and the various courtiers in charge of the falconers, the hunters, and the hares. These were all remunerative patronage jobs that offered places of influence in the court, as well as opportunities for exercising power and making money, usually by the sale of services. The playwright John Lyly spent his life fruitlessly trying to get the reversion of the mastership of the Revels (Hunter), and in 1604—05 the theatrical entrepreneur Philip Henslowe and his son-in-law, "famous Ned Alleyn," managed to get themselves appointed joint Masters of the Bears. They made enough money from this lucrative post, along with their theatrical income, piously to found and endow the College of God's Gift at Dulwich.

Revels was controlled by the master of the king's household, the Lord Chamberlain, one of the most influential nobles in the kingdom. The place was a patronage plum, and the devious and powerful Thomas Howard, earl of Suffolk, was Lord Chamberlain during the time of Shakespeare's service in the

Stuart court. The Lords Chamberlain took their authority in theatrical matters, as in other affairs of the household, seriously. In 1637 Archbishop Laud tried to suppress playing during Lent, arguing that the plague was still about, but Philip Herbert, 4th earl of Pembroke and of Montgomery, who was then Lord Chamberlain, objected mightily to the church meddling in an area that he clearly considered his to control. It was a power struggle between two politicians, and Pembroke, with a long history of family patronage of the arts and theater behind him, remarked sharply that he hoped "his Grace would not meddle in his place no more than he did in his; that the players were under his command" (Wickham, II, part 1, 92).

Until 1608 the Master of the Revels directed the considerable staff of his office not from Whitehall but from a headquarters at St. John's Gate. After that he was at Blackfriars, in the center of theatrical activity in the city, where the King's Men had an indoor theater. Costumes were made and stored at the Revels' quarters, plays were read, selected, and adapted with an eye to suitability for performance at court, and professional players were interviewed and rehearsed for courtly performance. Hamlet performs the major functions of the Master of the Revels when he greets the players and welcomes them to Elsinore, listens to a recital of lines from their Dido and Aeneas play, chooses *The Murder of Gonzago,* modifies the play for court performance with his famous "dozen lines, or sixteen," lectures the actors on dramaturgy and acting style, arranges for the players to be housed, and, during the performance, ironically assures an uneasy king of the propriety of the play for the royal ear:

> KING: Have you heard the argument? is there no offense in't?
> HAMLET: No, no, they do but jest, poison in jest—no offense i' th' world.
> (3.2.232)

Even after their companies became servants to the royals, the players still spent most of their time in the London theaters. But public performance was treated officially as mere rehearsal for court performance. On several occasions when the Privy Council intervened on behalf of the players, as it often did, to free some obstreperous actor from prison or to keep rowdy playhouses open when the city authorities had closed them down, it was said to be necessary to continue to "use and practise stage playes," in order that the players might thereby "be the better enabled and prepared to shew such plaies before his Majestie as they shalbe required at tymes meete and accustomed, to which ende they have bin cheefelie licensed and tollerated" (Chambers, 1923, I, 304). In the 1630s the Lord Chamberlain gave a company playing in the Cockpit in Drury Lane into the charge of William Davenant to govern and operate in ways that would best serve the king and the Crown. The actors entered wholeheartedly into this fiction. J. Cocke in his 1615 character of a common player mocked a player who "pretends to have a royall Master or Mistresse," even though "his wages and dependance prove him to be the servant of the people" (Chambers, 1923, IV, 256).

In Stuart times activities closely related to the persons of the royal family were paid out of the Privy Purse, but public functions, like plays, were paid for by the Treasurer of the Chamber, whose regular accounts provide most of the dates and many of the names of the plays that were performed at the English court (David Cook). James's Treasurer of the Chamber, Sir John Stanhope, the brother-in-law of Nicholas Brend, the owner of the land on which the Globe Theater was built, entered numerous payments for "apparelling" and for preparing various rooms and buildings for plays, banquets, masques, and other official activities, as well as payments to individuals and groups, like the acting companies, for services rendered. It has been estimated that court payments of either £6.13s.4d. or, if the king were present, £10 per performance amounted to 10 to 15 percent of the income of a playing company (Beckerman); while court performance was an important source of income, therefore, public performance, where the take must have been enhanced by being able to advertise that the players performed "by appointment to his majesty, the king," was still, as Cocke made clear, the source of most of the company's income.

The importance that the Stuarts attributed to playing appears not only in the arrangements they made to use the theater for their own political purposes but in their increased efforts to make sure that it was not misused by others. The Master of the Revels was specifically charged with controlling all aspects of theater in both the palace and the city, where he was responsible for licensing every play offered for performance in the public theater. In 1607 the Crown tightened things up further by requiring that all plays, whether already printed or earlier licensed for performance, had to be read again and "allowed" by the office of the Master of the Revels before they could be performed (Patterson). The Crown never enforced ideological purity as efficiently as modern totalitarian regimes, but in his youthful book on the laws of poetry James I took a severe view of the political limits of art. "Ye man also be war of wryting any thing of materis of commoun weill," he advised the poet, "or uther sic grave sene subjectis . . . because nocht onely ye essay nocht your awin *Inventioun,* as I spak before, bot lykewayis they are to grave materis for a Poet to mell in" (*Ane Schort Treatise,* 221). In 1596 James was reading *The Faerie Queene,* 5.9.38, where he found his mother, Mary, queen of Scots, figured as Duessa, the false sorceress who was tried and executed by Mercilla (Queen Elizabeth). He was not amused, and Robert Bowes, the English ambassador to Scotland, reported to Burleigh on November 12 that "The [king] hath conceaved great offense against Edward Spenser publishing in print in the second book p[ar]t of the Fairy Queene and ix*th* chapter some dishonorable effects (as the k. deemeth thereof) aginst himself and his mother deceassed . . . he still desireth that Edward Spencer for his fault, may be deuly tried & punished" (*State Papers Relating to Scotland,* November 12, 1596).

The king's hard views on censorship were close to the official policy, but laws were as difficult to enforce then as now. Censorship operated in uneven and sporadic ways, and some thought that the players in James's time were dangerously out of control (Finkelpearl, 1986). Samuel Calvert, for example, wrote in disgust to Ralph Winwood early in James's reign that "the players do not forbear to present upon their stage the whole course of the present time, not sparing either Church or King, with such freedom that any would be afraid to hear them" (Winwood, II, 54). The Venetian ambassador, used to a tightly controlled state, took much the same view in 1620: "In this country . . . the comedians have absolute liberty to say whatever they wish against any one" (*Calendar of State Papers* [Venetian], XVI, 111).

But numerous playwrights found to their sorrow that censorship was no idle threat. Jonson and Chapman were imprisoned for satirizing the king and his Scottish followers in *Eastward Ho,* and stage censorship showed its teeth year after year. In the spring of 1608 the Children at Blackfriars presented "a play about the late Marshal Biron which is very offensively taken by M. de la Broderie, the French Ambassador, for not only doth it present all the French Court but also the Queen uttering harsh words to Madame de Verneuil [the French king's mistress] and giving her a buffet" (Harrison, 1958, 78). The play was "stayed," but in a few days it was being performed again with new scenes, more false and scandalous than before, and an outraged ambassador went to Cecil directly to demand that three of the players, presumably the responsible adults, be imprisoned (Chambers, 1923, II, 53; III, 257). The author, George

Chapman, fled. Samuel Daniel's *Philotas* was suppressed for coming too near the death of the earl of Essex and the failed coup designed to bring James to the English throne. The most notorious test of censorship came in 1624, when the Spanish ambassador, during the negotiations for a marriage of the Spanish infanta to Prince Charles, protested the performance of Thomas Middleton's *Game of Chess,* which portrayed the English political scene as a chess game in which English pieces were moved about by Spanish interests. The play, performed by the King's Men, was enormously popular among the anti-Spanish, anti-Catholic faction, and it filled the public theater for several days before the exertions of the Spanish ambassador managed to get it closed. Staging religious matters also seems to have brought particularly heavy punishments, and a £1,000 fine was imposed in 1639 on the players at the Fortune Theater for performing a mock mass onstage. Still, no playwright or player was actually mutilated or hanged in James's time for what he had written or performed on stage, and portrayals of corrupt courts and evil rulers seem to have been acceptable so long as they avoided treating particular policies, prominent courtiers, or the Scots who were the close companions of James I.

During the eighty-four years from the accession of Elizabeth to the beginning of the English Civil War (1558–1642), the extant Declared Accounts record payments for 969 plays at court. Of these plays, 271 were performed in the forty-five years of Elizabeth's reign, while 421 were paid for in James's reign, a period of only twenty-two years. That is to say, in Elizabeth's court an average of only six plays a year were performed, while the Jacobean court averaged nineteen a year, more than three times as many. The increased interest in theater at the Stuart court also manifested itself in the extension of the playing season, in part because Queen Anne and Prince Henry were theater buffs, and also because the Stuarts increasingly made use of plays for state ceremonies. Command performances for special occasions were always a possibility. The King's Men, for example, traveled to Wilton, the great house in Wiltshire of the earls of Pembroke, to play before the royal party in the fall of 1603, and they entertained James and his brother-in-law, King Christian of Denmark, at the palaces of Greenwich and at Hampton Court during Christian's official visit to England in the summer of 1606.

But theatrical entertainment was normally concentrated in the court season. In Elizabeth's time, playing at court had been limited for the most part to the twelve nights of Christmas, with only an occasional play on other special occasions. But in the Stuart court playing began earlier, when the monarch took up winter residence in London at the palace of Whitehall, around Hallowmas (November 1), and was gradually extended to Shrovetide and the beginning of Lent. Following Lent, the court left for its spring residence at Greenwich, before going on the progresses that occupied most of the summer. By way of comparison of the court theatrical season, it is interesting to note that in the seventeenth-century Spanish court of Philip IV, there were weekly theatrical performances throughout the year, Thursday night being favored. The Spanish comedia at court was in a number of other ways more progressive than the English: it used actresses, for example, and displayed them in stockings and tights in the frequent plots that involved cross-dressing.

But the Christmas festivities remained the occasion for the most intense and most important theatrical activity at the Stuart court. The King's Men traditionally opened the season on December 26, St. Stephen's Day. The other premier playing dates were December 27 (St. John's Day), December 28 (Holy Innocents' Day), New Year's Day, and January 6 (Epiphany, or Twelfth Night). In James's time, Michaelmas and Hallowmas, as well as February 2 (Candlemas, or Purification of the Virgin), Shrovetide, and Easter Monday and Tuesday, were also frequently occasions for theatrical performance. The liturgical calendar was still at least something of a reality in court, and an effort may have been made to see that plays related to the traditional religious themes or imagery appropriate to the day on which they were performed (Hassel). Shakespeare's *Twelfth Night*, probably played before Elizabeth on that day in 1601, is the obvious example of a play correlating exactly with the festival on which it was performed (Hotson). The play's primary plot of a journey through difficulties to incarnated love is a secular version of the epiphany theme, while the second plot of Sir Toby Belch and the steward Malvolio picks up the motif of the Feast of Misrule, the secular festival that dominated the Christmas celebrations (Barber).

Twelfth Night was the big occasion of the Christmas festivities; the theatrical event of the year, the elaborate and expensive annual court masque, was staged on this date. James himself explained, with characteristic pedantry, to the ambassador of the archduke of Tuscany the critical importance of the day and, "argal," of the masque given on that day: "Nay, if one would argumentize thereupon it might be alledged that the last day should be taken for the greatest day, as it is understood in many other cases, and particularly upon the Festivalls of Christmas wherein Twelfe day or the Festivall of the three kings which is the last is taken for the greatest day . . . wherefore the Mask at Court, compos'd for [Twelfth Night] being the greatest of all the Festivalls" (Finnet, 8).

Performance at the English court took place in any one of several areas in the palace. Most often the freestanding Banqueting House (43' x 120') or the Great Hall (45' x 100') at Whitehall was used, but sometimes it was the somewhat smaller and more private Great Chamber or even the as-yet-unreconstructed Cockpit (see figure 27). A stage was erected below the musicians' gallery at the end of the hall, before the screen fronting the pantry that provided a Green Room for the actors. Sometimes, as at Christ Church in 1605, the screen was at the rear and the stage at the upper end of the hall. Increasingly, performance at court involved the use of perspective scenery, consisting of painted backdrops and sliding side panels, which in England seems to have been restricted to performance at court and not used at this early date in the public theater except when royalty was present (Orgel, 1975).

Depending on the hall and the occasion, the auditorium was arranged in one of several ways. In one of the most common arrangements, bleacher seats were set up along the sides and at the back of the hall, with boxes arranged at ground level between the tiered seats on the sides (see figure 23). The most favored spectators sat in the boxes, while the other courtiers and their ladies, all in elaborate dress, had to clamber about the tiers and squeeze themselves (even allowing for people's smaller size then) into a seat that was 8 inches deep and 18 inches wide, with only 2 feet from the back of the seat to the footrest in front (Orrell, 1988). The best seats were not those from which the performance could best be seen but those nearest the king and queen, who were seated in what was the most prominent and important feature of the hall when it was used for theatrical purposes: the State.

The State was a raised area on which the king and the royal party sat with favored guests under a canopy. Nicolò Molin, the Venetian ambassador, writing to the Venetian Doge and Senate on January 12, 1605, describes what it was like to sit with the king in the State: "We entered a box by five or six steps; in it were two chairs; the King took one, the Queen the other, a stool was prepared for me on the King's right, and another for the Duke [of Holst, the queen's brother, Ulrich] on the Queen's left, but he would not sit down; he preferred to stand uncovered, for the three hours the masque and *ballo* lasted" (*Calendar of State Papers* [Venetian], X, 206).

Placement of the State in the hall varied. Sometimes it was at the center of the box seats, as seems to be the case on January 12, sometimes forward of them, sometimes elevated at the rear of the hall. Inigo Jones located it high up and at rear center when in 1629–30 he redesigned the Cockpit in the Court as a theater. But always its position in relation to the other seats was designed so as to make it possible for all the spectators to see the king while he talked or watched the play.

This arrangement of the hall-as-theater formalized James's famous image in *Basilikon Doron* of the true place of kings in the world: "A king is as one set on a stage, whose smallest actions and gestures, all the people gazingly do behold." The king's centrality was more tightly focused when perspective settings were used—as they increasingly were at court—by locating the monarch at precisely the point where he of all the audience had perfect vision (Orgel, 1975).

But being seen was still apparently more important than seeing. In the summer of 1605, in preparation for a performance before the king in the Great Hall at Christ Church, Oxford, Jones, adopting a plan by Sebastiano Serlio, designed a hall that placed the State only twelve feet from the stage. Jones himself thought that it should be much farther away, but the academic functionaries hotly defended their placement of the State against the complaints of members of the royal household. The king's party contended that the king's chair had been set so low and so far forward that "only His Majesty's cheek would be visible to the auditory." The college representatives "attempted to explain that, by the laws of perspective, the King would have a much better view [of the stage] than if he sat higher. There was a solemn debate in the council chamber, resulting in the decision that a King must not merely see, but be seen, and the state was moved to the middle of the hall, twenty-eight feet from the stage, which in fact proved too far, as he could not well hear or understand the long speeches" (Chambers, 1923, I, 228; see my figure 25 and Appendix B). This change resulted in the elimination of about half the good seats in the house, since no one could sit forward of the State with his back to the king.

The arrangements made in *Hamlet* for the presentation of the internal play, *The Murder of Gonzago* (3.2), in the Great Hall of Elsinore preserve the arrangement in which the king, not the play, was the thing in court performances. After the royal party enters and is seated, the queen commands her son, "Come hither, my dear Hamlet, sit by me." Her invitation is to join her in sitting in the State, to the left, on the queen's side. The prince refuses, preferring to sit by Ophelia, "here's metal more attractive," on one of the nearby "degrees" or in one of the boxes around the State, where she, as a member of the family of the king's first secretary, would have been entitled to sit. Hamlet tells Horatio that during the performance he will "rivet" his eyes on the face of the king, looking for signs of guilt, and Horatio, presumably sitting elsewhere — probably farther to the side and rear, as his lower rank would dictate — promises to watch so closely that, "If 'a steale aught the whilst this play is playing and scape [detecting], I will pay the theft." This kind of scrutiny assumes the raised visibility of the king, and the intensity of Hamlet's observation of the king's face as he watches the play allows us still to feel something of the closeness with which the court concentrated on the person of the monarch during theatrical performance.

In time James wanted a more impressive theater than the various halls, the court cockpit or the large semi-temporary banqueting houses that were built one after another in the yard at Whitehall to accommodate such special theatrical occasions as masques and feasts for ambassadors. In 1619 he commissioned Inigo Jones to build a permanent Banqueting House in the solid and proportional classical style that the architect had brought to England.

To compare with Spain again, when a court theater, the Coliseo, was built into the new palace of Buen Retiro in Madrid in 1635, it was designed to admit not only members of the court but, through external doors, the public as well, since the king and queen liked to see what their people looked like. But at Whitehall, seating at court performances was by invitation only, and the scramble for precedence among the courtiers was intense. Performances were given in the late evening, ten o'clock or later, following receptions and elaborate banquets. Who ate with the king, and whether alone or in company, and who with the queen, and where at the table, were matters of the greatest social import. Getting a seat in the hall for the performance afterward, even with an invitation, was never easy, and there was always a great crush at the entrance causing "the white stafes" — the Lord Chamberlain's officers — to lay about them with their rods of office. The Venetian ambassador's chaplain, the observant Orazio Busino, drew a wonderfully full picture for his masters in the Most Serene Republic of what went on in the palace on the night of a theatrical performance before six hundred guests:

A large hall is fitted up like a theatre, with well secured boxes all round. The stage is at one end and his Majesty's chair in front under an ample canopy. . . . The ambassador was near the king; others with gold chains round their necks sat among the Lords of the [Privy] Council. . . . Whilst waiting for the king we amused ourselves by admiring the decorations and beauty of the house. . . . From the roof . . . hang festoons and angels in relief with two rows of lights. Then such a concourse as there was, for although they profess only to admit the favoured ones who are invited, yet every box was filled notably with most noble and richly arrayed ladies, in number some 600 and more according to the general estimate; the dresses being of such variety in cut and colour as to be indescribable; the most delicate plumes over their heads, springing from their foreheads or in their hands serving as fans; strings of jewels on their necks and bosoms and in their girdles and apparel in such quantity that they looked like so many queens, so that at the beginning, with but little light, such as that of the dawn or of the evening twilight, the splendour of their diamonds and other jewels was so brilliant that they looked like so many stars. (*Calendar of State Papers* [Venetian], XV, 111)

Having described the audience, Busino turns to the cynosure of the occasion, the king, who, to the sound of trumpets, came at ten o'clock to the already filled hall, accompanied by several ambassadors, who took stools in the State with him. The nobles sat on nearby benches. The stage area was carpeted with green cloth, a golden tent appeared on a drape, and a blue background canvas, bright with stars, provided a backdrop.

The Master of the Revels had the prime responsibility for making sure that what was presented on such occasions played well. Duke Theseus' question to Philostrate, the Athenian Master of the Revels in *A Midsummer Night's Dream*, who was modeled on Edmond Tilney, pretty well sets out what was expected:

> Say, what abridgment have you for this evening?
> What masque? what music? How shall we beguile
> The lazy time, if not with some delight?
> (5.1.39)

In what Philostrate had to offer on that occasion, we can still hear the sophisticated dramatic poet William Shakespeare laughing at the kind of junk theater that ordinarily made up the theatrical bill of fare at Elizabethan palaces: "the battle with the centaurs to be sung by an Athenian eunuch to the harp," "the riot of the tipsy Bacchanals" once again tearing the poet, poor old Orpheus, to pieces, and the nine Muses still "mourning for the death Of Learning." Theseus has heard it all before and is weary of it, but he is not sufficiently alert to avoid the fatal mistake of choosing to watch the only alternative, the "tedious brief scene of young Pyramus And his love Thisby" to be put on by the Athenian workmen led by Bully Bottom.

Sometimes so august a figure as the Lord Chamberlain involved himself in the choice of entertainments, as Lord Hunsdon, dying of syphilis, did in a memo about a play for Twelfth Night 1602, to be performed before Queen Elizabeth to honor the Russian ambassador and an Italian duke. Hunsdon reminded himself "To Confer with my Lord Admirall and the Master of the Revells for takeing order generally with the players to make choyse of [a] play that shalbe best furnished with rich apparell, have greate variety and change of Musicke and daunces, and of a Subiect that may be most pleasing to her Maistie" (Hotson, 15). If Shakespeare's *Twelfth Night* was "preferred," as seems likely, its costumes, music, dance, and romantic story would have satisfied the Lord Chamberlain's requirements perfectly.

More elevated Stuart tastes and increased political interest in the arts required increasingly sophisticated kinds of plays. The ideal theater of an absolutist monarchy—the theater that caught the essence of absolutism in spectacle and action—was embodied in the series of masques that were produced annually by Inigo Jones and Ben Jonson for performance before the king and his court on Twelfth Night. There had been masques, usually quite modest ones, long before James came to England; but with the king's arrival Jones and Jonson, designer and poet, were encouraged and paid to create between them a magnificent spectacle of absolute monarchy, ablaze with light, manifesting the wealth and the power of the king and symbolizing in music, poetry, intricate stage machines, spectacular scenic effects, and elaborate dance the claims of a divine-right monarchy to be able to bring into harmony the conflicting interests of the nation (Orgel, 1965). Professional actors were hired for the speaking parts, but the spectacle focused on a group of young aristocrats, often including the queen and sometimes the young prince, who moved through intricate dance steps to the sound of appropriate music, dancing out the complex but coordinated movement of life under royal authority. Forces of chaos and discord of the kind that actually threatened the kingdom would appear at the beginning of a Jonsonian masque, but by the king's power they were always banished magically from the stage or brought into the general harmony with which the masque concluded.

At the end, the stage opened out to include the court, and the noble dancers chose partners from the audience to dance out the revels of earthly and heavenly order in the ultimate theater of the court.

The tradition of festival playing in the court that climaxed with the Twelfth Night masque lasted until 1641, as civil war approached, when the court was dark on January 6 for the first time in many years, and the masque was performed at the houses of the earl of Chesterfield and Lord Strange.

Masques offered the high moments of the Christmas season, but the staple of courtly theatrical entertainment was provided by the transportation to court of plays from the public playhouses that were in some cases designed, in others adapted, for court performance. Let us see if we can now come closer to some of those occasions, beginning with the Christmas season of 1603—04, when the King's Men—Lawrence Fletcher, William Shakespeare, Richard Burbage, Augustine Phillips, John Heminges, Henry Condell, William Sly, Robert Armin, and Richard Cowley—took their repertory upriver to Hampton Court to perform before their royal patron at the first Christmas festivities he celebrated in England.

2

BLOOD REVENGE IN ELSINORE

AND IN HOLYROOD

HAMLET, HAMPTON COURT

CHRISTMAS 1603

The Christmas season of 1603–04 was the first celebrated in England by the new English king, James I, aged thirty-seven (see figure 7), and his dark-fated family. His queen was Anne of Denmark, formerly a beauty but now, at age twenty-nine, "a bony sallow woman, sharp-nosed and tight-mouthed," as one contemporary described her (see figure 8). Prince Henry, the heir apparent, aged nine, would die in 1612 (see figure 9), rumored to have been poisoned by his father, who was jealous of his popularity. Seven-year-old Elizabeth, the only surviving daughter, would marry the Elector Palatine in 1613 and become for a brief time the romantic Winter Queen of Bohemia (see figure 10), before spending nearly fifty years in exile. Charles, three, who would succeed to the English throne and in 1649 become the first English king to be publicly executed by his people, was as yet too young and sickly, with heavy iron braces on his legs, to be brought from Scotland. Two other children, named with unerring political purpose (as all James's children were) after Margaret Tudor and Robert Bruce, had died in Scotland. Two more born in England would die in infancy before James abandoned the connubial bed for good.

Queen Elizabeth had died on March 24, 1603, and, after what had seemed to him a lifetime of waiting, James VI of Scotland became James I of England as well. He progressed southward in a leisurely way into his new kingdom, perhaps to avoid attending

Elizabeth's funeral, for his fear of death was so great that later he would even avoid the funerals of his oldest son and his queen. He enjoyed entertainment in towns and great houses, marveled at the riches of his new kingdom, seemingly knighted everyone who welcomed him, and, out of his newfound wealth, bestowed gifts freely on his favorites, particularly the large train of Scots who followed him. Arriving in London in May, he soon left the city, where the plague, which was endemic in London throughout most of the seventeenth century, was raging. Three thousand people died in the last week of August, and by the end of 1603, thirty-eight thousand were dead, one-sixth of the citizens of the city. The pestilence continued until March 1604, when it stopped abruptly.

Postponing the traditional procession of the new monarch from the Tower through London until the following year, the king returned to the city only briefly, to be crowned in an abbreviated coronation ceremony at Westminster on July 25. The summer was spent on a progress through the south of England with his court; they traveled from one great house to another and were lavishly entertained at each. A number of ambassadors of various nations arrived to bring greetings from their royal masters, distributing rich gifts to the courtiers to win favor—"some with Boxes, and others with Buttons, caps of Feathers, Rings, and chains of Gold and Diamonds: Several Ladies also received Rings and Pearl Necklaces" (Sullivan, 192).

At Winchester a trial for treason was held for several plotters, including Sir Walter Raleigh, who were charged with having planned to seize the king and to crown the king's cousin, Arbella Stuart—who had as dangerously good a claim as James to the throne but was all innocent of the plot—as head of a regime that would be more tolerant to Catholics. Her innocence established, Arbella cheered up considerably and, after years of peevish exile under the firm hand of old Bess of Hardwick, enjoyed to the fullest her recall to court and her newfound prominence as a kinswoman of the king. Like one of Shakespeare's waiting women playing with young Prince Mamillius—"a sad tale's best for winter"—Arbella wrote amusingly and lightly about

> how we spend our time on the Queen's side? . . . Theare weare certaine childe-playes remembered by the fayre Ladies, *viz.* "I pray, my Lord, give me a course in your park." "Rise, pig, and go." "One peny follow me," &c. And when I came to Court they were as highly in request as ever cracking of nuts was. So I was by the Mistress of the Revelles not only compelled to

play at I know not what, (for till that day I never heard of a play called Fier,) but even persuaded, by the princely example, to play the childe againe. This exercise is mostly used from ten of the clock at night to two or three in the morning; but, that day I made one, it began at twilight and ended at supper-time. Theare was an interlude; but not so ridiculous (ridiculous as it was) as my letter. (Nichols, IV, 1061)

The royal progress came at last to Wilton, where Mary Herbert, sister to Sir Philip Sidney, was the dowager countess, her eldest son, William, who was unmarried, having succeeded to the title. It was the countess of Pembroke who in 1595 had published her brother's *Apologie for Poetry,* the preeminent English statement of neoclassical poetic principles, which Sidney, disdaining that it should "florish in the Printers shoppes," had left unprinted. Among those who contributed elegies after Sidney's death was James VI of Scotland, who was himself a poet of considerable, if unremarkable, talent. He shared Sidney's neoclassical principles of correctness, and as a young man, to please his tutor—the great humanist scholar, poet, and theologian George Buchanan—the king had written and published a similar type of poetics, *Ane Schort Treatise conteining some Reulis and Cautelis to be observit and eschewit in Scottis Poesie* (1584), which in a way characteristic of so authoritarian a king warned poets to obey the established rules of poetry.

Levinus Muncke, James's newly appointed chief of protocol, bored with the country, wrote to Ralph Winwood on October 29, "from the Court at Wilton near Salisbury: The Plague ceaseth apace in London; there dyed this week in London of all diseases but 600 and odd. I would to God the King would draw nearer to it, for in these arrant removes we endu[r]e miserie apace, and want of all things, which I never thought the country so unable to supply us" (Nichols, IV, 1059).

To relieve the tedium, and to entertain the recently arrived Venetian ambassadors, the king's players were paid £30 to come to Wilton in early December and perform a play. There is a nineteenth-century description of a letter, since lost, in which Mary Sidney, anxious to put in a word for Raleigh, tells her son to bring the king to Wilton with him to see *As You Like It,* adding that "we have the man Shakespeare with us" (Hannay, 124). Since the letter was accurate in those details that can be checked, it seems at least possible that it was also right about the play performed. *As You Like It,* a light comedy about another group of exiles living out their lives in the country waiting for a return to the court, fits the actual circumstances so exactly that it would be easy to surmise that it was written for the occasion. Lines like "To fright the animals and kill them up In their assign'd and native dwelling-place" may not have much amused a king obsessed with hunting deer on horseback, but satiric comparisons of country and courtly life would have found response in Levinus Muncke: "And how like you this shepherd's life, Master Touchstone?"

In a normal year, following custom, the royal party would have returned to London as winter set in, to celebrate Christmas at Whitehall. But because the plague continued, the king's party, not sharing Muncke's view that six hundred deaths in one week was only a trifle, went for Christmas to Hampton Court, twenty-some miles up the Thames from London.

Sir Dudley Carleton, later ambassador at Venice and The Hague and eventually chief secretary to Charles I, was in the party as the controller to Henry Percy, the ninth earl of Northumberland, who was destined to spend much of his later life in the Tower. (Carleton himself made one disastrous slip in 1605, when he was briefly confined to the Tower for unknowingly leasing to Guy Fawkes and his plotters the vault in which they assembled their gunpowder to blow up king and Parliament.) An observant and an intelligent man who was cleverly making his way in the court world, Carleton was a writer of numerous letters, corresponding all his life with the greatest letter-writer of the age, that inveterate gossip about courtly affairs, Mr. John Chamberlain. On December 22 Carleton informed Chamberlain that

> we have left Salisbury plains to the frost and snow, and the pleasant walks at Wilton to as good dirt as ever you saw in Smithfield when it is at the best, and coming to Hampton Court were there welcomed with fogs and mists, which make us march blindfold; and we fear we shall now stumble into the sickness which till now we have miraculously scaped. . . . We shall have a merry Christmas at Hampton Court, for both male and female masques are all ready bespoken, whereof the Duke [of Lennox, Lodowick Stuart, cousin of the king] is *rector chori* of the one side and Lady Bedford of the other. After Christmas, if the sickness cease, we shall come to Whitehall.

The royal palace of Hampton Court had been built in the country by Henry VIII's Lord Chancellor Cardinal Wolsey, in the short time of two years

(1514–16), by Lawrence Stubbs, his Surveyor of Buildings. The energies and tensions of court society can still be read out of the architecture of the redbrick palace of Hampton Court, intended to dazzle the world with its splendor and the elaborate design of its extensive gardens and grounds (see figure 12). Its cost and expanse spoke for the new world of the Renaissance courts, dispensing with all the architectural marks of medieval feudalism except for one last decorative remnant, a vestigial moat. A two-story building erected around two main courts, the Base Court and the Clock Court, and numerous smaller courts, the royal palace of Hampton Court contained upward of 1,000 rooms, including 280 apartments for guests.

On the north side of the Clock Court is the only surviving Tudor theater, the still-brilliant Great Hall, where spectacles and plays were staged (see figure 11). From the back of the dais at one end to the screens beneath the minstrel gallery at the other, it measures 92 feet 9 inches in length (105 feet 6 inches if the passageway behind the screens is included) by 40 feet in width, and 60 feet up to its gilded hammer beams (92 to the gable; see Appendix B). When Henry VIII grabbed the palace from Wolsey after his fall from favor in 1529, the Great Hall was redone to symbolize the magnificence and power of the Defender of the Faith and the Tudor dynasty. The stained-glass windows in the east wall depict the descent of Henry VIII from Edward III, as well as the union of the two houses of York and Lancaster, which was the origin of the Tudor royal line. The upper lights carry the arms of the realms ruled (at least at one time) by the English kings: France, England, Ireland, and Wales. In the west window, Henry himself stands in the center, surrounded by his arms, badges, and ciphers, along with some of his wives and children. The walls were hung with tapestries, which are still there, that depict the life of Abraham, as if to say that the Tudors stood in the same sacred relationship to their people as the biblical patriarchs did to theirs.

The Christmas festivities of 1603 held in Henry's great palace were splendid beyond memory. Earlier, the English courtiers had rushed north to greet James on his spring progress through his new kingdom, and now everyone who was or hoped to be anyone had to be at Hampton Court to see and greet the new king and queen during the Christmas festivities. Arbella Stuart was tremendously excited by the prospect. She bubbled in a letter to the earl of Shrewsbury on December 18 that the queen had arrived at Hampton Court on the sixteenth and that "the King will be heare to-morrow. The Polonian Imbassador shall have Audience on Thursday next. The Queene intendeth to make a Mask this Christmas, to which end my Lady of Suffolk and my Lady Walsingham hath warrants to take of the late Queene's [Elizabeth's] best apparell out of the Tower at theyr discretion. Certein Noblemen (whom I may not yet name to you because som of them have made me of theyr counsell,) intend another. Certein gentlemen of good sort another. It is said theare shall be 30 Playes. The King will feast all the Imbassadors this Christmas" (Nichols, IV, 1061).

Not everyone was as excited at the prospect of the coming festivities as Arbella. Robert Cecil, the "little beagle" (as, to his dreadful mortification, James called him, in reference to his height of little over a humpbacked five feet), but still the most powerful man in the realm and the politician who had made James king, longed to be elsewhere when he contemplated all the formal dinners he would have to attend while struggling with the problems of dealing with a court full of ambassadors. He complained to Shrewsbury on December 23, 1603, "Other stuff I can send yow none from this place, wheare now we are to feast seven Embassadors; Spain, France, Poland, Florence, and Savoy, besydes Masks, and much more, during all wch tyme, I would, wth all my hart, I were wth that noble Lady of yours by her turf fire" (Nichols, I, 301).

But most of the court could not imagine being elsewhere. All the beds were filled, the guests overflowed into the countryside, tents were set up in the park, and there was continual bickering about precedence and quarters. There were receptions, balls, banquets, masquerades, tennis matches, running at the ring, a grand tilt, mumming, and gambling for large sums. At the center of the festivities were the three masques that various court groups had been planning for months, and there were, if not the thirty plays mentioned by Arbella, nevertheless a large number, which were performed by no less than three companies of players in succession, first the King's Men and then the two other major London companies, which would shortly be patronized by Prince Henry and Queen Anne. The Office of Works recorded the making of "foote paces [footrests?] in the presence and great Chamber on the kinges syde and in the presence Queenes side and in the hall, making of degrees and a Cupboord in the great Chamber for the plate, making of the stage and setting up degrees and pticons [partitions] for the playe in the hall" (Wilson, 19). The plate had to be locked up lest it be stolen! Performances were in three places: the Great Hall, the Great Watching Chamber, and the still smaller Presence Chamber, the latter two located behind the dais at the head of the Great Hall (see figure 23). The first holidays, Carleton wrote to Chamberlain, "we had every night a public play in the great hall, at which the king was ever present and liked or disliked as he saw cause, but it seems he takes no extraordinary pleasure in them. The queen and prince were more the players' friends, for on other nights they had them privately and have since taken them to their protection. On New Year's night we had a play of Robin Goodfellow" (January 15, 1604).

The road to Hampton Court had been a long and difficult one for the King's Men that year. The public theaters had been "restrained" by officials on March 19, out of respect for the dying Queen Elizabeth, and the closing had been extended by the plague. The company had done what players usually did when the town theaters were closed, gone on tour in the countryside, with reduced numbers and cut-down plays and wardrobes, performing in make-do theaters, on trestle stages in public squares near market crosses, in front of the pantry screen in the halls of colleges, towns, and guilds, and in the country houses of the gentry and nobility. While the new king was making his way south (and signing the warrant on May 19 that made them the King's Men), the company had visited Cambridge and Oxford, performing *Hamlet* in one of the college halls. They went on to Coventry, then to Ipswich in the east, and ended up at Bath and Shrewsbury in the west before spending some time in the London suburb of Mortlake, whence they went on December 2 to Wiltshire to put on their first play before their royal patron at Wilton.

By December 26 the king's players had arrived at Hampton Court, where they performed on the first night of the festivities for their new master and his court in circumstances that no doubt were, as we shall see in the final chapter, much like those portrayed in *Hamlet* when the players arrive in the court of Elsinore to put on *The Murder of Gonzago* before the Danish court.

During the holidays they performed not only *A Midsummer Night's Dream* (which is more than likely what Carleton called "Robin Goodfellow") but Ben Jonson's new play *Sejanus* and an anonymous play, *The Fair Maid of Bristow*. They were paid for other performances as well, but the titles of the plays they performed on those occasions were not specified. Drawing on their repertory of sixty or seventy plays, none previously seen by the king except probably *As You Like It*, they must have put on, as they did in other years, their newest and biggest hits by their most popular playwright, which in late 1603 meant Shakespeare's *Twelfth Night, Troilus and Cressida*, the first and second parts of *Henry IV, Henry V*, and, most surely, *Hamlet*.

Hamlet would have been the likely choice to open the season on the night after Christmas. It was still fairly new—no more than a year or two old—and it was popular enough to have been worth pirating earlier that year. The title page of the 1603 pirated version of the play—"As it hath beene diverse times acted by his Highnesse servants in the Cittie of London: as also in the two Universities of Cambridge and Oxford, and else-where"—makes it certain that it was in the current repertory of the King's Men when they went to Hampton Court. Furthermore, the plays performed at court in the next year, 1604–05, are named, and the list does not include *Hamlet,* meaning that *Hamlet* must have been performed the year before. In 1604–05 the King's Men put on their new plays, *Othello* and *Measure for Measure,* and reached back into their repertory for *The Merry Wives of Windsor, The Comedy of Errors, Love's Labour's Lost, Henry V,* and *The Merchant of Venice,* plus Ben Jonson's two humour plays and the anonymous *Spanish Maʒe.* That *Hamlet* had already been played at court before 1604–05 is further made likely by a letter from Cecil's man Sir Walter Cope, in which Cope notes that by January 1605 the queen had seen all the plays in the repertory of the King's Men except *Love's Labour's Lost.*

Hamlet is a tragedy of state, the type of play suitable for kings and courts, something worthy the dignity of the occasion and the noble audience. It was also "relevant" in a number of quite striking ways. The words of the sentries on the battlements, "'Tis bitter cold," would have gotten a wry smile from an audience trying to keep warm in the winter damp of the Thames valley, and the sacramental description of Christmas would have struck the right holiday note:

> Some say that ever 'gainst that season comes
> Wherein our Saviour's birth is celebrated,
> The bird of dawning singeth all night long,
> And then they say no spirit dare stir abroad,
> The nights are wholesome, then no planets strike,
> No fairy takes, nor witch hath power to charm,
> So hallowed, and so gracious is that time.
>
> (1.1.158)

Besides, the Danish setting of the play complimented Queen Anne. The royal couple had, in fact, honeymooned in Elsinore, the Danish Kronborg, while waiting for favorable winds to return to Scotland, and from there the king ended one of his undated letters of early 1590, "From the castle of 'croneburg' where we are drinking and driving our [o'er?] in the old manner" (Letter 38). The castle had memories not only for James and Anne but for the actors as well, since several recent members of the company—Will Kempe, George Bryan, and Thomas Pope—had played there with a small company that was traveling on the Continent in the summer of 1586.

In addition, *Hamlet* held the mirror up to the present moment in a striking manner. In the second scene of the third act, the play within the play, King Claudius and Queen Gertrude sit in their State at the rear of the trestle stage and watch a Player King and Player Queen perform for them in the Great Hall of the palace of Elsinore. Directly facing Claudius and Gertrude, in a perfect mirror arrangement, King James and Queen Anne sat in their State in the Great Hall of Hampton Court watching, down the aisle formed by trestle seats on both sides of the hall, the King's Men perform *Hamlet* (see figure 23). It must have been one of the great moments in Western theater, a true coup de theatre, delighting everyone and causing all thoughtful spectators then and since to wonder which world was stage and which reality.

Claudius saw an image of his own guilt in the play he watched—"O, my offense is rank"—but what did James, watching from the other side of the stage, see in *Hamlet?* Probably not the baffled rationality and social alienation that modern audiences have since found in the philosophical and melancholy prince of Denmark, although James was certainly intellectually capable of under-standing "to be or not to be." More surely, however, his eye would have been caught by the play's dramatization of a succession crisis not unlike the one he had just been through and its exploration of the question "Who is the true king?"

In his handbook on kingship, *Basilikon Doron,* James had advised his son that a king should always come to the throne "by right of due descent." His Scottish legitimacy was clear once his mother was dead, but the claim to the English throne that he had pressed for many years was still questionable. His claim came through his grandmother, Margaret Tudor, daughter to Henry VII and sister to Henry VIII, but there were several others, some also watching *Hamlet* that night, like the hapless Arbella Stuart, with as strong a hereditary claim as James had. But right really had little to do with how he had gotten to the throne. There being no law of succession in force in England at that time, everything depended on the will of his cousin, the childless Elizabeth, and she, in a way that was characteristic of her treatment of suitors of any kind, had kept James (whom she persisted in calling "that little urchin") obsequiously dangling when he was king of Scotland, doing her bidding for many years in the hope that she would eventually name him heir to her throne. For sound political reasons, Elizabeth had held James's mother in prison for many years before agreeing in 1587, with many tearful protestations, to her execution, in order to forestall further plotting on Mary's part at the time of the Armada.

The execution of his mother had put James in a bind, and the letter he wrote to Elizabeth in response to her explanation of why it had been necessary is still painful to read in its sweating effort to maintain the appearance of a little dignity while at the same time letting Elizabeth know that he would not cause any trouble:

> Madame and dearest sister, Whereas by your letter . . . ye purge yourself of yon unhappy fact, as on the one part considering your rank, sex, consanguinity, and long professed goodwill to the defunct, together with your many and solemn attestations of your innocency, I dare not wrong you so far as not to judge honourably of your unspotted part therein. So, on the other side, I wish that your honourable behaviour in all times hereafter may fully persuade the whole world of the same. And as for my part I look that ye will give me at this time such a full satisfaction in all respects as shall be a mean to strengthen and unite this isle, establish and maintain the true religion, and oblige me to be, as of before I was, your most loving and dearest brother.
>
> J. R. (February 1587, Letter 27)

This is the way great princes handle awkward difficulties like "yon unhappy fact," and in the end it worked. Elizabeth most likely never did name James her successor, but she did not block him either. Her chief councillors, Cecil and Northampton, were the leaders of a political faction that wished to avoid civil war by bringing to the throne a Protestant king who would at the same time be acceptable to Catholics. James fit the bill, and the plotters had engaged in a childishly coded correspondence with him for years. When Elizabeth died they told a story about asking her on her deathbed who should succeed her. The dying queen was reported to have responded, "Who but a king?" This was immediately assumed to refer to James, and in a few hours messengers were on their way to Edinburgh, and Cecil and his supporters were out in the streets proclaiming the new monarch to a population that was itself hoping desperately for a peaceful transition of power. How risky a thing it had been appears in the fact that soon after he came to the throne for which he had waited for so long, James pushed an ex-post-facto act of succession through Parliament legitimizing his kingship.

To the expert eyes of the new king—who more knowledgeable?—*Hamlet* offered an extended succession struggle, nearly as complicated and as bloody as what he himself had just been through. Coming from what was still in many ways a feudal barony only beginning to take on the contours of a national state, James would have recognized at once the old-fashioned medieval warrior prince, Old Hamlet. Wearing complete armor, "cap-a-pe," courteous, religious, and chivalrously concerned that women, no matter how base their conduct, not be physically harmed, the old king is an idealized composite of the chiefs of an older heroic age with the rulers of the more immediate feudal past, when kings like himself and Old Norway determined the fate of kingdoms in single combat conducted in front of their armies and honored their pledged word on the outcome. He is the old-style father as well as an old-style king—representing the individual's past, as well as the nation's—and the force of his energy and the certainty of his morality are menacing to son and subject alike, as he crashes his heavy battle-ax in fury on the Baltic ice and commands the younger Hamlet to honor the ancient code of blood revenge and murder the uncle who has killed his father. Old Hamlet's religious views, which take for granted the importance of the Catholic sacraments he was denied before death ("unhousel'd, disappointed, unanneal'd") and the necessity of purging his sins in the fire of a Catholic purgatory, are as old-fashioned as is his death in a biblical garden, poisoned by a serpent who is also the first murderer, Cain killing Abel—"A brother's murder, It hath the eldest primal curse upon it." James would have been suspicious of the ghost, for, like the good Calvinist he was, he believed in heaven and hell, but "As for Purgatorie and all the trash depending thereupon, it is not worth the talking of" (*A Premonition*, 125).

The writs of the old legitimate kings who ruled by commanding presence and strength of arm, while powerful once, no longer ran in the Renaissance palace of Elsinore, any more than they did in Holyrood or Hampton Court, where the wardrobe of the dead Eliza, the Faerie Queene, was being altered to "coldly furnish forth" the gowns for the new queen's Twelfth Night masque. In Elsinore, as across Renaissance Europe, a new type of prince had come to power: the absolutist despot whose legitimacy went back only one or two generations at the most, like the English Tudors or the Valois and Bourbons of France. Although James Stuart claimed to be the descendant of the longest line of royal kings in Europe and insisted that there was no stain on his English title, he was in consideration of his English title both de facto and de jure one of the new type of European usurpers. And forced in his rude Scottish kingdom, as in England, always to rule by guile rather than force, he would have had the keenest appreciation of the Machiavellian "king-craft" by which Claudius maintained his throne.

As brother to the old king, Claudius has usurped the throne by poisoning the legitimate king and pushing aside the legal heir, whom he eventually tries to murder. Intelligent, crafty, never appearing to be doing what he is actually doing, affable, relentless in his drive to power, Claudius is cynical and pragmatic. And like the new-style ruler Machiavelli idealizes in *The Prince,* Claudius understands the necessity of legitimizing his rule by all available means. He creates the appearance of an uninterrupted continuation of the old order by marrying the queen of the brother he has killed and treating the rightful heir as his son and successor. Usurpation and murder are concealed by a carefully fostered ideology of divine right. Those two sycophantic courtiers Rosencrantz and Guildenstern, fervidly and earnestly assuring Claudius of their support for whatever action he chooses to take, allow us still to hear how such ideas sounded in the palace:

> The cess of majesty
> Dies not alone, but like a gulf doth draw
> What's near it with it. Or it is a massy wheel
> Fix'd on the summit of the highest mount,
> To whose [huge] spokes ten thousand lesser things
> Are mortis'd and adjoin'd, which when it falls,
> Each small annexment, petty consequence,
> Attends the boist'rous [ruin]. Never alone
> Did the King sigh, but [with] a general groan.
> (3.3.15)

Claudius acts out the part of God's deputy on earth magnificently. When threatened by a rebellious subject, he bravely confronts him with the bold words "There's such divinity doth hedge a king That treason can but peep to what it would, Acts little of his will" (4.5.124). And even as he dies he projects the invulnerability of annointed majesty, "O, yet defend me, friends, I am but hurt." In the manner of other Renaissance absolutists, Claudius stages his greatness on all possible occasions. Each time he drinks, a cannon is fired, forcing the gods in the skies to speak back to him in the echo, as if they were confirming his authority.

It was not by ceremony, show, and mythology alone that new kings like Claudius and James Stuart validated their claims to absolute power in the state. Shaky thrones were stabilized by new skills, political alertness, shrewd understanding, and careful attention to affairs of state, as well as by personal force. Philip II of Spain represented the ideal, sitting in his dark study above the chapel in the Escorial, the great palace he had built for himself, reading and writing extensive notes in a fine hand on every report that reached his desk from an empire that stretched around the world. James was anything but a compulsive administrator, regularly escaping to his hunting lodge and leaving affairs of state to his underlings, but he too had a shrewd, up-to-date understanding of how to manipulate men and events in the exercise of power.

Legitimacy in the Danish state, as in the English, derives from several different sources: natural authority and battle courage in Old Hamlet, skill in statecraft and ruthlessness in Claudius, and legitimate descent plus intelligence and sensitivity in Prince Hamlet, who is Plato's philosopher-king. In young Hamlet is concentrated all that was most idealistic and optimistic in Renaissance humanism: he is a student at Wittenberg—the university of Dr. Faustus and Martin Luther—a critic of the arts and frequenter of the theater, a lover, and a poet. He is the ideal courtier, the *uomo universale* fashioned by Castiglione and so admired by Ophelia,

> Th' courtier's, soldier's, scholar's, eye, tongue, sword,
> Th' expectation and rose of the fair state,
> The glass of fashion and the mould of form,
> Th' observ'd of all observers.
>
> (3.1.151)

Along with Renaissance painters like Michelangelo and Raphael, he exulted in the glory of the natural world—"this goodly frame, the earth ... this brave o'erhanging firmament, this majestical roof fretted with golden fire" (2.2.298). He shared with such humanistic philosophers as Pico della Mirandola a feeling of limitless human potentiality: "What [a] piece of work is a man, how noble in reason, how infinite in faculties, in form and moving, how express and admirable in action, how like an angel in apprehension, how like a god! the beauty of the world; the paragon of animals" (2.2.303).

Hamlet can see and speak, as no one else in the play can, to the heroic past in the figure of the father-king, Old Hamlet, but the old sureties, particularly about blood revenge, are no longer real for him. Caught between two worlds, for most of the play Claudius is able to manipulate him easily, and although in the end Hamlet becomes the instrument for bringing Claudius to his death, he can never fulfill his early promise to become the philosopher-king of Denmark. The election passes to the Norwegian prince, Fortinbras, an honest and straightforward soldier, but totally lacking in the sensitivity and intelligence that distinguish Hamlet.

James would surely have been interested in this dramatic analysis of rule, commenting as it did on his own experience and theories of government, the latter books having been published for the first time in England in 1603 to make his views known to his new subjects. But as he watched this dramatization of a succession struggle in the Renaissance palace, certain remarks and the configuration of the characters around the revenge theme would have suggested some of the deepest and most intense events in the history of his strange family.

Hamlet had been written in 1601, before James became king of England, and it could not have been designed to offer him a reprise of the Stuart scandal, although "some dozen lines, or sixteen" could easily have been added for the Hampton Court performance in 1603. But Roland Frye has convincingly shown how events in Scotland in the 1560s that had been the talk of all Europe for a generation provided material for the *Hamlet* plot.

Mary Stuart (see figure 6), raised in France and married to its young king François II in 1558, aged sixteen, returned to Scotland and its throne after his death in 1560. There, violently infatuated—"why she would hang on him as if increase of appetite had grown by what it fed on"—she married in 1565 with her distant cousin, Henry Stewart, Lord Darnley, like herself descended from Henry VII of England (see figure 1). Their combined claim to the English throne was powerful enough to make Elizabeth, just across an uneasy border, very nervous. James was born to Mary on June 19, 1566; he may have been Darnley's or he may have been the son of David Riccio, Mary's Italian secretary and familiar. At least this was the common gossip. A street mob once taunted James by calling him "thou son of seigneur Davie," and Henri IV of France cruelly and wittily remarked that James was truly Solomon—to whom James liked to be compared—the son of David. (James's delight in the Solomonic role was well known and played to in, for example, an entertainment at Theobalds in 1606, as we shall see, when a figure designed for the queen of Sheba came to him bearing gifts. Inigo Jones's design for a new palace at Whitehall was supposedly based on Solomon's Temple, and when James died Bishop Griffith Williams' funeral sermon was entitled "Great Britain's Solomon.")

Darnley may have thought the same thing as the French king, for he was so angry at someone—perhaps Riccio, perhaps his queen, who, possibly from fear of syphilis, no longer shared his bed—that in early 1566 he allowed himself to be used by certain Protestant lords, who were worried about the queen's Catholicism. He went to Holyrood Palace with a group of thuggish nobles to murder a pleading Riccio, who was clutching the pregnant Mary's skirts. Riccio cried out, "Madonna, io sono morto, giustizia, giustizia." Mary, heavy with child, was herself in great danger. She was imprisoned for a time until she managed to charm the mercurial Darnley once more and fled the palace with him.

For this act of lèse majesté, and for other failures, Mary came to loathe the weak and vicious Darnley. Soon she took up with the sinister James Hepburn, 4th earl of Bothwell, simian in appearance and violent in action—"ay, that incestuous, that adulterate beast." Mary and Bothwell conspired to murder Darnley, perhaps trying first to poison him. His body when found was covered with black pimples—"Most lazar-like, with vile and loathsome crust, All my smooth body"—which may, however, have been the product of advanced stages of syphilis, suggested also by the pits in his skull (Pearson; see figure 2). He was finally killed on February 9, 1567, after being brought to a house outside Edinburgh, where Mary arranged to be seen visiting him, as if there were no difficulties between them, and left shortly before the house was blown up. Darnley's body was found unclad, lying *in horto*—"sleeping within my orchard"—strangled, alongside the dead body of a naked attendant. A charge of homoeroticism? John Knox, the head of the reformed Scottish Kirk, reported, falsely, that Darnley's corpse was hurriedly interred beside the tomb of David Riccio to signal the completion of Mary's revenge for Riccio's death. In fact, Darnley was embalmed in the manner of the ancient Scottish kings and buried in the royal vault, where he properly belonged, alongside the corpse of James V, the queen's father, in the Abbey Church of Holyrood, where the body remained until the roof collapsed in 1776 (Pearson). The tombs were looted at that time, and

Darnley's skull was carried off, to be passed through several hands, going first to the Rooms of the Society of Antiquaries in Edinburgh, and ending in 1869 in the Museum of the Royal College of Surgeons, where a Victorian phrenometrician, like so many historians anxious to blame Mary's enemies for all that happened, examined it and declared that "not even the men of the early Paleolithic period had worse frontals than Darnley, but they compensated for it in their parietal dimensions" (Pearson, 52). Other scientists used this same evidence to argue that the skull was not authentic, but the question became moot in 1941 when a portion of the Hunterian Museum, which contained the skull, was destroyed by fire as a result of an air raid (Allen).

Mary never admitted any part in the murder—"As kill a king!"—but like Gertrude she scarcely bothered with the formalities of mourning and was seen everywhere with Bothwell, who, though it was never proven, was universally believed to have murdered her husband. On May 15, three months and one week—"nay, not so much, not two"—after Darnley's death, Mary and Bothwell married. "Thrift, thrift, Horatio, the funeral bak'd meats did coldly furnish forth the marriage tables."

The royal scandal, like those of the love lives of the British royal family in the late twentieth century, spread throughout Europe. Mary was hastily condemned by pope and kings alike. Even the French and the Spanish, normally the Catholic allies of the Scottish queen against Protestant England, remonstrated with her, and the queen of England wrote in careful but strong terms, "horrified at the abominable murder of her husband," piously advising Mary to act like "a noble princess and a loyal wife." Mary's subjects, who had previously worshiped her, turned on the queen of Scots in the streets and called her "whore," threatening to kill and burn her as an open adulteress and murderer. Within a month the Scottish church and the Protestant nobility, seeing an opportunity to rid themselves of a Catholic ruler, rose against her and Bothwell, defeated them at the battle of Carberry, and sent Mary in flight to England, where Elizabeth imprisoned her.

After his mother fled Scotland, James at the age of one was made king by the party of the Kirk and the Protestant barons. Raised from birth by a succession of substitute fathers, stern guardians and demanding tutors, his life was lonely and terrifying. In a kingdom where clan chieftains still ruled in the highlands and feudal barons regularly raided, murdered, poisoned, besieged, and kidnapped one another in the rest of the kingdom, the young king, a pawn in the struggle for power between the barons, was blooded in one terrible event after another. The "carnal, bloody, and unnatural acts, . . . accidental judgments, casual slaughters, . . . deaths put on by cunning and [forc'd] cause" of Elsinore would have held no surprises for a king who had grown up amid Scottish politics and in what his tutor George Buchanan aptly called "the bludie nest" of the palace of Holyrood. At a young age (see figure 3) James saw his grandfather killed in a coup attempt. He himself was kidnapped and sequestered at various times. His first two regents were assassinated, the third died of natural causes, and, having matured a bit himself, he had the fourth executed.

The duty of revenge for the murder of his father, King Henry I of Scotland (Darnley), was explicitly laid on James as a child by his grandparents. To prevent James from forgetting his responsibility, the Lennox family commissioned in 1567—68 a remarkable painting, *The Darnley Memorial,* by Livinus de Vogelaare, that showed the tomb of King Henry, with his effigy on top, in full armor—"armed cap a pe." Before the tomb the youthful James and members of the Lennox family pray for revenge in words that appear on labels issuing from their mouths. A plaque on the wall in the background commands the king of Scots to remember his father's death until God uses him as the means to avenge it. The details of the murder appear in relief on the front of the tomb (see figure 5).

After he fled Scotland, Bothwell turned pirate and ended his life chained to a pillar in a Danish prison. He died insane in 1578, but not before exonerating Mary of any involvement in the murder of the king. There was no good reason to believe the deathbed confession of a madman, but James and his ministers found it politically convenient to do so. They declared Mary to have been innocent—"leave her to heaven"—thus clearing the royal family of criminal activity, and published the earl of Morton, who was being troublesome in various ways at the time, as the real criminal, immediately executing him for the crime, using for the purpose "the maiden," a crude guillotine Morton had invented.

This would seem to end it, but the spirit of revenge ran deep in these noble Scottish families, and it turned out to be useful in subsequent political maneuvers. Certainly James was relentless in avenging any slight to his family and person. His mother, six months pregnant when Riccio was murdered, is reported to have said that she had "that within in her belly" which would avenge her on the Ruthven family. The elder Ruthven died soon after, but his son, William, the first Earl Gowrie, kidnapped James in 1582 and held him hostage for a year. James in turn executed Gowrie in 1584 and brought the house to extinction in 1600 after what he called "the Gowrie conspiracy" occurred. James claimed, in a story that has always seemed suspicious, that he had been lured (with a tale of buried treasure!) to Gowrie House and attacked there. He called for help, and in the ensuing struggle the last two Ruthvens were killed. James made his escape from the trap the occasion of a national holiday, August 5, Gowrie Day, first in Scotland and later in England.

Death also pursued with extraordinary thoroughness all those lords, like Morton, who had been involved in one way or another in the murder of Darnley and in the subsequent deposition of Mary. James, earl of Moray, was assassinated; Archbishop Hamilton was hanged; the earl of Lennox was stabbed in the back by his jailer; William Maitland, "Secretary Lethington," poisoned himself to avoid trial; John Stuart, 4th earl of Athol, was poisoned at a banquet; George Gordon, 6th earl of Huntly, had a seizure at a football game and died seeing ghosts; the earl of Argyll died in agony from the stone (gallstones); Kircaldy of Grange was hanged; and the brutal Gilbert Kennedy, 4th earl of Cassilis, was fatally thrown from his horse. James's hand was not always visible in these deaths, but the revenge was spectacularly gory and complete.

Mary and her son never saw each other after his first year, and the letters they exchanged were proper and cool. As James grew older, his mother became more and more of a political embarrassment. So long as she lived, her rights to the Scottish throne were legally prior to his, and dissident nobles from time to time could and did cause trouble in Scotland by taking up her cause. Furthermore, by antagonizing Elizabeth with her plotting, Mary kept jeopardizing James's hopes to be named heir to the English throne. But when Elizabeth began to feel that her life might be significantly simplified by getting rid of Mary, James had to protest, as a son and as a king, in a letter to the English queen:

> What thing, madame, can greatlier touch me in honour that [am] a king and a son than that my nearest neighbour, being in straitest [friend]ship with me, shall rigorously put to death a free sovereign prince and my natural mother, alike in estate and sex to her that so uses her, albeit subject I grant to a harder fortune, and touching her nearly in proximity of blood. What law of God can permit that justice shall strike upon them whom he has appointed supreme dispensators of the same under him, whom he hath called gods and therefore subjected to the censure of none in earth, whose

anointing by God cannot be defiled by man unrevenged by the author thereof, who, being supreme and immediate lieutenants of God in heaven, cannot therefore be judged by their equals in earth? What monstrous thing is it that sovereign princes themselves should be the example-givers of their own sacred diadems' profaning. (January 26, 1587, Letter 26)

This was a good line of argument, for Elizabeth was extremely skittish about setting unhappy precedents by executing any of the Lord's anointed rulers. But once Elizabeth and her councillors had concluded in 1587 that it was necessary to kill Mary, James made it clear in secret that he would not play his ace and ally Scotland with the Catholic powers on the Continent. *Mortui non mordent,* "the dead don't bite," his cynical emissary, the Master of Gray, remarked privately to Elizabeth when they discussed how James would respond to the death of Mary. Polonius describes the procedure perfectly, "And thus do we of wisdom and of reach, With windlasses and with assays of bias, By indirections find directions out" (2.1.61).

Perhaps James was still playing the role of avenger of the death of his father when he did nothing to prevent the execution of the mother who was complicit in that death. Perhaps he was merely allowing a difficult political problem to solve itself. Very likely both. But in the world of smooth political surfaces a blood feud that encompassed the death of one's mother could not appear openly. Like a pious son, James tried, not entirely successfully, to persuade the antiquarian William Camden to include a favorable view of Mary in those of his *Annales* dealing with Elizabeth's reign. He also had his mother's body removed from Peterborough Cathedral in 1613, where it had been brought earlier at his command from the hasty tomb at Fotheringay, to Westminster Cathedral and placed it in a chapel directly across from the tomb of her executioner, Elizabeth Tudor. Work on a tomb of equal grandeur to Elizabeth's began in 1606, under the direction of the earl of Northampton, but it was not until 1613 that the work was done. Only ten years after his accession had James felt secure enough on the English throne to risk outraging public opinion, which still demonized Mary. History's ironic comment on the whole bloody business of the death of princes appeared with the opening of Mary's crypt in the nineteenth century, when it was found to contain beside her own corpse those of twenty-seven other bodies, including, among a number of Stuart royal infants, her grandchildren, Prince Henry and Elizabeth of Bohemia; her grandson, the hero of the Civil War, Prince Rupert of the Rhine; and her cousin, the unhappy Arbella Stuart.

The severed heads of the Stuarts seemed to end up in London with fatal regularity. The skull of James's great-grandfather, James IV of Scotland, resided in Jacobean times as a grisly trophy in Saint Michael's Church in Wood Street, where it had been brought after he had been killed on Flodden Field in 1513 by the English army of Henry VIII (Stow). The famous tiny, egglike head of Mary (see figure 6), that dropped out of its red wig after her beheading at Fotheringay, presumably still lies in the lead wrapping that contains her body in Westminster Cathedral. As we have seen, the skull of her husband Darnley resided for a long time at the Museum of the Royal College of Surgeons, and Charles I lost his head outside the window of the Banqueting House his father commissioned.

The revenge plot in *Hamlet* never follows the Stuart revenge plot so closely that it would have caused James to feel that the personal history of his family in its most intimate details was being handled on the stage. Too close a parallel would have brought the performance as quickly to an end as it did in Elsinore, where Claudius, frightened by the mirror *The Murder of Gonzago* held up to him, rose, called for lights, and rushed out to pray for his sins in the royal pew of the nearby chapel. Still, the pattern fits loosely: a legitimate king murdered by his wife and a usurper who soon marry, a son on whom lies the responsibility for revenge. And although young Darnley and Old Hamlet appear to have little in common, there is a good deal of the clever Machiavel in Bothwell and in Claudius; and a Gertrude whose only way of dealing with men is seduction is not a world away from Mary, queen of Scots. If this left James to play the part of the educated and philosophical Hamlet, no one would have been surprised, and certainly the pedant king would not have been offended by so noble a version of his studious nature.

Nor would the handling of the revenge plot have been uncongenial to the new king. Centuries of overly scrupulous interpretations of the play have thoroughly confused our understanding of where it stands on the matter of revenge, but in the simplest and most direct sense it comes out pretty much where orthodox religious and state views of the matter rested at the time: "Vengeance is mine, saith the Lord." The blood feud is attractive to Hamlet when the Ghost first commands it—"Haste me to know it that I may sweep to my revenge"— but impediments of conscience and occasion prevent the revenge until it is arranged, not by Hamlet, who becomes only the agent in the final scene, but by "some divinity that shapes our ends."

Whatever his private interests—and they were very private—James was officially at one with this view of revenge in *Hamlet*. Revenge remained a major fact of life in a still-primitive Scotland, and Keith Brown's study of the subject estimates that in any given year in James's reign there were upward of fifty major blood feuds going on simultaneously. In attempting to make Scotland into a modern, orderly state where the king's peace was kept, James, like other Renaissance monarchs of advanced views, did what he could to stop the feuding. Without paltering, he analyzed blood revenge as a "naturall sicknesse that I have perceived this estate subject to in my time, [it] hat beene a fectlesse arrogant conceit of . . . greatnes and power; drinking in with their very nourish-milk, that their honor stood in . . . for anie displeasure, that they apprehend to be done unto them by their neighbors, to take up a plaine fied [feud] against him; and (without respect to God, King or commonweale) to bang it out bravely, hee and all his kinne, against him and all his" (*Basilikon Doron*, 24).

There was nothing in *Hamlet* to embarrass the king, though much to intrigue him, but perhaps as he rose from the play to go on to the banquet and the gaming tables on the morning of December 27 he may have allowed himself a small "Ah, weel."

The King's Men put on another five plays in the following days amid many intrigues and celebrations. Carleton wrote Chamberlain on January 15 that "We have had here a merry Christmas and nothing to disquiet us save brabbles amongst our ambassadors, and one or two poor companions that died of the plague." Masques, not plays, were the centerpieces in the extended celebration of the Christmas festivities, and they were deeply concerned with Spanish and French politics that year. James was genuinely dedicated to the cause of peace with Spain, after many years of war, and despite his French family connections and his familiarity with French culture—his French was at least as good as and antedated his English—he was concerned from the beginning of his reign to establish good relations with Spain's Philip III. Raleigh, who represented piracy and the long naval wars with Spain, had already been sacrificed at Winchester to this end, and now it was planned to give Juan de Tassis, the newly arrived Spanish ambassador, special treatment. He was feasted by the king on the first night of the Christmas festivities, December 26, when *Hamlet* was likely presented, and he was to be the guest of honor at the queen's masque on Twelfth Night, the high point of the season.

The French ambassador Beaumont, however, expected that as the representative of England's long-standing ally against Spain, he would be given precedence over de Tassis at the Twelfth Night festivities. The situation was most awkward, and critical, so some ingenious diplomat tried to solve it by honoring Beaumont first, giving him the place of honor beside the king at the performance of a masque of the Chinese Magician performed by the male courtiers on the night of January 1. Carleton describes to Chamberlain how the "younge Lordes and chief Gentlemen," using the familiar device of being travelers from a far country (similar to the masque of the Muscovites in *Love's Labour's Lost*), pleased the king and Beaumont with

a maske brought in by a magician of China. There was a heaven built at the lower end of the hall out of which our magician came down, and after he had made a long sleepy speech to the king of the nature of the country from whence he came, comparing it wth ours for strength and plenty, he said he had brought in clouds certain Indian and China Knights to see the magnificency of this court; and thereupon a traverse was drawn and the maskers seen sitting in a vaulty place with their torchbearers and other lights which was no unpleasing spectacle. The maskers were brought in by two boys and two musicians, who began wth a song, and whilst that went forward they presented themselves to the king. The first gave the king an impresa in shield wth a sonnet in a paper to express his device and presented a jewel of £40,000 value which the king is to buy of Peter van Lore. But that is more than every man knew, and it made a fair show to the French ambassador's eye, whose master would have been well pleased with such a maskers present but not at that price. The rest in their order delivered their escutcheons with letters, and there was no great stay at any one of them save only at one who was put to the interpretation of his device. It was a fair horse-colt in a fair green field, which he meant to be a colt of Bucephalus race and had this virtue of his sire that none could mount him but one as great at least as Alexander. The king made himself merry with threatening to send this colt to the stable, and he could not break loose till he promised to dance as well as Banks his horse. The first measure was full of change and seemed confused but was well gone through withal, and for the ordinary measures they took out the queen &c. (January 15, 1604)

It no doubt did make a fair show to the French ambassador's eye, but when Beaumont, a touchy man at the best of times, learned that the Spanish ambassador was to be the honored guest at the queen's Twelfth Night masque, Samuel Daniel's *The Vision of the Twelve Goddesses*, he went to pieces at this indignity to himself, to his king, and to his nation. He went so far as to threaten "at the hazard of my life to kill the Spaniard . . . at the feet of the king" (letter to Henri IV, January 23, 1604; in Sullivan, 193).

Seeking to placate him without giving in altogether and offending de Tassis, the king's political advisers came up with the not-so-good idea that the queen's Spanish sympathies—she was in the process of becoming a Catholic and probably converted in early 1604—could be blamed for her preferring de Tassis. After all, it was her masque and, besides, it could be pointed out that (as was plain for all to see) the king had difficulty controlling her. To placate Beaumont still further, the queen's masque would be postponed for two days, to the night of January 8. In its place on the critical Twelfth Night, another masque put together by the male courtiers, a minor affair combining performance of a play, a running at the ring, and some kind of enhanced Scottish sword dance, was performed. Neither ambassador was officially invited to this *Gesamtkunstwerk*, but both were free to attend in a private capacity. Understandably, neither did. Carleton describes what happened without any enthusiasm: "at night there was a play in the queen's presence, with a masquerade of certain Scotchmen who came in with a sword dance, not unlike a matachin, and performed it cleanly; from thence the king went to dice into his own presence and lost £500, which marred a gamester, for since, he appeared not there, but once before was at it in the same place and parted a winner" (January 15, 1604).

At the end of these awkward diplomatic maneuvers, the king's advisers felt that they had placated Beaumont sufficiently and now were free to massage the Spanish ambassador's ego, giving him the full treatment on January 8 when *The Vision of the Twelve Goddesses* was at last performed. The Polish ambassador was also invited to this performance, along with the staffs of the Florentine and Savoyard embassies, but the hotheaded French ambassador was barred from the hall to avoid any unpleasant scene.

Daniel's masque was a rudimentary piece of theater but a masterly piece of patronage writing, providing roles as goddesses for the queen and eleven of the great court ladies. The queen herself took the part of Pallas Athena, and other noble ladies of her circle—among them Lady Penelope Rich (Sidney's Stella), the countess of Hertford, and Lucy, countess of Bedford—danced the other divinities. A paradisiacal mountain was constructed, probably at the screen end of Hampton Court's Great Hall, since the king's apartments were at the dais end and he would have entered from that direction (see figure 23). Down this mountain the goddesses—costumed in the gowns of the dead Eliza, the Virgin Queen—descended in threes to the sounds of stirring music, until they came to a temple, where they spoke with a "Sibylla," who praised the new king and his kingdom in sonorous, mystical terms. Queen Anne was especially striking for the shortness of her dress—which was probably not, therefore, as might have been expected from someone who loved fashion, one of Elizabeth's—which revealed her ankles and her legs to close to the knee, as well as for her red favours, which declared her sympathy with the Spanish cause. Carleton was mildly scandalized and remarked ironically, "Only Pallas had a trick by herself, for her clothes were not so much below the knee but that we might see a woman had both feet and legs, which I never knew before" (January 15, 1604).

The goddesses had only a few brief lines, dancing rather than speaking being their skill. Then they proceeded down the hall to the front of the State, where the king and the Spanish and Polonian ambassadors sat. After they made their curt-seys to the king, the revels began in the "piazza," the open area between the State and the stage. Prince Henry, still awake, was "tossed from hand to hand like a tennis ball." Although the Catholic and pro-Spanish queen could not dance with that country's ambassador (this would have been too open an insult to the strong anti-Spanish faction at court), her favorite lady-in-waiting, Lucy, countess of Bedford, "took him out," while Lady Susan Vere danced with the Polonian ambassador. The two ambassadors

bestirred themselves very lively, especially the Spaniard [dressed in splendid red] for his Spanish galliard shewed himself a lusty old reveller. The goddesses they danced with did their parts, and the rest were nothing behindhand when it came to their turns; but of all for good grace and good footmanship Pallas bore the bell away. They retired themselves toward midnight in order as they came and quickly returned unmasked but in their masking attire. From thence they went with the king and the ambassadors to a banquet provided in the presence [chamber], which was dispatched with the accustomed confusion; and so ended that night's sport with the end of our Christmas gambols. (Carleton to Chamberlain, January 15, 1604)

Nursing his grievances at home, Beaumont was not in the slightest deceived by all this and wrote bitterly to his king about dark insults to the honor of France. Henri IV, who was used to such indignities and knew exactly what they were worth, accepted it all with sangfroid and looked for another ambassador.

By Twelfth Night the King's Men had already packed their costumes in their hampers and, the London public theaters still being closed by plague, had gone off to perform on January 6 in Essex at Maldon. They were back at Hampton Court, however, by Candlemas, February 2, when they put on a play before the Florentine ambassador. The king must have been pleased with their services that Christmas for he made them a "free gift" of £30 on February 8 to help make up some of the losses they suffered from being unable to play in the city.

With the plague at last abated and their patron returned to Whitehall, the king's players followed him there and performed before him on February 19. Ben Jonson's *Sejanus*, the last play in which Shakespeare is recorded to have been an actor, was one of the plays known to have been performed in court that season, and there are reasons to think that it was the last play put on by the King's Men that season. It caused trouble. Jonson had already been asked to leave a performance at court for obstreperous behavior, and his play about the Roman emperor Tiberius, who spent all his time in depraved pursuits on Capri and left the business of government to his favorite, the cruel and ruthless Sejanus, was too easily applied to James. His generosity to his favorites (particularly his Scottish followers), his already-apparent reluctance to engage in the tedious business of government (he would leave business to his council and frequently withdraw with his cronies and his beloved dogs to hunt the stag at Royston or Theobalds), and perhaps even his open pleasure in young men, all identified him with Tiberius. Jonson told Drummond years later that the sinister earl of Northampton, by now the second most powerful man in the kingdom, had held a grudge against him for brawling with one of his attendants and had had him "called befor ye Councell for his Sejanus & accused both of popperie and treason" (Jonson, I, sec. 325, 141). The playwright talked his way out of trouble this time, but *Sejanus* revealed a tendency on Jonson's part toward risky satiric games in his plays that would land him in trouble time and again.

All in all it had been a rewarding and exciting season for the King's Men, but they must have been happy to escape the power struggles and intrigues of the court. On April 9, with the end of Lent, the public theaters opened again, and they were back in business at the Globe.

One of the most romantic of the European royal families, the Stuarts boasted that they traced their lineage back before the Christian era, farther than Habsburgs, Tudors, or Bourbons, to a time when there were no people in Scotland. In truth, they had ruled Scotland only for several generations, and their succession was as filled with murder and violence as that of any of the other Renaissance princes.

Mary, queen of Scots, raised in France, returned to Scotland in 1561 and married her cousin Henry Darnley in 1565. Jealous of her reputed affair with her Italian secretary, David Rizzio, Darnley terrified her by killing Rizzio in her presence while she was pregnant with James Stuart, and she probably avenged herself shortly afterward by murdering him. A few months later she married her lover, the ferocious earl of Bothwell, and the scandal drove them both out of the country. Mary fled to England, where Elizabeth, fearing her claim to the English throne, imprisoned her and eventually sent her to the block, in 1587, on the eve of the invasion by the Armada, when Mary's plotting with the English Catholic party grew too dangerous to be tolerated any longer. Shakespeare adapted this story for his plot in *Hamlet*, 1600, where Gertrude resembles Mary in her infatuation and "o'erhasty marriage" with Claudius.

James succeeded his mother in Scotland at the age of one, and was soon sworn by the Lennox family to avenge his father's death. Lonely and frightened as a child, he had many male lovers, probably beginning with Esmé Stuart when he was in his early teens. In 1599 he married Anne, a Danish princess. Three of their many children survived infancy: Henry, who died in 1612; Charles, who succeeded his father; and Elizabeth, who became the Winter Queen of Bohemia. James succeeded Elizabeth I to the English throne in 1603, but the Stuart line did not last long in England: his son Charles was beheaded in 1649, and his grandson James II, the last of the Stuart kings, was driven from the throne in 1688. In 1745 Bonnie Prince Charlie led the last Stuart attempt to recapture the throne.

1 Lord Darnley and Mary, queen of Scots, Elstracke engraving
(Courtesy Trustees of the British Museum)

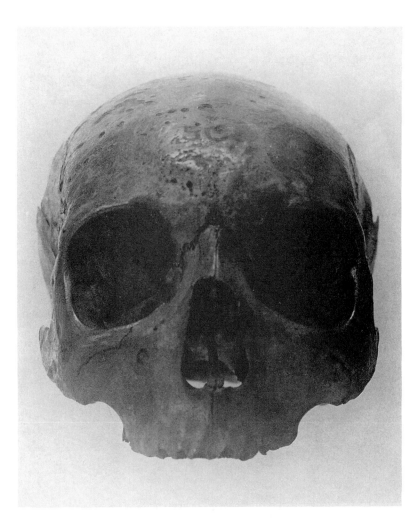

2 Skull of Henry Stewart, Lord Darnley, in the Museum of the
Royal College of Surgeons before its destruction in a bombing
raid in 1941 (From Pearson, *The Skull and Portraits of Henry
Stuart*, 1928)

3 James VI of Scotland, age 8,
attributed to Rowland Lockey after
Arnold van Brounckhorst, 1574
(Courtesy National Portrait Gallery)

4 Esmé Stuart, anonymous drawing, ca. 1580 (Enlarged; courtesy
Trustees of the British Museum)

5 The Darnley Memorial: George Vertue's engraving of a painting commissioned by Darnley's family to memorialize the death of
their son, by Livinus Vogelaare, 1568 (Courtesy the Collection of
Roland Frye)

6 Mary, queen of Scots, anonymous
anamorphic portrait (Courtesy
National Gallery of Scotland)

7 King James I, by Daniel Mytens, 1621 (Courtesy National Portrait Gallery)

8 Anne of Denmark, queen of England, attributed to William
Larkin, ca. 1612 (Courtesy National Portrait Gallery)

9 Henry, prince of Wales, by
Robert Peake, ca. 1610 (Courtesy
National Portrait Gallery)

Queen of Bohemia

10 Elizabeth Stuart, queen of
Bohemia, by Gerard Honthorst,
1642 (Courtesy Trustees of the
National Gallery, London)

3

THE KING'S PREROGATIVE

AND THE LAW

MEASURE FOR MEASURE, WHITEHALL

DECEMBER 26, 1604

Meeting the new king on his long and dilatory journey south from Edinburgh in the spring of 1603, a group of Puritan churchmen presented James with a thousand signatures, the Millenarian Petition, requesting consideration of various religious questions at issue between themselves and the more conservative powers of the Anglican state church. Having been raised as a strict Calvinist, James was theologically a Puritan, but having struggled as a king to control the Kirk, he distinctly favored the state religion in matters of church government. Yet James agreed to give the Puritans a hearing, and now, shortly after the end of the Christmas festivities in 1604, he fulfilled his promise at the Hampton Court Conference, setting up a debate between the high and low churchmen, with himself in his favored stance of learned judge observing and commenting, from slightly to one side, on the heatedly arguing adversaries.

The Scottish Solomon displayed his Latin, which was eloquent, quoted Scripture with the ease of someone who had been a close student of the Bible in some of its original languages from childhood, and dealt learnedly with subtle theological issues. Robert Cecil told the French ambassador that "I would wish my master read fewer [books] than he doth" (Major, 143), and James often neglected business to engage in long, drawn-out discussions with learned doctors and bishops about "whether a man, once in a state of grace, could ever thereafter be damned either 'totaliter' or 'finaliter' or both" (Major, 142). Much of the conference was taken up with the kind of trivial legalities that intrigued the donnish king, such as the questions of whether a woman or a lay person could legitimately perform baptisms, whether the sign of the cross should be used in baptism, whether the clergy should wear cap and surplice, whether a ring should be used in marriage, and the exact meaning of the words "with my body I thee worship" in the matrimonial service. Marriage was much discussed at the conference, and its problematics were picked up in one of Shakespeare's new plays that year, *Measure for Measure*, which featured a bed trick, sex before marriage but after verbal contract *de praesenti*, the death penalty for adultery, a debate on whether charity or chastity is the prior virtue, and forced weddings at the conclusion.

New laws governing marriage were put into effect as a result of the conference. Only a duly licensed cleric, in a parish church, between 8 a.m. and noon, and after the banns had been read on three consecutive Sundays or festival days, could legally pronounce a man and a woman husband and wife. Exception from these rules required a bishop's license. The most lasting consequence of the conference came without much discussion, after the Puritans requested an adequate translation of the Bible. James agreed, almost casually, and the result was the 1611 King James Authorized Version, the greatest prose work of its time, and a book that has reverberated ever since throughout the English-speaking world.

Having listened to the arguments at the conference, the authoritarian James was not impressed with the Puritan case, and he laid down the law as head of the church in no uncertain terms: "I shall make them conform themselves, or I will harry them out of this land, or else do worse." He well understood the close connection between established religion and the absolutist state: if you, he said to his bishops, "were out and [the Puritans] in place, I know what would become of my supremacy. No bishop, no king." In the end, he thoroughly enjoyed the part of supreme arbiter he played in the conference, writing to Lord Henry Howard, "We have kept such a revel with the Puritans here these two days as was never heard the like, where I have peppered them as soundly as ye have done the Papists there" (Letter 101, 1604). The conference, not Shakespeare's plays, had apparently been the entertainment high point of the king's Christmas.

By the beginning of Lent the plague had abated sufficiently for the court to return to Westminster, where the royal family took up residence in the great straggling palace at Whitehall, which covered twenty-three acres of jumbled gates, gardens, and public and private apartments, and even included a Whalebone Court, which was entered through an arch formed by a whale's jaw. As York Place in the Middle Ages, it had been the official residence of the archbishops of York and was greatly expanded by Wolsey. When that churchman fell from favor in 1529, requesting his royal master to "call to his most gracious remembrance that there is both heaven and hell," Henry VIII confiscated Whitehall and made it, rather than Westminster, the royal palace in London. Improvements were made by building to the west a sports complex containing a cockpit, tennis court, and tilting yard, which was connected to the main part of the palace by two gates, Holbein Gate and Whitehall Gate. These bridged King Street, which ran down from Charing Cross toward the Abbey, Westminster Hall, and Parliament (see figure 28). Holbein Gate was not designed by the painter, but Hans Holbein the Younger had rooms there, where he stayed when he was painting those hard-jawed wary-eyed portraits of the Tudor courtiers and putting a huge, dominating image of Henry, his parents, and Jane Seymour on the wall of the Privy Chamber (Thurley, 210). Shakespeare, who often performed in one of the halls of the palace, was knowledgeable enough about its history to have one of the gentlemen in his play *Henry VIII* remind another that it was no longer to be called York Place, "for, since the Cardinal fell that title's lost. 'Tis now the King's, and call'd Whitehall" (4.1.95).

An Italian visitor noted that the palace was "nothing more than an assemblage of several houses, badly built at different times and for different purposes," and it clearly lacked the overall design that made Hampton Court a figuration of the absolutist state. In the expansive spirit of Stuart court culture, James made numerous improvements, ranging from new stables and elaborate sundials to a new Banqueting House (43' x 120'), "strongly builded with brick and stone" in 1606, to replace the temporary Elizabethan structure that had burned earlier that year. But it was impossible to make the extensive palace of Whitehall symbolize divine-right monarchy in stone and space, and James always disliked the place. He commissioned a vast new palace from Inigo Jones in the latest neoclassic style, to rival the Escorial and the Louvre, but though a drawing exists, only the new Banqueting House was built after the 1606 Banqueting House burned in 1619.

As well as being the royal residence, the palace housed the executive offices of government in the time of the Tudors and Stuarts, until it too burned, after numerous earlier fires, on January 4, 1698, leaving behind only the two gates, which stood for many years, and Jones's Banqueting House, which still stands.

Whitehall Stairs and the River Gate gave access from the Thames to the central area of the palace, fronted by the Royal Chapel and the Great Hall, from which steps led up to the Great Chamber and the king's side of the central terrace, with the Pebbled Court and a "preaching place" in the center.

In the time of James I, Whitehall contained no area designed primarily as a theater, but there were several spaces in which plays were regularly performed. The Great Hall and the smaller Great Chamber were often used for performances, and the free-standing Banqueting House across the Pebbled Court from the Great Chamber provided a place for large-scale state entertainments. Across King Street was a cockpit, where James attended cockfights twice a week, and this was sometimes adapted for playing. After James's time the cockpit was reconstructed by Jones and his assistant John Webb specifically as a royal theater, in a manner that reveals paradigmatically all the basic physical arrangements of theater in the court (see figure 27).

On March 4 the long-delayed procession that should have occurred at the coronation moved from the Tower through the city of London to Westminster, giving many citizens their first chance to see and welcome their new king. The procession of the monarch through the city was one of the traditional ceremonies of state, and although the new king disliked crowds and expressed himself with vulgar vehemence on the subject, he rode his white jennet through the entire city, stopping at one triumphal arch after another to ponder the arcane symbols marked on them and endure the speeches delivered at each. The court marched with him, and in the parade were the King's Men, who as grooms of the chamber had each been issued four and a half yards of red cloth to make their liveries for the occasion.

James's first parliament met on March 19, and the Scottish king became entangled in English law almost at once, when the Crown tried to exercise its prerogative by declaring void a Buckinghamshire election to the House of Commons. This raised the question of ancient parliamentary privilege, and the House forced the king to accept that it had long been and still was the sole judge of its own returns. Encouraged by this success, the House proceeded to attack, unsuccessfully, several particularly galling royal privileges left over from feudal times. Worse still, it began meddling with religious matters, and while constantly protesting its loyalty, it refused to get on with ratifying the union of Scotland and England under the name of Great Britain that James so greatly desired. The king did not understand the workings of the House of Commons and years later complained petulantly to the Spanish ambassador Sarmiento that it was a disorderly body filled with cries, shouts, and confusion. He was surprised, he said, that "my ancestors should ever have permitted such an institution to come into existence," but since it was in place when he arrived, there was little he could do about it.

The king found particularly upsetting the Commons' insistence time and time again on the supremacy of ancient law over the royal prerogative, and from the outset of his reign his major power struggles centered on his belief that *la loi c'est moi*. In matters of church and state he continued to insist that he was the final authority, though forced regularly in practice to retreat from his absolute position.

The king did not, however, fancy direct confrontation with issues or opponents; he preferred to see himself as working always like Vincentio, Shakespeare's "old fantastical duke of dark corners" in *Measure for Measure*, indirectly to find directions out. Godfrey Goodman, bishop of Gloucester, observed that "the disposition of King James ... was ever apt to search into secrets, to try conclusions" (I, 3), which, "the actions of kings being written in such dark characters," was to be expected of the ruler. James Stuart liked to position himself to one side of the main action, while still controlling it, as he had at the Hampton Court Conference and earlier, as we shall see in the next chapter, at the trial of the Witches of Lothian in Scotland. Throughout the trials of the Gunpowder Plotters in the spring of 1606 he listened to the proceedings unseen, from behind a hanging in Westminster Hall, sending in questions and notes. But his control was none the less firm for his remove from center stage. He participated even in the interrogations of the plotters—sending questions, for example, to Father Henry Garnet, the head of the Jesuits in England, after the man had been tortured, about such matters as whether a priest who hears of treason in confession is bound to report it if the person confessing persists in his treasonous activities (Caraman). So much did James take this indirectness for granted as one of the tools of kingcraft that in *Basilikon Doron* he advises his heir to take care to always spy upon his court and be ever watchful of what was going on.

But despite all his cunning, the king could not, it seemed, manipulate the law, criminal or civil, without getting into grave trouble. The state trial of the Elizabethan swashbuckler Sir Walter Raleigh and the others who had been brought to the bar at Winchester in November 1603 on charges of high treason backfired badly, despite the extraordinary care with which the king had micromanaged it. The trial was political, and its main target was Raleigh, who had offended the new king by pursuing the death of the king's supporter, the earl of Essex, in 1601. In the transfer of dynasties from Tudor to Stuart, Raleigh, insolent but usually surefooted, lost his balance on the slippery ice of the court. The new king frowned on him when Raleigh rushed north to greet him on the progress from Scotland to London, for Raleigh was too violent, too closely associated with the old queen, the war party, and the anti-Spanish faction. Perhaps even Raleigh's fashionable association with tobacco offended a king who in 1604 published a polemic, the *Counterblast to Tobacco,* against the new vice of smoking. Raleigh's monopolies and his offices were removed when he was charged in 1603 with having knowledge of the foolish and hopeless plot that aimed to put Arbella Stuart on the throne and, with Spanish aid, to force more favorable treatment for English Catholics. Raleigh was not deeply involved, but he almost surely did angle for a pension from the funds that were to be raised from Spain to support the plot, and he failed to report to the authorities, as the law required, that treason was afoot. And so the trap closed on him.

Raleigh was an important counter in James's foreign policy. From the time he had arrived in England, the king had attempted to make peace with Spain and bring an end to a long generation of war. That he was able to sign the peace treaty in the summer of 1604 was in some part due to the fact that in 1603 he scapegoated Raleigh, the old scourge of the Spanish fleet, to show the Spaniards that England was in earnest about peace in the new era.

Although they had once cheered his victories over Spain, the people had conceived by 1603 a violent hatred for Raleigh as an atheist and a Machiavel, a man, proud as Lucifer, who had pressed for the execution of Essex, the popular hero who was his rival for Elizabeth's favor. A government mob shouted insults, threw mud and stones at him, and tried to overturn his carriage when he was brought to Winchester for his trial.

The government was taking no chances on the outcome of the trial. In addition to a jury of carefully selected knights brought in from London, a backup commission, which included Cecil—who had also urged the execution of Essex but had hedged his bets by corresponding with James—and Howard, oversaw the trial to ensure the right verdict. Lord Chief Justice Sir John Popham, the same judge who had interrogated Shakespeare's company about its performance of *Richard II* during the Essex rebellion, presided. A Falstaffian tun of a man, Popham had been kidnapped by Gypsies as a child and learned from them the art of thievery. As a judge, he grew rich and fierce, taking bribes from and then handing out maximum sentences to the wretches who came before him (Wallace).

The prosecutor was the attorney general, that great spokesman for the common law, Sir Edward Coke. In time Coke would become the king's mortal enemy for asserting the superiority of the law over the king, but for the moment he was trying to ingratiate himself with his new sovereign, hoping to be made serjeant and chief justice of one of the king's courts, in both of which ambitions he succeeded, largely because of his success as prosecutor of Raleigh and later of the Gunpowder Plotters. He attacked Raleigh with the full force of moral indignation that a man on the make can muster: "Well, I will now lay you open for the greatest traitor that ever was. This, my Lords, is he that hath set forth so gloriously his services against the Spaniard, and hath ever so detested him! . . . I will make it appear to the world that there never lived a viler viper on the face of the earth than thou! I will show you wholly Spanish, and that you offered yourself a pensioner to Spain for intelligence. Then let all that have heard you this day judge what you are, and what a traitor's heart you bear, whatever you pretended" (Bowen, 211).

It was outrageous, but it worked. The chief justice was a thief and a sadist, and the prosecutor was determined to write his name on the world with the blood of the accused. When Raleigh insisted that he had the right to be confronted by his accusers, the judge refused on a technicality. Raleigh replied sarcastically, "I know not, my Lord, how you conceive the law; but if you affirm it, it must be a law to all posterity." Popham's response has become a legal classic, "Nay, we do not conceive the law, we know the law" (Wallace, 208). Not only the procedures but the charges were brazen. Raleigh had been and remained the leader of the anti-Spanish party, and for him to be accused of plotting with Spain against England was crazy on the face of it. But even more ludicrous, the Crown was itself engaged in making peace with Spain at the time, and was using Raleigh as a part of that plan by charging him with collusion with Spain. Within a short time two of the overseeing commissioners, Cecil and Howard, like many other courtiers, would accept pensions from Spain that were many times larger than the amount Raleigh was accused of seeking.

In the face of this legal violence, Raleigh bore himself superbly, sardonic and amused always. But it did him no good, for he and the others charged with treason were all found guilty and sentenced to that dreadful fate reserved for common felons and traitors of higher rank: "You shall be had from hence to the place whence you came, there to remain until the day of execution; and from thence you shall be drawn upon a hurdle through the open streets to the place of execution, there to be hanged and cut down alive, and your body shall be opened, your heart and bowels plucked out, and your privy members cut off, and thrown into the fire before your eyes; then your head to be stricken off from your body, and your body shall be divided into four quarters, to be disposed of at the king's pleasure: And God have mercy upon your soul" (Wallace, 216). Figure 14 shows this sentence being carried out on the Gunpowder Plotters.

At nearby Wilton, whence he was masterminding the trial, James decided to let two priests involved in the plot be, as Carleton, who observed the event, remarked, "very bloodily handled." One simple-minded conspirator, George Brooke, was favored with beheading, but the crowd, which usually gathered in a holiday mood at the scaffold, had doubts about his guilt, and when Brooke's severed head was held up, as required by law, by the executioner, they refused to join the sheriff in crying "God save the king!"

On December 10, a week after the King's Men had come up to Wilton to lighten the atmosphere of the court with *As You Like It*, the remaining conspirators, excepting Raleigh, whose execution date had not been set, were brought to the scaffold. The king, sensitive to the change in public opinion, openly discussed his reasoning and his mercy at great length with an admiring court, and then spared the lives of the conspirators; but he directed his writ to be delivered and read only at the last moment. Like the czar's reprieve of Dostoevski, the scene of punishment and pardon was stage-managed for the maximum effect. There was unplanned additional drama when the messenger was late and had trouble until the last moment making his way through the crowd to the sheriff with the king's instructions. Raleigh, able to see but not to hear the proceedings, watched from a window in his prison nearby on a gray, rainy day, as the first conspirator was taken to the scaffold. After some delay, the poor wretch was told that his death was to be postponed for a short time, and he was led away and left to pray in private. As he moved off, the next conspirator was brought up and the grotesque farce was repeated. And so with the third. Only after the maximum suspense had been milked from this device (and the maximum psychological strain imposed on the traitors) were they returned to the scaffold together where, as Dudley Carleton, who was again watching the scene, put it in a letter to Chamberlain from Salisbury on December 11, 1603, they "looked strange one upon the other, like men beheaded and met again in the other world. Now all the actors being together on the stage (as use is at the end of a play)," they were told that their sentences had been commuted to exile or imprisonment. The crowd was vastly pleased. Carleton extended his theatrical metaphor by going on to say that "there was then no need to beg a plaudite of the audience, for it was given with such hues and cries that it went from the castle into the town and there began afresh." In time Raleigh, too, was reprieved from death but sentenced to spend the rest of his life in the Tower.

It seems to us a legal outrage, but there was nothing unusual in the procedures or the handling of Raleigh's case; this was in these times the standard course of law. In fact, if not in theory, the legal system of early modern England was a "theater of punishment," operating not only to render justice but to demonstrate the absolute power of the state and the helplessness of its subjects before that unlimited force. The criminal statutes defined as felonies punishable by death many acts that would nowadays be considered minor transgressions, such as poaching, stealing a loaf of bread, or, as in the only slightly exaggerated case in *Measure for Measure*, getting an unmarried woman with child. And in the law no mitigating circumstances, such as the fact that Claudio and Julia were engaged to be married, were admitted. *Measure for Measure* hardly exaggerates the state of the law. Judges like Popham were as absolute as Angelo and Escalus, and Newgate and the Clink were filled with condemned men and women in circumstances as wretched as those of the eternal prisoner Barnardine. Torture was a regular feature of legal proceedings. Even the reasonable Escalus thinks of the torture chamber immediately he scents resistance to authority: "Take him hence; To th' rack with him! We'll touze you Joint by joint, but we will know his purpose" (5.1.311). Executions were public spectacles in which the victims confessed their crimes, asked forgiveness, forgave their executioners, committed their souls to the next world, and in general made as good a show of it as they could. The bloodiness of the executions—the beheadings, the burnings alive at the stake, and the hanging, drawing, and quarterings—made shatteringly memorable the power of the state. After the bloody theater of justice administered, the heads of the executed were held up for all to see and later impaled on spears and displayed on the tops of nearby towers.

Mercy was necessary in such a violent system if it was to remain at all bearable, but the frequent pardons that manifested forgiveness also served to reinforce the life-and-death powers of the magistrate:

The pardon [was] important because it often put the principal instrument of legal terror—the gallows—directly in the hands of those who held power. . . . Discretion allowed a prosecutor to terrorize the petty thief and then command his gratitude, or at least the approval of his neighbourhood as a man of compassion. It allowed the class that passed one of the bloodiest penal codes in Europe to congratulate itself on its humanity. It encouraged loyalty to the king and the state. . . . And in the countryside the power of gentlemen and peers to punish or forgive worked in the same way to maintain the fabric of obedience, gratitude and deference. (Hay, 48)

"Rawley" 's bravura performance in the theater of punishment turned him overnight from a villain to a national hero. Queen Anne took him up to spite the king. Prince Henry, looking for another way to distinguish his warlike and princely self from his cowardly, peace-loving father, became Raleigh's patron, visiting him in the Tower and encouraging him to write his history of the world. The court began to suspect James's deviousness, and meanness whispered, among other strange rumors, that he was a jealous author who hated Raleigh and wanted to get rid of him because his literary reputation was much higher than that of the king. In the end Raleigh became a cult figure, as he still remains, and many years after his eventual beheading Goodman, bishop of Gloucester, could write, "I know where [Raleigh's] skull is kept to this day, and I have kissed it" (I, 69).

The King's Men had gone back to the Globe in the spring and early summer. They traveled to Oxford sometime during the summer but were back in town in August, where they were paid £21.12s. by the Crown for attending the Constable of Castile and his party, who arrived in England that month to sign on August 19 the peace treaty with Spain that James hoped would bring to an end the dirty, undeclared war that Raleigh and his kind had practiced for many decades (see figure 15). The Crown's confidence that the players made a good impression on visitors was underlined when the queen's players were assigned to another ambassador.

There were difficulties as well as successes for the players that year. Lord Say and Sele proposed on October 30 to give Cecil 1,000 marks as a gift and £40 annually to the king if he were granted the right to charge a penny a head on all admissions to the playhouses. This tax seemed perfectly reasonable to Say and Sele "since interludes and common playhouses are unnecessary and yield no penny to the King" (Harrison, 1941, 164), but the players had by now gained enough influence at court to fight off this threat to their business.

In December the King's players tried to please their royal patron by presenting at the Globe a lost play, author unknown, that portrayed the strange events at Gowrie House in Perth on August 5, 1600, where James charged that traitors had made an attempt on his life. The whole thing sounded fishy; it may have been a set-up in which James went to Gowrie House and then cried out that he was being attacked, in order to get his host, the earl of Gowrie, and his brother (against whose family, as we have seen, he had a blood feud) killed. Palace gossip, interested, as always, mostly in sex and romance, said that Ruthven, the earl, loved Queen Anne, or, more likely, that James had made a pass at Ruthven but been rebuffed. Whatever the truth, as a part of James's ongoing construction of a totem of kingship, Gowrie Day became a day of national celebration, just as what ironically came to be known as Guy Fawkes Day would become later a British holiday to commemorate the king's escape from the Gunpowder Plot.

Since James had himself made such good political use of the event, no doubt the players thought that putting the Gowrie affair on the public stage would please their royal patron. But they were new to big-stakes patronage, and although they drew a large audience, they made a serious error by putting a figure of the living king onstage in shadowy events that he would just as soon not have illuminated by the bright light of dramatic performance. John Chamberlain tells us what happened: "The tragedie of Gowrie with all the action and actors hath ben twise represented by the Kings players, with exceding concourse of all sortes of people, but whether the matter or manner be not well handled, or that yt be thought unfit that princes should be plaide on the stage in theyre life time, I heare that some great counsaillors are much displeased with yt: and so is thought shalbe forbidden" (December 18, 1604). *Gowrie* was closed down, as Chamberlain thought it would be, and no copy has survived. This misstep must have taught the players a great deal about the necessity of indirection in putting the king's interests onstage.

The 1604–05 theatrical season at court began early at Whitehall that year, and the titles of the plays given are recorded along with the exact dates of performance. The King's Men came up at Hallowmas to put on their new play *Othello*. As a young man, James had been so stirred by the great victory that the Christian alliance had won over the Turks in the naval battle at Lepanto in 1571 that he published in 1584 an epic poem in ballad meter on the subject, "The Lepanto." It was translated into French by Guillaume Du Bartas, who had stayed for a while at the Scottish court, and whose *Semaines,* the story of the first and second week of Creation, influenced James, no less than John Milton, to provide for his own poem a prologue in Heaven. Whether Shakespeare read "The Lepanto" is not known, but *Othello* portrays the war against the Turks and picks up many of the themes of "The Lepanto," along with its Venetian setting, its great heroes from many nations, its storm at sea, and its scenes in Cyprus. There are a number of verbal parallels as well, particularly a striking anticipation of the "malignant and turbaned Turks" and "circumcised dogs" whom Othello "smote":

> A bloodie battel bolde,
> Long doubtsome fight, with slaughter huge
> And wounded manifold
> Which fought was in Lepantoes gulfe
> Betwixt the baptiz'd race
> And circumsised Turband Turkes.
> (l. 6)

On November 4, the King's Men performed again, putting on that old favorite *The Merry Wives of Windsor.* The king's Privy Council, the highest executive body in the government, became concerned at this time about the cost of the masque planned for the coming Christmas and its propriety as a vehicle for Queen Anne, who was six months along with a short-lived child who would be called Mary after the king's dead mother. That Anne had appeared as an actress at all, and especially in such a short skirt, had been bad enough the year before, but now it was rumored that she, pregnant as she was, had asked the new writer of masques, Ben Jonson, to provide her and her attendants with parts of blackamoors, in which they would scandalously wear blackface. The Council got its nerve up and wrote to his majesty on December 17, "that in time past many Christmases have passed without such mark of note, dancing, comedies and plays being thought sufficient marks of mirth except some great strange Prince or extraordinary marriages fell at that time" (Harrison, 1941, 171). They took the further risk of adding, "As for the Queen's intention to take a part in a masque wherein there shall be fine ballets and dancing, they are bold to say it were a ready way to change the mirth of Christmas to offer any conditions where her Majesty's person is an actor." Ancient prejudices against actors and women on stage here combined and added to the fear of a scandal in court, but the council ended lamely by saying that they would not have the masque canceled, even though it would save a great sum, because "the ambassadors of foreign Princes will believe that the masque has been forborne because the King or the Queen lack £4000."

Carleton was again at court that Christmas, and wrote (January 7, 1605) that when Cecil's oldest son, William, was made a knight of the Bath, the queen's young and awkward brother, the duke of Holst, tried to persuade others to help him pay for an entertainment, which was not, Carleton thought, "bien séant à un prince." The various ambassadors, as usual, vied in shows of favor, and the Spanish ambassador feasted the duke and many of the court ladies, presenting them with fans and gloves at a banquet that ended with a play.

The King's Men and their playwright "Shaxberd," as his name is spelled in the warrant for payment that year, opened the Christmas festivities before the king at Whitehall on St. Stephen's Day with *Measure for Measure*, a sophisticated new comic version of the old tale of the corrupt judge who exchanges justice for sex with a beautiful young woman. The title may well have been suggested by the conclusion to James's *Basilikon Doron*, where he advises Prince Henry in biblical language: "And above all, let the measure of your love to everyone be according to the measure of his virtue."

Modern audiences have found *Measure for Measure* a difficult, complex play, and it has long been known as one of Shakespeare's "dark comedies," or one of his "problem plays." Interpretation has been busy over the years, and the lenient Duke who turns the enforcement of the laws over to "the prenzie Angelo" has been said to figure everything from God leaving humans the freedom to work out their own salvation, to the Freudian ego—the scene *is* Vienna—withdrawing from the psychic conflict and leaving the id (the sexual instincts that are so pronounced in Vienna) and the superego (the puritanical Angelo) to confront each other directly, as they do in analysis. But whatever modern ingenuity has found in the play, on the night after Christmas at Whitehall in 1604 it must have seemed to most of the audience a witty, fast-paced, and bawdy comedy, a romp almost, with lots of good low-humor scenes in brothel and jail, a wonderful malapropistic clown—"Peter Elbow and it please your honor"—a clever intrigue plot, and such sophisticated moral puzzles as whether the heroine's maidenhead was of greater value than her brother's life.

Shakespeare, as usual, had borrowed and improved his story of a lenient duke, who, finding it impossible to enforce the laws, has turned his authority over to his deputy, the puritanical Angelo, and his assistant, the elderly Escalus, and left the city. Angelo, a man so cold he was said to urinate ice water, condemns Claudio to death for getting his fiancée, Juliet, with child, but he is smitten with Claudio's sister, the virginal Isabella, and offers her her brother's life in return for sex. Isabella refuses and Claudio's death seems certain, when the duke reenters in disguise and arranges for the lady of the fascinating name, Mariana of the Moated Grange, who had once opened her chaste treasure to Angelo only to be abandoned by him, to substitute for Isabella in the darkness. The "bed trick" deceives Angelo, but he reneges on his word and requires Claudio's head sent to him instantly. The duke, however, arranges for the head of a pirate who has opportunely died that day to be substituted for Claudio's, and then resumes his old identity. In a big final scene he reveals the truth, punishes the wicked, and plights in marriage everyone in sight, including himself to the frigid Isabella.

While writing, at Prince Henry's command, his *History of the World* in the Tower, Raleigh observed that "whosoever, in writing a modern history, shall follow truth too near the heels, it may haply strike out his teeth" (*Works*, II, lxiii). The players knew the force of this remark only too well from their recent experience with *Gowrie*, where they had learned the hard way what James had earlier made emphatically clear in print: it was out of bounds to represent directly onstage a living monarch or his undisguised interests. But it was possible to get at these matters obliquely, and this they immediately proceeded to do in *Measure for Measure*, where they opened up onstage the primary concern of their royal patron at that moment, the relation of the ruler to the law.

Duke Vincentio of Vienna was not King James I of Great Britain, but everyone in the original audience would have noticed that they shared a number of personality traits, problems with the law, and ways of transcending the law to achieve justice. Most personally, both disliked the crowds who pressed around great ones and pulled at their persons and clothing on public occasions. James made no bones about his feelings on this matter, perhaps because of his terror of assassination, as well as of the endemic plague, and there had been a bad scene during the procession through London the previous spring in which the King's Men had marched. When his councillors urged the necessity of, if not "pressing the flesh" like a modern politician, at least showing himself to his people, James exclaimed furiously that he would pull down his breeches and show his arse to the throngs that were pressing for a glimpse of him. His phobia worsening, James would in later life issue a proclamation expressing "our high displeasure and offence at the bold and barbarous insolency of multitudes of vulgar people" (Law, II, 61). Duke Vincentio is not so vehement, but he takes care when giving his city over to the governance of Angelo to remark that

> I love the people,
> But do not like to stage me to their eyes;
> Though it do well, I do not relish well
> Their loud applause and aves vehement.
> (1.1.67)

His concern is stated even more tactfully a few scenes later where we hear of a loving people "subject to a well-wish'd king," who

> in obsequious fondness
> Crowd to his presence, where their untaught love
> Must needs appear offence.
> (2.4.27)

If, watching the play, the king saw something of himself in the stage duke's dislike of crowds, he could have also recognized some of his own problems with the administration of the law in Vincentio's difficulty in providing justice to his people. James often said that he was too lenient in dealing with malefactors; in addition, he must have known that some of his magistrates were untrustworthy, and he must have grimaced feelingly at the difficulty of administering the law through instruments as fallible as the stage constable Peter Elbow, who gets everything so confused that it is impossible to untangle it sufficiently to get it wrong: "If it please your honor, I am the poor Duke's constable, and my name is Elbow. I do lean upon justice, sir, and do bring in here before your good honor two notorious benefactors. . . . Precise villains they are, that I am sure of, and void of all profanation in the world that good Christians ought to have" (2.1.47).

But the problems with the law in 1604 after the fiasco at Winchester extended far beyond an inefficient police force to more basic problems of corrupt hanging judges, merciless statutes, and human nature itself. *Measure for Measure* picks up all these major issues. About the need for the law there is no question in the play. Human nature is fallen as far in Shakespeare's Vienna as in James Stuart's kingdom. At the very bottom of the human heap is Barnardine, a hardened criminal, who spends his days in jail drinking. He refuses to allow himself to be executed, no matter how reasonably his betters explain to him that the greater good of society requires his death. This is the old Adam that Freud called id: "A man that apprehends death no more dreadfully but as a drunken sleep, careless, reakless, and fearless of what's past, present, or to come; insensible of mortality, and desperately mortal" (4.2.142). When his jailers nervously try to force him out of his cell in order to execute him, they encounter something very resistant and very primitive; "He is coming, sir, he is coming; I hear his straw rustle," says the turnkey hopefully, but Barnardine refuses to die that day, or any other.

The rest of the population of the jail, which like those in our modern penal system seems to hold a large part of the citizenry, is less desperate but morally not much better than Barnardine: "Here's young Master Rash, he's in for a commodity of brown paper and old ginger. . . . Then is there here one Master Caper, at the suit of Master Three-pile the mercer, for some four suits of peach-color'd satin, which now peaches him a beggar. Then have we here young Dizzy, and young Master Deep-Vow, and Master Copper-spur, and Master Starve-lackey the rapier and dagger man, and young Drop-heir that kill'd lusty Pudding, and Master Forth[r]ight the tilter, and brave Master Shoe-tie the great traveller, and wild Half-can that stabb'd Pots, and I think forty more" (4.3.4).

Shakespeare's Viennese, resembling Freud's in this as in other ways, are as incurably sexual as they are foolish, venal, and violent. Those not in jail are to be found for the most part in whorehouses, associating with drabs, knaves, and bawds. There is Lucio the whoremaster, Pompey Bum the tapster cum pimp, and the ultimate "john," Master Froth, who gives his business to the whore Kate Keepdown and to Mistress Overdone the brothel keeper, married nine times and overdone by the last. Even a nice young man like Claudio beds Juliet before marriage. The puritanical judge Angelo has seduced Mariana, and Isabella's icy chastity, rather than preserving virtue, raises an untutored lust. It is indeed the "bawdy planet" that one of Shakespeare's characters styles it in a later play.

James had little to learn from his players about the failings of human nature in Edinburgh, London, or Vienna, but Calvinist that he was, he must have been struck by the play's startling image of original sin:

> Our natures do pursue
> Like rats that ravin down their proper bane,
> A thirsty evil, and when we drink we die.
> (1.2.128)

Shakespeare's view of human nature is, however, broader than Calvinist theology. It is not just that humanity in *Measure for Measure* is tainted with sexuality from birth; people also have a love affair with life, and a fear of death, so
deeply instinctive as to overwhelm all abstract considerations of morality and
honor. Claudio's instinct for self-preservation is more eloquent but no less fundamental than Barnardine's. When Claudio's sister, Isabella, comes to him in
death row, to tell him with loathing about Angelo's offer to exchange his life for
sex, she expects a heroic response and a big speech about death before dishonor.
But in a travesty of the courage with which a hero like Raleigh eventually died
on the scaffold in 1618 (first testing the edge of the ax with his thumb), Claudio,
facing death, has some very real doubts about the weight of his sister's maidenhead when set in the scales against his own oblivion: "Sure, it is no sin; Or of the
deadly seven it is the least." Death by contrast is, after all, so final, so complete:

> Ay, but to die, and go we know not where;
> To lie in cold obstruction, and to rot;
> This sensible warm motion to become
> A kneaded clod; . . .
> . . . 'tis too horrible!
> The weariest and most loathed worldly life
> That age, ache, [penury], and imprisonment
> Can lay on nature is a paradise
> To what we fear of death.
> (3.1.117)

In the face of the voracity of human appetites and the overwhelming fear of
death, the law seems necessary but futile. Willy-nilly, human beings will, as one
of Shakespeare's clowns had said, "hearken after the flesh," and Pompey Bum
says equally truly when he tells Escalus what would be required to control sex
in old Wien: "Does your worship mean to geld and splay all the youth of the
city?" (2.1.230). Good-natured tolerance such as the duke used in the old days
results only in liberty that "plucks Justice by the nose," but the law is too savage
to be strictly applied. The Viennese law punishing adultery by death is the kind
of ridiculous, inhuman law that regularly appears at the beginning of comedy,
where it blocks the young lovers for a time from marrying the persons of their
choice. But it also represents, in an almost literal way, the tendency of early
modern legal systems to make of very human slips felonies punishable by death.

The law overcompensated, then as now, for its difficulties in enforcing statutes by the excessiveness of its penalties.

Not only is the law too cruel to be applied to fallible human beings, those who administer it are inescapably, in modern police-speak, "perpetrators," hypocritical, self-seeking, ignorant, and corrupt. Angelo is a no-nonsense, law-and-order type, brushing away, as the law of his time did, all extenuating circumstances, running a court where mercy tempers justice not in the slightest.

In the end justice in the play comes not from the law but from the disguised duke, who, working obliquely (in something like the manner James also preferred), uses a series of tricks to bring about if not absolute justice then at least a comic ending. He cuts through the legal tangle not only with his perspicacity, good judgment, and clever machinations but by the use of mercy, the virtue suggested by the play's title, which ultimately derives from Christ's words in the Gospel of Matthew, that read in Shakespeare's Geneva Bible, "Judge not, that ye be not judged. For with what judgment ye judge, ye shall be judged and with what measure ye mete, it shall be measured unto you again."

But the power of the monarch still has its limits. What the duke can do by the exercise of his judgment and his absolute powers is captured in the kind of marriages that he arranges onstage at the end of the play. The duke himself is to marry the cold Isabella, who would rather go back to the convent; the hypocritical, ruthless, and unrepentant Angelo is paired with the doting Mariana; the fashionable man-about-town Lucio is tied to the whore Kate Keepdown. Only the marriage of Claudio to the pregnant Juliet offers some hope. This is the best that the duke's mercy and absolute power can achieve, and while the marriages are better than the death and depravity that threatened for a time, the ending of the play is obviously far from ideal.

Measure for Measure puts onstage, through the exaggerations of the comic lens, a justification of the king's justice and the dangers of the law that the Raleigh trial had made scandalously clear at Winchester. The criminal law inspired terror, with harsh arbitrary statutes inconsistently enforced. It was administered by corrupt judges and merciless prosecutors, who arranged public spectacles of bloody executions *pour encourager les autres.* Only the king's justice, coming from an absolute ruler like the duke or James, who operates above the law, penetrates all pretenses, is concerned for all the people, and is able to temper strictness with mercy, can turn leaden law into something that vaguely resembles golden justice. It may not have worked at Winchester, and the House of

Commons may have been skeptical about the king's superiority to the law, but the king's players could make it, almost, work on the stage.

Plays were by no means the only amusements at court that season. After many practical jokes, "sewing into the sheet, casting of the bride's left hose, and twenty other petty sorceries," Sir Philip Herbert, a great favorite of the king's, married the Lady Susan Vere, daughter of the earl of Oxford, on December 28, with high solemnities. The king himself, like Duke Vincentio, gave the bride away with many pretty compliments and a strange follow-up. The couple was married "in the chapel, feasted in the great chamber, and lodged in the council chamber, where the king gave them in the morning before they were up a *reveille-matin* in his shirt and his nightgown and spent a good hour with them in the bed or upon, choose which you will believe best" (Carleton to Chamberlain, January 7, 1605).

Later, Carleton further informed his correspondent, a number of male courtiers put on a masque of the "four seasons of the year and *Hymeneus*, which for song and speeches was as good as a play. Their apparel was rather costly than comely, but their dancing full of life and variety; only Sir Thomas Germain had lead in his heels and sometimes forgot what he was doing." On Innocents' Night, December 28, the King's Men performed an old play, presumably revised, *The Comedy of Errors*.

How playing could become the instrument of politics in a practical way appears in a trifling event that took place shortly after the first court performance of *Measure for Measure*. Robert Cecil, recently made Viscount Cranborne, and head of the queen's household, wanted to provide a banquet for Queen Anne at his mansion in the Strand, James having gone off hunting, and needed some entertainment to make the occasion more festive. He commissioned his adviser on patronage matters, the antiquarian Sir Walter Cope (whom Chamberlain mocked as "the idle oracle of the Strand"), to arrange for something suitable. Cope did not like his task, any more than did Polonius when Hamlet commanded him to see the Elsinore players well bestowed, and complained in a note to his master, "I have sent and bene all thys morning huntyng for players Juglers & Such kinde of Creaturs, but fynde them harde to finde." Annoyed, he left a note for these "creatures" to come to him. One of the Burbages, either Richard or Cuthbert, soon appeared but told Cope that "ther ys no new playe that the quene hath not seene, but they have Revyved an olde one, Cawled *Loves Labore*

Lost, which for wytt & mirthe he sayes will please her excedingly." There was still a problem, however. That play was already "apointed to be playd to Morowe night at my Lord of Sowthamptons, unless yow send a wrytt to Remove the Corpus Cum Causa to your howse in Strande. Burbage ys my messenger Ready attendying your pleasure" (Chambers, 1930, II, 332).

Cecil and Southampton, two powerful courtiers, close to the king, were by early 1604 competitors for royal favor, and each was trying to advance his cause by feasting the queen, and needed a play for the occasion. A new play would have been best, obviously, but a refurbished old one had to do. Southampton had the inner track in one way, having long been Shakespeare's patron, but Cecil was the most powerful man in the kingdom, and everyone, particularly the king's players, depended on his favor. Some kind of compromise was worked out, for another letter from Carleton on January 7, 1605, to John Chamberlain records that "the last nights revels were kept at my Lord of Cranbornes, where the Q. with the D. of Holst and a great part of the Court were feasted, and the like two nights before at my Lord of Southamptons."

The great occasion of the season was, as always, Twelfth Night. During that day, Prince Charles, still wearing heavy iron braces on his weak legs but well enough to be brought from Scotland at the queen's insistence, was installed as the duke of York with great ceremony, his "ornaments carried by nine earls," attended by eleven new knights of the Bath, including Cecil's son and a number of the king's favorites. "A public dinner was made in the great chamber, where was a table for the little duke and the earls and another apart for these new knights" (Carleton, January 7, 1605).

In the evening Ben Jonson's first masque was performed for the court. A great crush occurred at the beginning of the performance. The white staffs laid about them with their rods of office, and in an effort to keep order they locked a number of spectators out of the hall in the gallery until the performance ended. *The Masque of Blackness,* despite the earlier efforts of the council, was danced by the queen and her ladies made up as blackamoors, their faces and bare arms painted up to the elbows. Carleton was scandalized and felt that this "was a very loathesome sight and I am sorry that strangers should see our court so strangely disguised." "The presentation of the mask at the first drawing of the traverse," he went on, "was very fair and their apparel rich, but too light and courtesan-like." Things got out of hand at the end of the performance when "in the coming out, a banquet which was prepared for the king in the great chamber was overturned, table and all, before it was scarce touched. It were infinite to tell you what losses there were of chains, jewels, purses, and suchlike loose ware, and one woman amongst the rest lost her honesty, for which she was carried to the porter's lodge, being surprised at her business on the top of the terrace." (January 7, 1605).

In Elizabeth's time, Christmas festivities, like her court, were more seemly, and they had ended at the conclusion of Twelfth Night, but now they continued so long that even Carleton complained, "It seems we shall have Christmas all the year." The king's players had their part in the continuing festivities. Shakespeare's company was back at court on January 7 with a patriotic play, *Henry V*, and on the following night put on Ben Jonson's *Every Man Out of His Humour*. They came back to the palace on February 2, Candlemas, with the other Jonson humor play, *Every Man In*. On the following night they were ready to perform still again, but for some reason their performance was put off until Shrove Sunday, February 10, when they appeared for the first of three nights in a row, opening with *The Merchant of Venice*. For the only time on record the king commanded one of their plays to be repeated, and *Merchant* was on the boards again on the night of the twelfth. Did the king fall asleep at the first performance? Did he so like the clever courtroom arguments of Portia and Shylock, which were just his kind of thing, that he wanted to hear them again? Years later he would go back to see for a second time a Cambridge play, *Ignoramus,* that tickled his fancy with its satiric portrait of the lawyer who had been his prosecutor in the Raleigh trial, Edward Coke.

4

THE POLITICS OF MADNESS

AND DEMONISM

MACBETH, HAMPTON COURT

AUGUST 7, 1606

The king's players struggled in the autumn of 1605. Plague once again closed the theaters on October 5, before the winter season was well begun, and the company was on the road in the following months, at Oxford on October 9 and later at Barnstaple and Saffron Walden. These journeys kept them out of town in late autumn during the excitement of the discovery of the Gunpowder Plot, in which Guy Fawkes and a group of disaffected Catholics—including some acquaintances of Shakespeare's—tried to blow up the king and Parliament on the opening day of the new session, November 5. Unproven charges have since been made that the government itself set up the Gunpowder Plot, or at least allowed the plan to proceed after it had been discovered, in order to whip up patriotic support for the king and fury against the papists. Whether these charges are true or not, the occasion was exploited, like the burning of the Reichstag in the 1930s, to supercharge loyalty and increase hatred for a religious group already identified as the national enemy. James well understood how to manipulate public opinion in this way. Provocative posters were engraved and printed (see figure 19), and Parliament soon declared a national holiday celebrating the cult of royalty and its miraculous escape from its treacherous enemies.

By the middle of December, the King's Men were back at the Globe, and on December 26 they went up to the palace as usual to open the Christmas season at Whitehall, putting on a play in the Banqueting House. Trials of the surviving Gunpowder Plotters were going forward, and it was a time for high patriotism, for congratulating the king and the country on their narrow escape from disaster, and for damning the Catholics once again for their unreasonable attempts to bring down a Protestant government that never ceased persecuting them.

The King's Men were paid for ten plays at court that season, but titles were not specified in the warrants for payment. Presumably the company would have put on Shakespeare's new plays, as in previous years, and filled in with old plays that the court had not seen. They were called on again to perform that summer, twice at Greenwich and once at Hampton Court, on August 7, 1606, at the end of the visit of the royal bother-in-law, King Christian of Denmark, who had come to England to see his sister, who was pregnant for the last time. It is most likely that the play on this latter occasion was Shakespeare's new play *Macbeth* (Paul). The absence of swearing in the play indicates that it was either written or cleansed of profanity at some time after the Acte to Restraine Abuses of Players was passed by Parliament on May 27, 1606. The act imposed a fine of £10 on anyone who might "in any Stage play . . . jestingly or prophanely speake or use the holy Name of God or of Christ Jesus, or of the Holy Ghoste or of the Trinitie, which are not to be spoken but with feare and reverence" (Chambers, 1923, IV, 338).

King Christian also came to firm up his relations with England in anticipation of a war with Sweden, which his more practical council managed to delay until 1611. Not everyone was delighted with the visit. Sir Henry Neville remarked dryly, "We are in dayly expectation of the King of Denmark's arivall and the Queen's delivery, charges that we have little need of" (Nichols, II, 50). When Christian's ship arrived at Gravesend on July 17, James was at Oatlands hunting, and the Danish king had to wait aboard for a day until the English king came to greet him. Upon James's arrival there were welcoming entertainments in Latin, and, although Christian did not speak English, the rising playwright John Ford read two poems composed—in English—for the occasion, "The Monarch's Meeting" and "The Applause Song."

Once ashore, to James's annoyance, great patriotic crowds followed the monarchs and Prince Henry everywhere. At Eltham on July 21 there were "continual cries to God for His blessing, and to preserve them, their states and dignities, from all mallice and traytors' practises for ever." Going on July 24 to the sumptuous country house at Theobalds that James had by then extracted from Cecil, they were met with "such multitudes of people as were not to be

numbred" (Nichols, II, 62). They were welcomed with "The Song at
Theobalds," sometimes attributed to Ben Jonson, sung by a group of choristers
directed by John Lyly, the old playwright and inventor of Euphuism who long
ago had been the most fashionable writer in Elizabeth's court. After the song, the
kings walked under "a goodly Tree with leaves cut all out of greene silke, and
set so artificially, that . . . as the Kings Maiesties passed away, even in a trice, all
the leaves showere from the tree, both uppon the heads and Garmentes of both
the Kinges, and of a great multitude of their followers upon everie leafe beeing
written in golde Letters this word (*Welcome*) and uppon some twice (*Welcome*)"
(Allde, 12). Epigrams of greeting were tacked to the walls. Then came a pageant
written by Jonson, which opened with the figures of three Hours sitting above
the porch in the clouds, the first bearing a sundial, signifying law, the second carrying a clock, signifying justice, and the last an hourglass, signifying peace.

Then the party got down to serious pleasures. Sir John Harington, though
himself far from prudish, was considerably shocked by what now began to take
place. Writing to his friend Secretary Barlow he reported:

I came here a day or two before the Danish King came, and from the day
he did come untill this hour, I have been well nigh overwhelmed with
carousal and sports of all kinds. The sports began each day in such manner
and such sorte, as well nigh persuaded me of Mahomets paradise. We had
women, and indeed wine too, of such plenty, as woud have astonishd each
sober beholder. Our feasts were magnificent, and the two royal guests did
most lovingly embrace each other at table. I think the Dane hath strangely
wrought on our good English nobles; for those, whom I never could get to
taste good liquor, now follow the fashion, and wallow in beastly delights.
The ladies abandon their sobriety, and are seen to roll about in intoxication.
In good sooth, the parliament did kindly to provide his Majestie so season-
ably with money, for there hath been no lack of good livinge; shews,
sights, and banquetings, from morn to eve. (I, 348)

Later there was a "representation," paid for by Cecil and others, of the queen
of Sheba coming to Solomon. A drunken Sheba offered the kings rich foods, jel-
lies, and creams, but spilled them in the lap of the Danish king, and when he,
unfazed, rose to dance with her, he was so tipsy that he fell and had to be carried
off to bed. Faith, Hope, and Charity were by now totally smashed, and after
mangling their speeches reeled about and vomited before collapsing in the hall

in a stupor. Victory then approached in armor with a sword, which, as the champion of peace, James put aside, but she got so befuddled that she had to be led away to sleep on the steps of the chamber. "Now did Peace make entry, and strive to get foremoste to the King; but I grieve to tell how great wrath she did discover unto those of her attendants; and, much contrary to her semblance, most rudely made war with her olive branch, and laid on the pates of those who did oppose her coming" (Harington, I, 351).

The stay at Theobalds that began as a country house party ripened toward an orgy. The Danes were, as Hamlet lamented, noted for drunkenness, and their king was, like Claudius, a deep drinker, who on one occasion in later years pledged thirty-five toasts before being carried off in his chair by his admiring attendants. Matters came to a crisis when Christian, thinking he was being funny, made the cuckold's horns at the aged Charles Howard, earl of Nottingham, the Lord Admiral of England who was the legendary victor over the Armada (see figure 15) and who had recently married a young wife, Margaret Stuart, a distant cousin of King James. Violent protests by defenders of the lady's virtue and the earl's honor followed this boorish act. The lady herself was so deeply wounded that she continued to protest the insult to her honor through diplomatic channels for years. The shamed Danes promised to control their drinking and showed their delicacy by putting silver chains on the thumbs of anyone who imbibed too much and then nailing the chains to a post.

On July 28 the kings returned to the queen's palace at Greenwich and there saw two plays, titles unknown, by the King's Men. On the 31st, in a huge spectacle of state, the kings rode in a procession through London. "With great admiration passed these famous Kinges till they came to Cheapside, viewing the numbers of people which stood in windowes, the streetes, and other places; shewing lovely and gracious acceptance of their loves, by their favourable countenance" (Nichols, II, 68). John Marston, the fashionable satirist of the day and a rising playwright, wrote the Latin dialogue for the first pageant offered on that occasion, an allegory of Concordia, London, and Neptune. A second pageant, a "Pastoral Dialogue," written by John Lyly (who had not lost his court touch though he no longer had its favor), flattered the two monarchs shamelessly through the words of a shepherdess who told a shepherd she could only love him "when she could behold two Sunnes at one time of equall brightnesse when there were two Majesties of like splendour or two Kings in one state, with many such like imagined impossibilities, which now he shewed her were come to passe, approoving those two kings glorious Suns, two Majesties, and what else she had reputed impossible" (Allde, 25).

At Greenwich again on August 5, the holiday commemorating James's escape from the Gowrie plot, Lancelot Andrewes, the bishop of Chichester and the king's almoner, who was the most noted preacher of the time, took as his text Psalm 144, verse 10, "It is He that giveth salvation unto Kings, Who delivereth David His servant from the hurtful sword." Sermons were not only prime entertainments, attracting far larger audiences than plays, but they were, like plays— and not always so indirectly—instruments of state. Andrewes, who was James's particular favorite for his ascetic life and his dense, intellectualized rhetorical style, had chosen his text with care to celebrate not only James's escape at Gowrie but his more recent deliverance from the Gunpowder Plot. By this time all the Gunpowder conspirators had been tried and bloodily executed, including the leader of the English Jesuits, Father Garnet. But the fury against the Jesuits was not assuaged, and Andrewes condemned the Society of Jesus as locusts— "a kind of creatures who have a man's face, women's hair, but lions' teeth, and their tails the stings of scorpions" (*Sermons*, V, 235).

Later on the same day, and also on the next, a running at the ring and tilting took place, part of the court's encouragement of the fashionable cult of chivalry and of its own pretensions to being Camelot restored. Christian prided himself on his tilting, delighting to cut a knightly figure. Challenges had earlier been sent as far as France by four knights errant, James's favorites all: Lennox, Arundel, Pembroke, and Montgomery. Each knight now defended against professional tilters (like Master Forth[r]ight in *Measure for Measure*)—who were paid to lose to their noble adversaries—one of four "indisputable" propositions:

1. That in service of Ladies no Knight hath free-will.
2. That it is Beauty maintaineth the world in Valour.
3. That no fair Lady was ever false.
4. That none can be perfectly wise but Lovers. (Nichols, II, 50)

John Ford wrote a little piece, *Honor Triumphant,* praising the four challengers, and dedicated it to the countesses of Pembroke and Montgomery.

On August 7 the two kings and their parties went upriver to Hampton Court. In the evening the King's Men arrived with a play, probably *Macbeth,* designed specifically to display their patron's greatness to his fellow king. It is one of only two plays that Shakespeare obviously designed in the first instance for Stuart

performance—the other being *Henry VIII*—and it probably was written especially for this important occasion. Consideration for the queen's Danish sensibil-
ities and those of her brother required replacing the Danish invaders of Scotland
in Shakespeare's primary historical source, Raphael Holinshed's *Chronicles*, with
"Norweyan banners [that] flout the sky" (1.2.49).

The hot politico-intellectual topic of the day, "equivocation," was also picked
up. In defending himself at his trial in March 1606, Father Garnet in his desperate circumstances had made use of the practice known technically as equivocation—saying something in a way that misleads the questioner but still avoids
lying by stating in some obscure way the truth as the speaker understands it.
When caught out, Garnet defended equivocation as legitimate in cases where
the need was great and the law unjust, which was certainly true for him. The
concept caught the popular interest, and Dudley Carleton wrote Chamberlain
unfeelingly on May 2 that Garnet "will be hanged without equivocation," as he
shortly afterward was, though through the king's mercy he was not drawn and
quartered. Shakespeare too picked up the fashionable word and played with it in
Macbeth in a grim and unsympathetic way. In the famous "knocking-at-the-
gate" scene, the Porter lists among the other sinners knocking on the gate of
Hell "an equivocator, that could swear in both the scales against either scale,
who committed treason enough for God's sake, yet could not equivocate to
heaven" (2.3.8). Pity for the king's enemies was not wise in his friends.

Touching for the King's Evil, another sensitive matter at the time, was also
handled in the play in a way to please the king. The power of the English kings
to cure the King's Evil—scrofula or tuberculosis of the skin—by touching the
lesions on the neck and cheek (Samuel Johnson was one of the last people
touched) had been asserted and practiced as far back as the days of Edward the
Confessor. That English king was contemporary with the events in *Macbeth*,
where his curative powers are described in some detail:

> strangely-visited people,
> All swoll'n and ulcerous, pitiful to the eye,
> The mere despair of surgery, he cures,
> Hanging a golden stamp about their necks,
> Put on with holy prayers, and 'tis spoken,
> To the succeeding royalty he leaves
> The healing benediction.
>
> (4.3.150)

The matter had to be handled adroitly, and was. As one of the "succeeding roy-alty" James had inherited this power, yet as a realist who believed that the age of miracles had passed and who vastly disliked sickness and crowds, he had at first resisted touching the sores of the victims who crowded about him to be cured. But his councillors persuaded him that this was an important piece of public relations. Not only did it show his concern for his people, it also reinforced the mystical powers of a king who claimed his divine-right authority from the hands of God Almighty. James reluctantly yielded to these arguments, but he still refused to touch the victims, consenting only to what the play tactfully, but wrongly, ascribes to Edward: "hanging a golden stamp [coin] about their necks."

The "bending poet" played in *Macbeth* to a number of the marginal concerns of his royal patron, but centered on bigger, more permanent issues. The play dramatizes the Stuart Myth, a "mystical and legitimist version of Scottish his-tory" (Norbrook, in Sharpe and Zwicker), that James had constructed and pushed as one part of his cult of divine right. He commissioned the drawing of an elaborate family tree going back to Banquo, and elsewhere he traced his line back to 330 B.C. and King Fergus, the first ruler of Scotland and reputed founder of the nation. The line supposedly continued through Duncan and his son Mal-colm Canmore, who was crowned at Scone in 1057, and on through the myth-ical Banquo, from whom the Stuarts claimed direct descent. Although the Stuart name had historically become royal only eight rulers previously, James, by tracing his line back to Fergus, could boast in his address to his third Parliament in 1607 that "I am in descent three hundred years before Christ."

Shakespeare put this imperial boast onstage in *Macbeth* in a "line of kings that stretches out to the crack o' doom." What the stained-glass windows of the Great Hall at Hampton Court did for the Tudor lineage, *Macbeth* did in another art form for the Stuarts in act 4, scene 1. According to the original stage direc-tion, *"A show of eight Kings, [the eighth] with a glass in his hand, and Banquo last"* parades down time and across the stage, like a living family tree. In the mirror carried, presumably, by the last of the eight kings, the ninth Stuart king, James VI of Scotland and James I of England, was reflected sitting in his State on August 7, 1606. Nor did the line of Stuart kings end with him, for the play prophesies that he shall be the progenitor of "many more" who shall carry the symbols of rule over both England and Scotland, the "twofold balls and treble scepters" (4.1.21). Strictly speaking, the eighth king should have been a queen,

James's mother, Mary, or even the murdered Henry Darnley, but the coals under those ashes were still too hot for a playwright to walk on safely.

The history of Scotland tells, insofar as it can be known, a story of endless clan warfare in a land that took shape only very late as the feudal kingdom that James tried to modernize. Most often in the past one king had come to power by killing another and had held his throne only as long as his sword could keep him there. Nine of the ten kings who preceded Macbeth were murdered, and earlier times had been equally bloody. In this tribal struggle Macbeth had every right, whatever such a word might mean in these circumstances, to seize the throne and maintain it by whatever means came to hand. The same struggles had continued, though with less ferocity, on into Stuart times. The Stuart Myth, however, portrayed an unbroken succession that ran from Fergus. The time of Duncan and Macbeth in the mid-eleventh century was made the critical transformation point in Scottish history. It was then, the myth had it, that after centuries of near chaos an imperium was established, and the true kings from that point forward were determined by rule of primogeniture. Shakespeare's play dramatizes this critical point in the Stuart Myth, when Duncan names as his successor his son, Malcolm, prince of Cumberland, and Malcolm later creates the rank of earl, thus establishing the true principles of succession and hierarchy that, as natural law, had been struggling all along to emerge from the desperate events of Scottish history.

History was tidied up considerably in the process of staging this ideology of legitimacy. The information that Macbeth was Duncan's cousin with equal "right" to the throne and that Duncan was a weak king while Macbeth was strong and effective was suppressed. Banquo's complicity in the murder of Duncan was also ignored. In order to make the murder of Duncan, who is treated as a legitimate king, more heinous, Shakespeare grafted from Holinshed the story of another particularly unpleasant king killing, that of Duff, by a murderous thane and his ambitious wife, onto the Duncan-Macbeth story. Macbeth's torment from a guilty conscience was imported from the life of an earlier king who had poisoned his nephew. This is the synthesizing work of the propagandist, and through it Shakespeare transformed, to fit his patron's political myth, a petty power struggle in a primitive society between a weak and a strong warrior into a sacred event in the history of divine-right legitimacy. Elaborate family trees, national celebrations of thanksgiving for the preservation of the king, and plays like *Macbeth* were just some of the ways of making the Stuart Myth real.

The entertainments, pageants, poems, masques, and plays designed and staged for King Christian's visit show how greatly ideology and flattery, costly and clever, were the staples of patronage art. In retrospect, Shakespeare might appear to be above this kind of business, but in the Stuart court he differed little from his fellow artists in his basic patronage work. *Macbeth* treats ideas like "touching" and equivocation in a manner agreeable to the king; it stages the contrived Stuart family tree; and it historicizes the critical event in the Stuart Myth, the establishment of primogeniture as the natural and legal way of selecting the king.

But the greatest artists in the age of patronage, Shakespeare prominent among them, went beyond this kind of simple patronage work to produce an art that legitimated ideology in new and unexpected ways. Shakespeare was clearly learning how to work in the palace. *Gowrie* had taught him the dangers of directly representing the king and his business in the theater, and in *Measure for Measure* he had found a way to put a character onstage who resembled the king without being identical with him and to construct a fiction that explored the king's concerns about law and justice without seeming to go near actual affairs of state—which, the king had long ago said, were too dangerous for a poet to "mell" in. He may even have gone farther in developing his patronage art by including in his scene in *Measure for Measure* a powerful justification of Stuart claims of the necessity of the king's being above the law. So ingrained is appetite and self-preservation that the law can never control the people, only the king's justice can sort out the confusion, and only the king's mercy can make life bearable. By 1606 Shakespeare was pushing these ideas even harder, developing other ways to use the art of the theater to legitimate ideology.

Cosmicization is a social-construction-of-reality term for the familiar intellectual activity of validating ideas by working them into earlier established schemes of reality—Renaissance theories of kingship and hierarchy worked into the Aristotelean Great Chain of Being, Marx's economics inserted into Hegel's dialectical history of *geist*, or Freudian theories of the psyche contextualized in romantic art. Ideologies require constant recosmicization to be kept real, and a great patronage painter like Michelangelo recosmicized the Christian mysteries in his frescos of Creation and Judgment Day in the Sistine Chapel. The beginning and end of the story of human beings, creation and judgment, are juxtaposed in a startling way, eliminating the entire history of the world, which lay between these two events, to render overpoweringly the serene beauty of God making man and the tormented confusion that humankind in turn had made of God's creation. Orthodoxy is pushed to its limits here—Christian myth naturalized in a materialistic age—where the Word is made flesh with a beauty that almost explains the inevitability of damnation and that hints, momentarily, of some mysterious divine purpose in desire.

Macbeth works in something of the same way, if by different means, cosmicizing the Stuart Myth not by exploding the story into universals, but by working it into the crevices of nature and psychology until it becomes a seamless part of a deeply felt existential reality. When the playwright finished his work, the Stuart royal lineage and the divine right of kings were no longer dependent for their truth on strained readings of the Bible and old chronicles—the reinforcements James relied on in his political theory—but were at one with the workings of nature, with the flow of time and the normative functioning of the human mind.

Shakespeare had a genius for phrasing succinctly a simple familiar state of things, and nowhere more so than in *Macbeth:* "my single state of man," "thou sure and firm-set earth," "the good things of day," "the milk of human kindness." The natural ways of things at the heart of these phrasings are associated throughout *Macbeth* with the activities of Duncan and divine-right monarchy and with the hierarchical social order of which they are the apex. As the linkings accumulate, the Stuart Myth ceases to be myth and becomes as much a reality as any the most common things in nature. The restoration of the legitimate king after the usurper Macbeth is killed becomes not just a political act but a return to direct and inevitable ways of life:

> Give to our tables meat, sleep to our nights;
> Free from our feasts and banquets bloody knives;
> Do faithful homage and receive free honors.

(3.6.34)

The continuity of kings from oldest time to the present day was at the center of Stuart ideology—kings were there before the beginning of nations. Shakespeare visualizes the concept as fact in the line of kings stretching out to the crack of doom; in addition, he wrinkles it into time itself and into the inevitable ongoingness of all natural things. After his first encounter with the witches Macbeth exclaims, "Come what come may, Time and the hour runs through the roughest day" (1.3.146). The line is, I think, unparaphrasable in any full sense,

but throughout the play the old king Duncan and the forces of legitimate succession are associated with a natural order of time in which waters flow to the
sea, and things—men, or seeds, or kings—are planted, grow, and flourish in the
sun until they at last bear fruit. Duncan, expressing his gratitude to Macbeth for
his services in battle against the barbarians with which the play begins, welcomes him by saying, "I have begun to plant thee, and will labor To make thee
full of growing" (1.4.28). When Duncan tells Banquo that he has enfolded him
in his heart, Banquo, whose own heart is in the right place, responds, "there if I
grow, The harvest is your own."

This inevitable continuity of natural things, and of kings, in time extends to
human life and human history in a series of escapes into the future by the
younger generation, the seeds of the kingdom, from attempts to kill them and
thereby to stop time. King Duncan is killed; his sons and heirs, Malcolm and
Donalbain, escape to restore Scotland. Banquo is murdered, but Fleance gets
away in the darkness and confusion. Distortions of the natural parent-child
sequence can occur—Macduff's children are killed after he abandons them—but
in the long run time flows forward, taking with it the man who had himself earlier been blocked from birth but was released by a Caesarean section, "untimely
ripped" from his mother's womb. The apparitions the witches produce to show
Macbeth his future (an armed head, a bloody child, a child crowned with a tree
in his hand, and the parade of eight kings) are all images, however riddling, of
the forward pressure of nature in time. Even the riddles in which the witches
conceal Macbeth's fate, that no child of woman born can kill him and that he can
fall only when Birnam Wood comes to Dunsinane, are opaque descriptions of
living things moving forward in time. "The time is free," Macduff proclaims
after the death of Macbeth, and this odd line carries life on into the future, into
the succession of Scottish kings and a world where needful things will be performed, in the words of the new king, Malcolm, "in measure, time, and place."

The forces of evil in the play are identified by words and actions that momentarily obscure reality and impede, distort, and temporarily stop the flow of time.
The witches speak always in paltering terms that leave events indeterminate
and suspended in time: "fair and foul," "when the battle's lost and won." The
Macbeths have no future, having no children. Lady Macbeth chooses to
"unsex" herself, speaking of tearing an infant from her nipple and bashing its
head against the battlements.

The condition of being stopped in time, "cabined, cribbed and confined," as

Macbeth sums it up, becomes as the play proceeds as much a psychological as a physical condition. King killing and the rejection of natural authority lead to confusion, neurosis, hallucination, anomie, and suicide. Macbeth is always frantically trying to stop time, to grasp the moment, to catch the future in the instant:

> If it were done, when 'tis done, then 'twere well
> It were done quickly. If th' assassination
> Could trammel up the consequence, and catch
> With his surcease, success; that but this blow
> Might be the be-all and the end-all—here,
> But here, upon this bank and [shoal] of time,
> We'ld jump the life to come.
> (1.7.1)

Isolated on a shoal as the river of time flows by, the words are breathless with an effort to bring time to an end by preventing the inevitable consequences of regicide, the deed Macbeth cannot yet even name. But as he speaks, the consequences in time come flooding irresistibly through the rhythm of the passage and his mind: "But in these cases, We still have judgment here, that we but teach Bloody instructions."

In time he does appear to bring time to a stop, ceasing "on the torture of the mind to lie In restless ecstasy" (3.2.21), as the firstlings of his heart become the firstlings of his hand. But the violent, unreflecting actions that offer escape from time lead not into freedom but into the endless tedium of one vast empty feelinglessness in which he begins "to be a-weary of the sun." When time is stopped, life is felt as no more than the dull repetition of sameness: tomorrow and tomorrow and tomorrow. History is no more than an endless caravan moving toward death. Life has no more substance than an awkward actor playing a small part in a brief play. And it all means nothing, no more than the babbling of a madman, "a tale Told by an idiot, full of sound and fury, Signifying nothing" (5.5.26).

Lady Macbeth, who seemed so tough at first ("A little water clears us of this deed"), also ends up trapped and isolated in an unmoving time, but in a different way. Terrified of the dark, she must go over and over, again and again, never able to escape, that moment in the past when she and her husband killed the king. "Fie, my lord, fie, a soldier, and afeard? What need we fear who knows it, when none can call our pow'r to accompt? Yet who would have thought the old man to have had so much blood in him?" (5.1.36). Now she endlessly walks the night, hearing the bell, trying to remove the stains from her hands—"Out, damn'd spot!"—locked in the crime forever, suicide her only escape. In this way the king's playwright planted his Stuart patrons and "labored to make them full of growing" in the natural order of things, in the onward flow of time, and in normal, healthy psychology.

Their enemies are identified with the demonic, the chaotic, and the the infernal, a propaganda technique that James had already exploited and refined. The black arts are as old as humanity, and the Middle Ages were familiar with the village magic of spells and charms. Christianity did not take these practices seriously until about the time of the Renaissance, when witchcraft became not just harmful magic, *maleficium,* but a power derived from a compact with the Devil, who was taking up a more prominent role in religion and the affairs of the world at that time. Pope Innocent III issued a bull against unlawful magical practices and devil worship in 1484, and shortly afterward the Dominicans produced their famous handbook for identifying and dealing with witches, *Malleus Maleficarum.*

The Catholic Church developed elaborate rituals of exorcism, but the Protestant religions, though their heightened sense of evil at work in the world encouraged fear of witches and devils, denied believers any ritual defenses except prayer and fasting. The Bible, the source of all truth, spoke of demons like the Gadarene swine and the witch of Endor who practiced on Saul, and commanded that "Thou shalt not suffer a witch to live" (Exod. 22.18). Exorcistic ritual might have kept things from getting so intense, but in its absence a mass hysteria of witch hunting swept the Protestant countries of northern Europe. Something like fifty thousand people, it has been estimated, were executed for witchcraft throughout Europe between 1500 and 1700. The hysteria was at its height between 1550 and 1650 in Scotland, where there were perhaps five times as many executions—three to four thousand—as in England, often by burning alive (Thomas).

Even though the witch hunts were not so bloody, witchcraft was still very real in England, and a statute of 1604, passed shortly after James became king, made trafficking with the devil and the practice of witchcraft felonies punishable by death: "Hereby it is enacted that any person, that shall use any invocation or conjuration of any wicked spirit for any purpose, or shall take up any dead body or part thereof to be used for sorcery or enchantment, or shall practice witchcraft whereby any person shall be killed, wasted or lamed, shall suffer death as a felon" (Thomas, 443). This law stayed on the books until 1736, when enlightened opinion at last made it impossible to prosecute witches in the courts, although folk belief remained (and still remains) unconvinced.

Any calamity, sickness, drought, death of farm animals, or destructive storms could be blamed on witchcraft, and odd persons, midwives, and the mentally deficient were all suspect, particularly if they engaged in such practices as telling fortunes or making love philtres or medicines from herbs. The daughters of Eve the temptress, particularly poor old women, were charged with being witches more often than men, though there were male witches, known as warlocks. In this strange and terrifying chapter in the history of abnormal social psychology, the victims themselves not only often understandably confessed under the most dreadful tortures to practicing the black arts but came in many cases to believe they were in fact witches, able to call up the devil and to cast spells on those who harmed them. Victims often played their parts in the great witch-hunt as completely as their persecutors!

James Stuart may have been something of a pedant, but he also was a canny man, not much given to superstition. Yet he set himself up as an expert in witchcraft, publishing in Scotland his *Demonologie* in 1596, which was republished in London in 1603 (thus giving Shakespeare a chance to know what his patron thought about the black arts). James's views were by no means unusual. Women, he wrote, were ten times more often witches than men. Image magic — mutilating an image of the victim — was the most dangerous form of witchcraft. Pricking the "witch mark" to see if it bled and throwing the suspect into the water to see if she floated or sank were, he thought, surefire tests for possession.

James acquiesced to the 1604 English witchcraft statute, but after his arrival in England he frequently pardoned convicted witches and sent them to the learned doctors of Cambridge University for examination. He liked to play his Solomon role with accused witches, amusing himself at his hunting lodge by questioning and trying to trip them up. When faced once with a woman who had remained in her bed in a rigid trance, seemingly possessed by a devil, he reached over and flipped up her skirt, bringing her out of her trance instantly.

The overall evidence suggests that the king was a skeptic, but if so he knew well how to turn witchcraft to political purposes by setting it up as the devilish enemy of God's deputy, the king, and casting himself as its nemesis in writing and in practice. His favorite, Robert Carr, earl of Somerset, wanted in 1612 to marry Frances Howard, the notoriously loose countess of Essex, who was suing for divorce on the probably false grounds of her husband's inability to consummate the marriage. Essex agreed that he was impotent, but to save his reputation he insisted that he had this problem only with his countess. Witchcraft was used to construct a face-saving explanation of his difficulties, but when the archbishop of Canterbury was asked to provide an annulment on these grounds, he expressed doubts about the charge and drew on the Bible for evidence. James was outraged and wrote the archbishop at once, telling him that his theology was in error and that he should read *Demonologie* to bring himself up to date. Besides, the king added, too much reliance on the Bible smacked of Puritanism. The archbishop ought particularly to note that "if the Devil hath any power, it is over the filthiest and most sinful part thereof whereunto original sin is soldered" (*State Trials*, 801).

This was not the first time that Stuart politics and witchcraft came close together. In a sensational case in Edinburgh in August 1593, a coven known as the Witches of Lothian (which included Agnes Sampson, Gillie Duncan, Margaret Thomson, and five others, led by a schoolmaster, Doctor Fran) was charged with having conspired to keep James from returning from Denmark with his new bride, Queen Anne, in 1590, when the royal couple had been forced to wait in Kroneberg-Elsinore for months for a favorable wind from Denmark to Scotland. Under torture the witches revealed that they had practiced against the king's life as well. Pieces of dead bodies had been tied to cats, who were thrown into the sea; threads were prepared and unknotted to raise tempests; a black toad had been roasted, hung up for three days, and the juice from it collected in an oyster shell. Eventually, as the demonic coup, a handkerchief of the king's was obtained and an image made which was passed to the Devil at a Witches' Sabbath with the ominous words, "This is King James the Sixth, ordained to be consumed at the instance of a nobleman, Francis Earl of Bothwell" (Watson).

This sounds more like magistrate's language than the spell of a witch, but the name of Bothwell brought James himself scuttling down to the dungeons at once to sift the witches between torture sessions about what they knew of his feared and dangerous enemy, the earl of Bothwell. The witches didn't know much, but in time they implicated another conspirator, the warlock Richard Graham, and he revealed, again under torture, that he had been approached by Bothwell to cast a spell over James. The court of law, however, had some doubts and refused to convict the witches, at which James assembled the jury and lectured them to the effect that he knew witchcraft to be "a thing grown very common among us. I know it to be a most abominable sin; and I have been occupied these three quarters of a year for the sifting out of them that are guilty herein. . . . As for them who think these witchcrafts to be but fantasies, I remit them to be catechised and instructed in these most evident points" (Watson, 141). The king had his way, and Graham, after dreadful torments, recanted and was burned alive, as were five of the Witches of Lothian.

Francis Stewart, 5th and last earl of Bothwell, was the cousin of James Stuart and nephew to James Hepburn, the 4th earl, the lover of James's mother and probably the murderer of his father. A very wild and dashing Border Scot, more than a little crazy, Bothwell had kidnapped James on one occasion and frightened him for his life on others. These antics did not endear Bothwell to the cautious and fearful James, and they, rather than trading in the occult, were probably the earl's undoing. Witchcraft was just the hook to catch so popular and dangerous a man. Graham and the Witches of Lothian were not, most suspiciously, kept alive to appear as witnesses, but their forced confessions were used as the basis to try Bothwell for treason and witchcraft. Having had the foresight to fill the streets with his armed retainers, Bothwell was not convicted, though no one doubted that he had plotted against the king, but he escaped only narrowly and was never again the threat to James that he had earlier been.

The record is quite clear: James made use of witchcraft to serve his political ends. His playwright transferred this device to the theater in *Macbeth,* whose witches are exactly like those James had described in *Demonologie*. They are female, although masculine beards are their telltale demonic mark, and they have familiars, the cat Graymalkin and Paddock the toad. Like many witches of the time they beg food from door to door, and when a sailor's wife refuses one of them the chestnuts she is eating, the witch revenges herself by sending succubi to her husband — "I'll drain him dry as hay" — visiting insomnia on him, and (with a glance at James's difficulties in sailing from Denmark) raising contrary winds during his voyage to Aleppo. The witches spread disease among the animals ("killing swine"), they wind up charms of various kinds ("Thrice to thine, and thrice to mine, And thrice again, to make up nine"), and they mix strange ingredients ("Eye of newt and toe of frog, Wool of bat and tongue of dog") in their cauldron to produce a potent witches' brew.

But there are more serious matters. The *Macbeth* witches are not merely casting spells, they have compacted with the forces of darkness. The Devil does not appear in the play, but there is a hell-gate scene, and superior demons are represented by those the witches darkly call "our masters" and—though the scene may be a non-Shakespearean addition—by Hecate, the Greek goddess of darkness, night, and magic. Hecate is angry with the witches for trading with Macbeth on their own "in riddles and affairs of death," without allowing her a chance to display her own black magic. Then too, Shakespeare's witches play for large stakes: the soul of an honest man, the soldier Macbeth, snared to damnation by promising him a kingdom.

James was the expert, a king who had examined witches, sent them to the torture chamber and the fire, and written a book on the subject. He had found it politically useful throughout his life to cast the demonic as a major antagonist to himself and a threat to the well-being of his kingdom and his subjects. But Shakespeare was a quick study. *Macbeth* extended this policy, providing a theatrical version of the political strategy. Just as James had identified Bothwell with the forces of darkness, and would in the future identify the impotence of Essex with possession, Shakespeare portrayed Macbeth, the enemy of divine-right kingship and of the Stuart ancestors, as being controlled by witches and used by forces of darkness. Treason in this way became not just a political act but a form of possession, an action contrary to and destructive of the very order of nature itself. The forces of the netherworld seek for their own uncreating purposes the killing of the legitimate king in order to restore the realm of tyranny and chaos.

Shakespeare contributed to his patron's ideology of divine right even further by deepening this witchcraft theme. He psychologized it and traced its effects in the minds of its instruments, Macbeth and his murderous wife. Their mental processes degenerate throughout the play and come at last to total alienation and ennui ("I gin to be a-weary of the sun"), to madness ("Who would have thought the old man to have had so much blood in him?"), and to suicide. Murder of the rightful king and the destruction of the various kinds of orderly authority he represents and defends not only plunge the kingdom into disorder but create mental states of chaos and miasmic confusion, where sleep becomes impossible, where the real cannot be distinguished from the unreal—"Is this a dagger which I see before me?"—where consciousness becomes only "restless extasy," and where, finally, "nothing is But what is not." In Shakespeare's theater, treason becomes not only demonic possession, it is derangement and madness.

How much the Danish king who spoke no English understood of this consummate piece of patronage art at Hampton Court that August of 1606 is doubtful. But James Stuart must have been enormously pleased. *Macbeth* was the Stuart play, celebrating his ancient lineage, portraying the critical event in it and in Scotland's history, and making divine-right kingship identical with nature and sanity.

5

THE TRUE KING

LEAR, WHITEHALL

CHRISTMAS 1606

We think of it as the Age of Kings, when the great absolutists appeared, trying to look as if they had always been there, first as dukes in the Italian city-states and in Burgundy, then as rulers of Spain, France, England. These were monarchs of previously unknown strength of character and will to power who claimed to rule absolutely all parts of life by no less authority than God Himself, whose earthly deputies they claimed to be. These new-style kings were outsize personalities, sometimes introverted and darkly melancholy, sometimes energetic, violent, and brightly colored. Everything was on the heroic scale. They were intelligent, often learned in quirky ways. They were cultivated, and had a taste for the past as well as the future. They spent and built lavishly, changed the ancient ways of religious and secular life with a wave of the hand or a stroke of the pen, and disposed of their subjects and their enemies ruthlessly.

But the sixteenth and seventeenth centuries, far from belonging uncontested to the kings, seethed with competing political forces (Skinner). Machiavellian cunning and force majeure competed with constitutionalist views that held that the people and their rulers entered into contracts with each other. Arguments for the supremacy of the ancient laws of the land jostled against nihilistic arguments that nothing is unlawful, while anarchists, rejecting all forms of civil government, clamored for a hearing along with proponents of reformed religions like Huguenot Calvinism in France, which encouraged individuals to find ultimate authority only in their own consciences.

In this conflict of legitimacies, the big kings had to bend every effort to authenticate their right to rule, as well as to establish de facto authority. Renaissance rulers turned their households into big-government bureaucracies designed to extend their power to all areas of life—religion, education, law, finance. The Leviathan states they created for these purposes invaded ancient rights and weighed heavily on subjects unaccustomed to centralized governments that claimed the right to tax more and more heavily in order to finance their own expansion, maintain the prodigal expenditures of the court, and pay for standing armies to fight wars against other rising states.

As the state became more expert in imposing central authority on its subjects and extending its writ throughout the kingdom, resistance to kings who asserted that they ruled by divine authority did not disappear. People of all ranks defended their traditional liberties in a long series of revolutions throughout Europe (Zagorin). This extended political conflict was fought in privy councils, in religious convocations, in law courts, and in parliaments, as well as on the battlefields. But nowhere were the ideological wars more fierce in the age of Gutenberg than on the printed page. Among the kings' defenders, for example, Luther and Calvin located kingly authority in the Bible and made it an article of faith that the magistrate's power is not derived from the people or from brute force but from God himself. Had not Saint Paul enjoined the people in Romans 13:1—3, "Let every soul be subject unto the higher powers for there is no power but of God. The Powers that be, are ordained of God. Whosoever therefore resisteth the power, resisteth the ordinance of God and they that resist, shall receive to themselves damnation. For rulers are not a terror to good works, but to the evil"? Castiglione idealized the social organization and ethos of the court, Jean Bodin constructed a systematic apology for absolutism, and Thomas Hobbes grounded the authority of the Leviathan state in the absolute need for order (Skinner). When Oliver Cromwell was deciding in 1648 to execute James's son, King Charles I, he discussed with his advisers the theories of the Scottish humanist George Buchanan and of Juan de Mariana, a Spanish Jesuit, about "the nature of regal power" and the legality of regicide (Burnet). The decision to send Charles to the headsman was, of course, primarily a piece of realpolitik, but history and political philosophy were employed here as elsewhere to provide at least an appearance of legitimacy for critical decisions on matters of state.

Buchanan, James's old tutor, was the right authority for Cromwell. Kings were not for him the dominant central figures in the political scene. A former Catholic, a humanist scholar schooled in France and Spain beginning in 1539, and a noted author of Latin plays, Buchanan was at one point tried for heresy by the Inquisition in Portugal. He returned to Scotland in 1561, probably in the train of Queen Mary, and there entered the households of a series of great lords, the first one being that earl of Lennox whose son was Henry Darnley. Darnley's murder at Kirk o' Fields turned Buchanan into an active propagandist for the anti-Catholic, anti-absolutist party. He wrote a justification of the deposition of Mary which was offered to Elizabeth, "who did not relish it," and he worked for many years on his *Rerum scoticarum historia* (Edinburgh, 1582), with its history of Scotland in which kings were only the instruments of the people's needs. His Scottish history sounded the names of "all those mythological kings [Thereus and Durstus, Ferlegus and Ferquhard] whose names read like a roll-call of Acteon's hounds" (brackets in original). So deeply was he involved in this material that "he must have felt himself," as Hugh Trevor-Roper goes on, "almost a member of that Great Council whose solemn sessions had deposed 'twelve or more kings' of the house of Fergus; must have felt at home in every dark chamber, saturated with sex and crime, of the royal castle of Berigon on the western shore of Albion 'fornent the Ilis'" (1966, 24).

Buchanan's main source was an earlier, imaginative history of Scotland by Hector Boece, which was in turn derived from an even more doubtful chronicle by Veremund. The Welshman Humphrey Lhuyd had charged in *The Breviary of Britayne* (1572) that the Scots "far from being a nation of political philosophers who had perfected their constitution in the time of Aristotle and Alexander the Great, as Boece claimed, first appear in history at the end of the Roman empire when St. Jerome described them as cannibals dining off each others' breasts and buttocks and copulating like cattle" (Trevor-Roper, 1966, 27). But Buchanan dismissed Lhuyd's charges in true scholarly spirit as no more than "hodge-podge trash raked by him out of the dung-hill," arguing that the true and natural form of government had first appeared in antiquity in Scotland, where it had been an elective monarchy in which kings, though they might regularly be chosen from one family, need not be related, since they reigned only at the pleasure of the councils of nobles and of the three estates.

Buchanan's primitive Scots are originally "scattered in clanships, without king, or any certain form of government" (I, 154). Under the pressure of imminent attack by the Picts and the Britons, and only then, they applied themselves "to procure both foreign auxiliaries and a foreign prince. But as none of the chiefs of the islands, who were all of equal dignity, could be induced to yield precedence to another, Fergus, the son of Ferchard, who was esteemed the first of all the Scots for wisdom and activity, was declared king, in a full assembly of the people, and appointed to prepare an army, and lead it to battle, if necessary." Only after Fergus returned home victorious did "the Scots confirm the kingdom to him and his posterity by an oath" (I, 156).

Sovereignty, Buchanan's story of the mythical forty kings of Scotland is designed in all its parts to prove, belongs to the people, who confer it on a king only when they are in great danger and confirm it only so long as he provides the safety they require. Primogeniture was imposed by a trick: King Kenneth III killed his most worthy possible successor and then persuaded his nobles into agreeing, without realizing the implications, that his son be designated prince of Cumberland and future king. Primogeniture in this view was a usurpation of power that led to the establishment of an illegal hereditary system of kingship and of inequality among the nobility.

Regicide was therefore, in the view of Buchanan, God's cause. His reading of Scottish history treated its ceaseless struggles for power as episodes in the exercise of the natural right of a people to choose and overthrow kings, with only a secondary interest in continuity in the royal family. Macbeth thus had every right to claim the throne, to which Duncan had no privileged claim, and for which he had no right whatsoever to control the succession.

Although Buchanan's *History* was dedicated to him, James found his old tutor's political theories an abomination. In 1584, two years after Buchanan's death and the publication of the *History,* both it and Buchanan's treatise of political philosophy, *De iure regni,* were censured in the Scottish Parliament as "not meet to remain for records of truth to posterity," and all owners of printed copies were required, not to destroy them—no sense in wasting expensive books—but to turn them in to be purged of "the offensive and extraordinary matters among the contents" (McFarlane, 414). There was no second printing of either work in Scotland for a long time, but they were reprinted many times on the Continent.

James's childhood involvement with his tutor was proleptic, for no family was fated to have a more tragic role than the Stuarts in the history of divine-right kingship. The authority of Scottish kings had become even more precarious after the establishment of Calvinism in the 1550s and 1560s, with its claims for the unlimited authority of the Kirk in all affairs of life. Barons and presbyters were now united in their assertion of what they called the ancient right of the nobility, and later of the dominies, to "correct, chastise, banish or execute" kings who failed to satisfy them. The test came in 1567 when Mary was deposed and then in the following year driven out of the kingdom as a scarlet Whore of Babylon, a red rag of Rome, whose Catholicism threatened the Presbyterian settlement and whose flagrant immorality was said to outrage public virtue.

Mary's son, James, was raised as a Protestant and made to know painfully his own weakness in his dealings both with his nobles and with bishop-hating, king-despising clerics like John Knox. George Buchanan, by, as the old tutor put it grimly, "whipping the arse of the Lord's annointed," instructed him that political power originated in the people. Oligarchical Venice, as James told the Venetian ambassador years later, was held up as the model state in the royal classroom.

The Protestantism took, but the political theory did not. James acquired, probably from his French connections and familiarity with French culture— monarchist books like Guillaume Budé's *Le Livre de l'institution du prince* and Jean Bodin's *République* were in the royal library by 1577—and developed, perhaps as a compensation for his actual weakness, a theory of the absolute, unlimited authority of a king over his subjects, which he argued publicly in a series of pamphlets and books. That rare creature, a literate king, James was his own polemicist. He summarized his political theory for the English Parliament in his opening speech to that body in 1609:

> Kings are justly called Gods, for that they exercise a manner or resemblance of Divine power upon earth. For if you will consider the attributes to God, you shall see how they agree in the person of a king. God hath power to create, or destroy, make, or unmake at his pleasure, to give life, or send death, to judge all and to be judged not, accomptable to none, to raise low things and to make high things low at his pleasure, and to God are both soule and body due. And the like power have Kings, they make and unmake their subjects, they have power of raising, and casting downe of life and of death. Judges over all their subjects, and all causes, and yet accomptable to none but God only. They have power to exalt low things, and abase high things, and make of their subjects like men at the Chesse, A pawne to take a Bishop or a Knight, and to cry up, or downe any of their subjects, as they do their money. (McIlwain, 307)

Although revisionist historians have tried to soften his views, and though he well understood the art of compromise in practice, in his writings and public speeches James's absolutist theories of government were uncompromising. *Basilikon Doron* was published as advance propaganda in England on the eve of his arrival there where it became a best-seller, going through eight editions, plus some pirating, and 13,000 copies were sold in 1603 alone, a huge sale for the time (Wormald, 51). His other major political work, *The Trew Law of Free Monarchies,* an extended defense of divine-right kingship, was also published in England in 1603. The king's name appeared on the title page for the first time in two of the three English editions, in order to make his views "legible" to his new subjects. James was a learned but not a subtle author, and the legitimations of divine right that he offers in *The Trew Law* are more conventional than perspicuous.

Believing that every word of the Bible was "dited" by God, the Old Testament giving the law, the New telling of grace and forgiveness, James took from Holy Scripture the primary legitimation for the view that as God is to the cosmos, so the king is to the state. "*Monarchie* is the trew paterne of Divinitie," is the way he put it flatly (*Trew Law,* 54). This divine pattern he found everywhere in the Bible, especially in the books of Samuel and Kings, which told the history of the Hebrew monarchy, of Saul and David and Solomon. Using these books, which he knew in close detail, the learned James proved that God put kings on their thrones to rule in a godly fashion for the benefit of the state and the people, and that a bad king was God's punishment on the people for their sins. So absolute is the authority of kings, however, that even if the king is a tyrant, obedience is still required of his subjects, and rebellion, the most heinous of sins, is not justifiable by any excuse. Since God made kings, only He can unmake them.

In James's writings, secular history demonstrated the priority of kings as surely as biblical revelation. He was particularly anxious to prove what *Measure for Measure* had put onstage: that while the king used the parliaments to make the laws that he enforced in the courts, the king was above both parliament and law. "Rex est lex loquens" (the voice of the king is the law) was his text. He read history in a way exactly opposite to Buchanan's, and for him the kings preceded nations or laws. Nations were created by kings, and kings then gave them laws: "The Kings ... in *Scotland* were before any estates or rankes of men within the same, before any Parliaments were holden, or lawes made.... And so it followes of necessitie, that the kings were the authors and makers of the Lawes, and not the Lawes of the kings" (*Trew Law,* 62). Not only Scottish history but biblical history and the European chronicles provided James with historical precedents of kings making law and interpreting it to their subjects, not being bound by it. This historical fact, James argued, is sedimented in the universally acknowledged existing rights of the king. All land, for example, belongs to the king, whose subjects hold it from him. His authority is equally and obviously paramount in his control of wards, in his appointment of judges, and in the other unchallenged rights of sovereignty exercised by kings in all lands.

James's science is not even as impressive as his historical and biblical scholarship, but he undertook to demonstrate in an unoriginal way in *The Trew Law* that nature itself provides a model, and therefore a legitimation, for the hierarchically organized state. James schematized nature as the cosmic pattern we know as the Great Chain of Being, a succession of degrees or links descending from God and the angels to the meanest clod of earth. Each link in the chain is is a microcosm of the whole. As the king rules his subjects, so the father heads the family, the head the body, reason the passions, the lion the beasts, the oak the trees. Shakespeare's showpiece of Great-Chain ideology is Ulysses' speech on degree in *Troilus and Cressida*—"take but degree away, untune that string, and hark what discord follows"—and all of his old-style legitimate kings, Richard II, Old Hamlet, Duncan, Lear, and others, at the beginning of their plays assume the existence of some form of an infinite ladder of natural and social hierarchies.

But though in James's theory the world proclaimed the self-evident truth of divine right, in practice his subjects continued to resist. Along with the attempt to assassinate him in 1605 had come growing resistance in Commons and in the church to his prerogative claims, and establishing the antiquity and divine authority of kingship required constant ingenuity and effort. In this great business, he was as fortunate as was Louis XIV with Racine, in having as his official playwright the leading apologist for kings in his or any other time. Taken together, Shakespeare's political plays offer Western culture's most extensive narrative of the age of kings, broader in scope and deeper in character than any other history or theory of kingship. Richard III, Richard II, Henry Bolingbroke, Hal, Old Hamlet, Claudius, Duncan, Lear, to name only some of the most prominent kings in his plays, constitute a remarkable and varied portrait gallery of Renaissance kingcraft. A legitimist like Richard II is unable to comprehend that the social order which supports him is not an eternal and immutable fact of nature, but a usurper like Henry IV sees with the clearsightedness of Machiavelli that in the end the exercise of power comes to the ruthless use of force. If Brutus assumes that justice and truth govern politics, then the cool indifference of Richard III to the request for a payoff by a former ally for whom he no longer has any need, "Thou troublest me, I am not in the vein," weighs exactly what virtues like gratitude are worth in the political world.

At the apex of this monumental study of kings stands Shakespeare's paradigmatic political play and his most magisterial image of the true king, *King Lear*, which according to the title page of the first quarto was played in 1606 "before the Kings Maiestie at Whitehall upon S. Stephans night in Christmas Hollidayes." Shakespeare's patronage signature is to be found in this play, as elsewhere, in a number of topical details that advertise the play's concern with contemporary interests of the king and court. Lear's fool would immediately have caught the attention of an audience at a court where there had been no official fool since the time of Henry VIII until James, with his "pawky" sense of humor, brought with him from Scotland Archie Armstrong, who was no doubt fooling it in the audience that Christmas. *King Lear* glances at current politics in the opening act, where the old king of Britain makes the mistake of dividing his kingdom, thereby replicating the House of Commons' continuing refusal to end the separation of the kingdoms of England and Scotland. More daring by far, though he changed two sons to three daughters, Shakespeare selected from among the possibilities in his many sources and made the titles of the husbands of Lear's two older daughters identical with those of James's two sons at that time: Henry, not until 1610 prince of Wales but duke of Cornwall, and Charles, after 1605 duke of York but still, as from birth, duke of Albany. Obviously, Shakespeare, like Lear's fool—"Take heed, sirrah, the whip"—felt by this time that he could sail fairly close to the political wind in allowing the antagonisms in the House of Stuart between father and children to play about his story (Patterson).

At its political center, *Lear* stages James's conception of the absolute king. Like James's history of monarchy, the story of Lear begins in a primitive time when a king rules not by delegation of power (à la Buchanan) or by any contract with terrified subjects but out of innate unquestioned authority and his own essentially kingly nature. Lear towers above his subjects, a titanic personality, "every inch a king," a man who has in his countenance an inalienable authority that his followers "would fain call master." His will is locked, commanding, fearless, autocratic in every way. His natural right to rule is reinforced by time-honored custom and immemorial legitimacy. He is an old man, as old as Shakespeare can realistically make him, "fourscore and upward," and he emerges, as in James's theory of divine right, out of the mists of the ancient past, as if there had always been kings of this kind, from time out of mind, before there were people.

One of the legendary kings of ancient Britain, Lear calls upon the gods to do his bidding with all the confidence of James's belief that the royal and the divine wills are one—"by the sacred radiance of the sun, The [mysteries] of Hecat and the night." Like James, too, he assumes an unquestioned control over the natural order of things: "Hear, nature, hear . . . Suspend thy purpose." His own traditional ways of thinking and doing appear to him as the workings of nature itself—"Allow not nature more than nature needs, Man's life is cheap as beast's" (2.4.266). This identification with a divine nature confers an undoubted ownership of the sacred land and consequent right of transfer on him:

> even from this line to this,
> With shadowy forests and with champains rich'd,
> With plenteous rivers and wide-skirted meads,
> We make thee lady.
>
> (1.1.63)

Shakespeare exaggerates for dramatic purposes all the powers claimed for divine right, including what some political theorists, James Stuart included, considered the essential mark of kingship, namely, priority to the law. "The laws of a sovereign prince, although they be grounded on good and lively reasons, depend nevertheless upon nothing but his mere and frank good will," is the way the French monarchist Jean Bodin put it (156). Lear is the lex loquens actualized, resigning his duties without consultation, giving his kingdom to whomever he will, disowning and banishing any who cross him, acting as if his royal title were indelibly his, even after he has surrendered its power. In James's political theory kings are part of the world's reality, woven inextricably into God's schemes of nature and history.

However, in his living image of the divine-right king, Shakespeare, first in the old-fashioned moral way of humanist mirror-for-magistrates art, goes beyond the immediate prince-pleasing functions of palace art to lengthen the shadows cast by the sun king. In the arbitrary exercise of his prerogative, Lear puts power into the hands of the selfish and wicked. His motives, too numerous for certainty, in exercising his prerogative are tainted with selfishness—an inordinate desire to be loved and praised, a determination to have his own way, a longing to seek his own ease in retirement, susceptibility to flattery (all prominent weaknesses of James Stuart). The root trouble is phrased crisply by his daughter Regan, "he hath ever but slenderly known himself."

The consequences of an unchecked will and of putting the wicked and ruthless into power appear most dramatically in act 3. Tom o' Bedlam, the mad beggar (or the "poor, bare, fork'd animal," as Lear calls him), mankind stripped of all the personality and all the role coverings normally provided by society, appears first. Tom is "the thing itself," a crazed, superstition-ridden wanderer across the land, who stays alive by eating dead animals from the ditch and drinking the water from stagnant pools, in his fear seeing a world filled with devils and darkness. Tom is natural man—though not in Lear's idealized sense of that term—reduced to little more than biological existence.

The second heath image is of natural, not human, emptiness: a bare land and a titanic storm that batters anything in its path, simply raging, indifferent to human existence, pitying "neither wisemen nor fools." Human concerns and human values mean and are nothing in the face of this colossal power of a natural world that dwarfs in its energy—earthquake, flood, cyclone, fire—the puny powers of human beings. The human world as heart of darkness, all moral and social controls removed, provides a third image of a world from which the rule of the true king is gone. Off to the side of the heath is Gloucester's castle, usurped by the savage Cornwall and the sadistic Regan. This fortress was built to protect life, but now it contains the most fearsome terror on the heath. Here a man and woman use their unrestrained political and physical powers to rip out the eyes of a helpless old man, the earl of Gloucester, who has crossed them. They act with all the sadistic joy that a barbaric humankind has taken in the exercise of power and the infliction of pain and torture in gulag and concentration camp, from Auschwitz to Cambodia, Beirut, and Sarajevo.

In *Lear*'s existential heath images Shakespeare looks far deeper into the state of nature on which kingship ultimately rests than did his royal master in his political writings. "Yes, yes," James would have said, "these are excellent pictures of the kinds of suffering and savagery that God will visit on the land that revolts against the rightful king, or in which the king makes serious mistakes of judgment. But when the rightful king is restored, they will pass." The heath, in

James's political philosophy, is an unnatural state of things; true nature is to be found in the hierarchical state. But these boundary scenes, which are a regular feature of Shakespearean political theater—Richard II in his dungeon, Hamlet in the Elsinore graveyard—are not in *Lear*, or elsewhere in Shakespeare, mere passing disturbances of rebellion, they are visions of a human and natural reality always underlying the surfaces of civilized life. They become visible only when the social order breaks down, and they will be covered if it begins to function again, but they are always there.

To look unprotected at this ground of things is dangerous, but not to understand the reality in front of which political power must operate is to remain unaware of the full human condition. All of Shakespeare's kings come sooner or later to the heath in some form, and there their measure is taken by the fullness of their comprehension and their response to the primal scene.

The most desperate reactions in all Shakespeare to the emptiness and meaninglessness that lie on the heath just behind civil life are those of the two major characters of *King Lear,* the old king and his faithful noble, Gloucester. The villains of the play do not experience the heath in this play—what they see they ignore—and they remain therefore, as their deaths show, locked into a limiting rationalism that does not fully comprehend the depths of the world in which they live. The old king does experience it, fully and shatteringly. At first he rejects submission and tears for a defiance of evil that as it becomes more impotent drops off into madness. Shakespearean madness is never some clinical disorder, a nonfunctional way of thinking and acting, but rather a last-ditch defense of values that have become untenable but cannot be relinquished, the only way left to deal with terrors that cannot be denied but cannot be accepted. (R. D. Laing's analysis, though not his admiration, of schizophrenia as a defense against absurdity is close to Shakespeare's view.) And so Lear runs mad, defying all the terrible things that are implicit in what he saw on the heath and that now flood into his speech: the bestiality of human life, the foulness of sex, the cruelty and indifference of power to the suffering of others.

But still he continues to believe that he is somehow above this confusion and retains both the moral authority to denounce it and the power to punish it. All the conventional marks of sovereignty, even some of the slightest, "the power to legislate, to make war and peace, appoint higher magistrates, hear final appeals, grant pardons, receive homage, coin money, regulate weight and measure and impose taxes" (Skinner, II, 288), appear in Lear's disjointed mad speeches in an almost programmatic fashion. Though jumbled together in the ramblings of a madman, they are the powers of a man who still thinks he is "every inch a king": "There's your press-money"—"It were a delicate stratagem to shoe a troop of horse with felt"—"I pardon that man's life"—"None does offend, none, I say none, I'll able 'em"—"they cannot touch me for [coining], I am the King himself."

Suicide is at the opposite end from madness on the spectrum of human defenses against the intolerable, a surrender to the overwhelming while still protesting its injustice. This is the earl of Gloucester's response to being sadistically tortured, blinded, and cast out to wander on the heath. He crawls away from the explosion in his face feeling that he has no way and that he therefore needs no eyes. Feeling himself too weak to defy the power of evil gods who allow the torture of humans for their inexplicable amusement, even as humans in turn torture insects—and the insects torture some other life form?—he seeks to throw himself over the cliff at Dover in an attempt to be rid of a consciousness he can no longer endure.

After the abyss has been glimpsed on the heath, the minor characters try to moralize and philosophize what they have been through. "This shows you are above, You justicers." But their rationalizations are no more effective than the madness and suicide of the major characters. Tears are the things and "give me your hand" the gesture that carry the silently growing feelings of community that eventually lead the way off the heath. Gloucester tries to help Lear, and Cornwall's servant attempts to prevent his master from putting out Gloucester's other eye. Edgar guides his blinded father away from the heath, Cordelia succors and forgives the crazed Lear, the duke of Albany comes out on the king's side, and a French army appears to defend the king's party against the usurpers.

The bonds that are knitting together this new community are brought into close focus in act 4 in the parallel scenes in which Cordelia cures Lear's madness and Edgar momentarily restores his father's faith in life and willingness to live. That scene, so awkward always in the theater, in which Gloucester thinks he has jumped over Dover Cliff and is persuaded that he has been deluded into jumping by fiends and that his "life's a miracle," suggests that an illusion of a caring deity is necessary if people are to go on living. Cordelia's treatment of Lear—music, new clothing, rest, medicine, and, finally, forgiveness for past wrongs—renews the sense of an ineradicable goodness and harmony in, not outside, life.

The feeling of basic human sympathy emerging in these scenes swells to embrace a universal community that includes all the poor and helpless, when Lear in the midst of his own sufferings breaks through to a perception of the dreadful injustices of the world. The beadle lashes the whore he lusts after, the justice is a greater thief than the man he condemns. In time a society can be and is rebuilt on his pity for the "poor naked wretches, whereso ere you are that bide the pelting of this pitiless storm," and an acceptance of responsibility for their plight, "O, I have ta'en Too little care of this!" The old kingdom with its divine-right pretensions and hierarchical metaphysics is gone, but in its place is a new community held together by a need for mutual support and a sympathy for the suffering of others—"Give me your hand."

Everyone inside and outside the play would like for it to end here, with the mistakes paid for by suffering and something learned on which a new society can be built. But the plot sweeps on into the terrible last act, carrying away all attempts to manage history by thinking or feeling, madness or sanity, defiance or yielding. The army that would save the old king is defeated, and Lear withdraws from the world with Cordelia—"We two alone will sing like birds i' th' cage"—only to be followed by the murderer who kills her. Gloucester's heart bursts, and Lear at long last can endure no more.

In the usual Shakespearean manner a diminished world is put back together at the end of *Lear*. The wicked are punished, the good who survive (there are not many) are rewarded. But it all has a flat anticlimactic quality. Lear cannot extract any satisfaction from the retributive justice of killing Cordelia's murderer with his "biting falchion." Kent reveals himself and the faithfulness of service with which he has followed Lear all this way, and is now prepared to follow him into death, only to be met with the deflating "[You] are welcome hither." Albany promises justice, but even the death of the villains one after another seems somehow but a "trifle." With Lear dead, the kingdom is given to virtuous, decent men, Edgar and the duke of Albany, who, though they began the play as innocents, have been tested and toughened by going to the ends of the moral world. But each of them is in the final scene notably reluctant to accept the crown and oversee the restoration of the kingdom. Government and rule have become heavy burdens of necessity. Life is only bearable with illusions: "Look her lips, Look there, look there!" All that anyone is willing to assert is in Edgar's last flat words, "The oldest hath borne most; we that are young Shall never see so much nor live so long."

Understandably, there may have been some trouble about the play. *King Lear* exists in two quite different forms, the early quarto and the revised folio versions. It may be that the earlier version cut too close to the bone for comfort and had to be modified into something more politically suitable (Patterson). There has been speculation that Lear's line "Dost thou call me fool?" (1.4.148) was censored as lèse majesté (Taylor, 102) and that the mock trial in act 3 was eliminated as being too harshly critical a satire on official justice.

Whatever problems there may have been, King James got his £10 worth, though he must have wondered about it at several points during the course of the play. *Lear* fleshes out his abstract theoretical version of kingship, putting onstage a titanic divine-right king who stands astride his kingdom and his people, a king who speaks to the gods. The kingdom disintegrates when the true king no longer rules, but it is as perdurably enduring as its king, and though rocked to its foundations, it is still shakily in place, as is the institution of kingship, at the end of the play.

King Lear gave its patron a defense of kingship, but in doing so it drove the foundations of legitimacy to bedrock. In this play, Shakespeare was not simply extending the legitimation of his patron's theories, as he had in *Macbeth,* he was improving upon them. Whereas James took the king and his order as the prior reality, Shakespeare portrayed the moral emptiness of the heath as the primary fact of existence. For the playwright the established order with which his play begins is a social defense against an always threatening anomie, while for James that anomie is a temporary consequence of a breakdown in the natural order of kingship. Since the two views resemble one another if you do not look too hard, and since they move toward the same end—an orderly state ruled by a king— they would not come into open conflict in a theatrical presentation. But Shakespeare's true king is a far more human and tested figure than James's. He is the man who can endure the hammerings of history, look into the depths of himself and acknowledge his errors; who can feel for the sufferings of all of his people, who knows himself a man, not a demi-god, and who acts with courage and care for his people. The kingdom itself endures not because God and nature decree it, but because in the face of the terrors of existence people identify with others and band together in mutual defense. The refusal of the happy ending at the conclusion of act 4 and the bleakness of the end of act 5 drive home how shaky are any kind of social order or any sense of meaning in life. Shakespeare was not a revolutionary, but he penetrated far deeper into existence than did

James and the other divine-right theorists of the time in grounding king and state not in some mystical theory but in the primary feelings and experiences of living men and women.

In 1651 the country had been through a civil war and executed James Stuart's son, and in the light of these earthshaking events the royalist Thomas Hobbes published a philosopher's view of the grounds and nature of sovereignty, *Leviathan, or The Matter, Forme and Power of a Commonwealth Ecclesiasticall and Civil*. For Hobbes, divine-right kingship died with King Charles, even as in Shakespeare it died with King Lear. Both writers replace the old order with a new, far less joyous type of monarchy based on an assertion that life for human beings is unbearable outside an ordered state with a strong ruler. Shakespeare represents the unacceptable condition of anarchy with a maddened old man, stripped naked, accompanied by a fool, a few faithful followers, and a ragged, crazed beggar, wandering aimless across a bleak wasteland in the midst of a dreadful storm. If the old gods are present they do not reveal themselves, and the world seems to offer justification for everything and nothing, to be only a terrible place of struggle and suffering and emptiness. In the most famous passage of his book, Hobbes describes this same condition as one

where every man is enemy to every man; . . . wherein men live without other security, than what their own strength, and their own invention shall furnish them withal. . . . There is no place for industry; because the fruit thereof is uncertain and consequently no culture of the earth; no navigation, nor use of the commodities that may be imported by sea; no commodious building; no instruments of moving, and removing, such things as require much force; no knowledge of the face of the earth; no account of time; no arts; no letters; no society; and which is worst of all, continual fear, and danger of violent death; and the life of man, solitary, poor, nasty, brutish and short. (1, 13, 82)

Hobbes the rationalist has humanity respond to this fearful situation in a logical and practical manner by contriving a binding legal covenant with a ruler and with one another "as if every man should say to every man, *I authorize and give up my right of governing myself, to this man, or to this man, or to this assembly of men, on this condition, that thou give up thy right to him, and authorize all his actions in like manner.* This done, the multitude so united in one person, is called a *commonwealth*, in Latin *civitas*. This is the generation of that great *leviathan*, or rather, to speak more reverently, of that *mortal god*, to which we owe under the *immortal God*, our peace and defence" (2, 17, 112).

In neither *Leviathan* nor *Lear* does the world offer an absolute authority for kingship of the kind that James confidently invoked in his *Trew Law*. The state and kingship are legitimated only by what Lear calls "the art of our necessities," which Hobbes describes as the desperate need that human beings have to protect themselves from the rapacity of one another. Hobbes tries by a complicated argument to privilege religion from his skepticism; Shakespeare does not deal head-on with religion, but in *Lear* human political arrangements exist without metaphysical support. God may be present: on this question the play is understandably silent, but within the exclusively human world of the play the actions of mankind "must show the heavens more just" if sympathy and community are to shelter humanity within the state.

Shakespeare and Hobbes each saw the same problems in government, and the same necessity for founding a strong state and ruler on more solid rock than divine right and a mythical Great Chain of Being. But Shakespeare did not conceive of history in the logical terms of a philosopher like Hobbes, in which a problem is analyzed and a rational solution supplied. Whenever a Shakespearean character tries to grasp the future in the instant—Brutus pondering beforehand the effects of the murder of Caesar, Macbeth consulting the witches and trying to interpret their ambiguous symbols, Henry V justifying his war policy to his soldiers in the light of the camp fires before Agincourt—the result is not clarity but bafflement and error. There are in Shakespeare no epic prospects of history similar to the view of the future that Michael shows Adam in books 11 and 12 of *Paradise Lost*. There are, however, many scenes similar to that in *War and Peace* where Napoleon dispatches regiment after regiment into the darkness of the smoke-covered field, believing wrongly that he, the Great Man, is controlling the battle.

James was not as farsighted as either his own playwright or his son's philosopher. No matter how often he compromised, he continued to insist doggedly throughout his reign that he was king because God had made and kept him a king. But not everyone else thought so. John Chamberlain records the view of the man on the street that one of James's many speeches on the absolute authority of the king "bred generally much discomfort; to see our monarchicall powere and regall prerogative strained so high and made so transcendent every way" (May 24, 1610). But James himself may have felt the winds of change blowing over his kingdom, at least toward the end of his reign when so many of his hopes had soured. On January 13, 1621, in his opening address to the House of Commons, he peevishly said, "I have piped unto you, but you have not danced; I have mourned, but you have not lamented.... It may be it pleased God, seeing some vanity in me, to send back my words as wind spit into my own face" (McIlwain).

The court was the center of national life in the Renaissance, and here gathered all those in the nation seeking power, wealth, pleasure, and fashion. Great palaces like those of Hampton Court and Whitehall provided a regal setting for the "political nation" to conduct its affairs of state and of the heart. Under her strict control, Elizabeth's court had been relatively austere and frugal, but James Stuart was a peace-loving, tolerant, and self-indulgent man who hated the business of state and left political and economic concerns to his Privy Council and his chief secretary, the clever and scheming Robert Cecil. Only the most important affairs of state, like the Gunpowder Plot on his life in 1606, commanded his full attention.

While the king hunted the stag with his boisterous Scottish attendants, and toyed with favorites like Robert Carr, earl of Somerset, and George Villiers, duke of Buckingham, his court became notoriously and scandalously vulgar, licentious, dangerous, and corrupt. Enormous sums were gambled and given away, threatening to bankrupt the nation; faction ruled social life in a court where no one smiled "but from the teeth out"; sexual favors were exchanged for appointments; magicians and their arts were employed to influence affairs; and the sale of offices, graft, and bribery were standard. It was in this court that Shakespeare's Stuart plays provided both entertainment and social commentary. He portrayed, in an amused and sophisticated way, a court much like that of James, in the Egypt of Cleopatra and Mark Antony, but he also showed in the same play a more businesslike court, in the Rome of Octavius Caesar—to whom James was often compared—and showed it triumphing over Egyptian weakness.

11 The Great Hall at Hampton Court (40' x 105' 6" x 92'), 17th-
century woodcut (From Ernest Law, *History of Hampton Court
Palace*, 1888)

12 Hampton Court, engraving by Antonius van den Wyngaerde,

13 Whitehall Palace, Thames front, later 17th century (Courtesy
the Mansell Collection)

1558 (Courtesy Ashmolean Museum, Oxford)

14 Hanged, drawn, and quartered: execution of the Gunpowder
Plotters, engraving by Nicholas de Visscher, 1606 (Courtesy
Trustees of the British Museum)

15 The Somerset House Conference, at which a peace treaty was
signed with Spain, Flemish, perhaps by Pantajo de la Cruz, 1604.
The English noblemen are seated on the right side; *from left to
right:* Thomas, earl of Dorset, K.G., holding the Wand of the Lord
High Treasurer; Charles Howard, earl of Nottingham, K.G.;
Charles Blount, earl of Devonshire, K.G, Lieutenant of Ireland;
Henry Howard, earl of Northampton, Lord Warden of the
Cinque-Ports; Robert Cecil, Principal Secretary of State. The
Constable of Castile leads the Spanish embassy on the left.
(Courtesy National Portrait Gallery)

16 Robert Cecil, earl of Salisbury, by Jan de Critz the Elder, 1602
(Courtesy National Portrait Gallery)

17 Robert Carr, earl of Somerset, in
the style of Hilliard, ca. 1611
(Courtesy National Portrait Gallery)

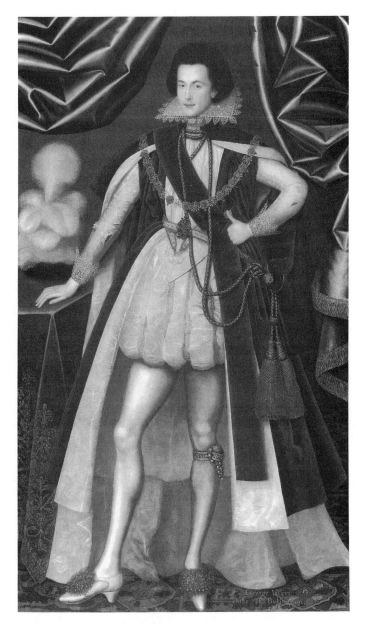

18 George Villiers, 1st duke of
Buckingham, attributed to William
Larkin, 1616 (Courtesy National
Portrait Gallery)

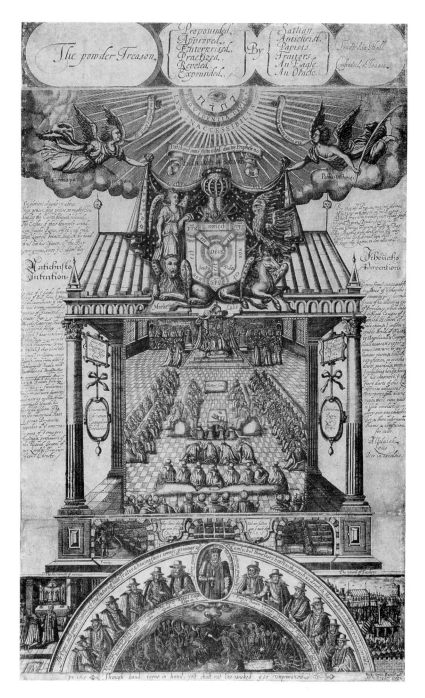

19 The Powder Treason, engraving by Martin Droeshout, 1606
(Courtesy Trustees of the British Museum)

20 The countess of Essex deals with the magus Simon Forman,
engraving by Martin Droeshout, 1612 (Courtesy Trustees of the
British Museum)

6

SEX AND FAVOR IN THE COURT

ANTONY AND CLEOPATRA, WHITEHALL

CHRISTMAS 1607

How good a king was James I? The Whig historians portrayed him as a failure: a stubborn, blundering, spendthrift, pedantic divine-right monarch out of step with his new country and locked in a struggle with the common law and the House of Commons that eventually brought England to civil war in the 1640s. Revisionist historians have recast him as a poor administrator but a fairly practical politician who cannily kept England at peace for the twenty-two years of his reign, preventing tinder-dry religious quarrels from flaring to open war and managing to get along on the antiquated economic arrangements that kept him always needy. True, his two greatest projects, the union with Scotland and the Great Contract—that would have traded in some of his various feudal rights for regular subsidies—failed, but he ended the long war with Spain and avoided a showdown with Parliament.

On the whole the nation seemed satisfied with his rule, and in a poll of the kind we run today his policies might have gotten an approval rating of, say, 53 or 54 percent. But he himself had what modern public-relations people would instantly recognize as an image problem. He had an intelligent and sensitive face and deep eyes, but he was not the charismatic or regal figure that Daniel Mytens made him in his official portrait (see figure 7). As he was described long afterward, and spitefully, by Sir Anthony Weldon, James

> was of a middle stature, more corpulent through his cloathes
> then in his body, yet fat enough, his cloathes ever being

made large and easie, the doublets quilted for steletto proofe, his breeches in great pleits and full stuffed; hee was naturally of a timorous disposition, which was the reason of his quilted doublets; his eyes large, ever rowling after any stranger that came in his presence, insomuch, as many for shame have left the roome, as being out of countenance; his beard was very thin: his tongue too large for his mouth, which ever made him speak full in the mouth, and made him drink very uncomely, as if eating his drink, which came out into the cup of each side of his mouth; his skin was as soft as taffeta sarsnet, which felt so, because hee never washt his hands, onely rubb'd his fingers ends slightly with the wet end of a napkin; his legs were very weake, having had (as was thought) some foul play in his youth, or rather before he was born, that he was not able to stand at seven years of age, that weaknesse made him ever leaning on other mens shoulders; his walke was ever circular, his fingers ever in that walke fidling about his cod-piece; he was very temperate in his exercises and in his dyet, and not intemperate in his drinking . . . he drank very often . . . rather out of a custom than any delight, . . . he was very constant in all things, (his favourites excepted,) in which he loved change . . . in his apparell so constant, as by his good will he would never change his cloathes untill worn out to very ragges. (II, 1)

James's oversize tongue and habit of speaking thickly, spraying spit around him, were probably symptoms of the disease porphyria, which he passed on through his daughter Elizabeth of Bohemia to his descendent George III, in whom it manifested itself as purple urine and the derangement that so long incapacitated him.

It was not only James's personal appearance that put his subjects off. They disliked his talking about having been made king by God Himself, even if he retreated when push came to shove, and they found the 158 hungry Scots he appointed to offices in the state and the household to be a set of voracious "locusts" and "horsleeches" (Levack, 61). He was also too "clerkish" for them, with his writing and his intellectual talk. He was believed to be a tricky Machiavel, who at the same time was, paradoxically, derelict in his duties, dedicating "rainy weather to his standish [writing desk], and faire to his hounds, or any thing else that owned the voice of pleasure" (Osborne, 168).

His avoidance of court business and ceremonies was notorious, and the court whispered that he spent all his time at one of his hunting lodges, where he drank, enjoyed his favorites, interrogated witches, and listened to the gossip purveyed by Secretary Lake, who controlled access to him and determined which papers he signed. Lake, who had been reading to Queen Elizabeth when the countess of Warwick told him that she was dead, was hated for his power, and it was whispered that his wife, a passionate woman, beat him. In the country James hunted the stag from horseback. (His favorite hound, Jowler, was once kidnapped and sent back with a petition tied to his collar asking "Good Master Jowler" to intercede with the king since the dog saw him more than did any of his poor subjects.) The king, whose weak legs caused him to be tied to his mount, hunted with such intensity that he would piss in the saddle rather than dismount, and he delighted in practicing such ancient rites of venery as "taking the assay of the stag" by thrusting his hand into the entrails of the freshly killed beast.

The king's family life was as messy as his person. He no longer liked his wife who had, it was cruelly said, little "to make the king uxorious" (see figure 8), and he fondled in public the handsome young men with whom he was infatuated. She returned the dislike with interest and had in Scotland entered into factional politics in stubborn and dangerous ways. She fought the king over control of their eldest son and embarrassed him frequently on occasions of state, suggesting her Catholic sympathies by refusing to take communion at their coronation, for example, or by her performances at the court masques. There was a story—nothing more, but nonetheless telling for that—that once when she went hunting she purposely overshot the deer and killed old Jowler. She was not popular in the court, but one diplomat, the Venetian Nicolò Molin, in his summary report to the Most Serene Republic for the year 1607 spoke of her tactfully as understanding that "those who govern desire to be left alone, and so she professes indifference. All she ever does is to beg a favour for some one. She is full of kindness for those who support her, but on the other hand she is terrible, proud, unendurable to those she dislikes" (*Calendar of State Papers* [Venetian], X, 513). Prince Henry openly disliked his father, and by 1607 was, like many other heirs to the English throne, setting himself up as his father's mirror opposite: martial, businesslike, smartly princely in all respects (see figure 9).

From the distance of Jacobean England, Elizabeth's court began to look increasingly splendid and moral, presided over by the wise old Burleigh, its style set by Robin Dudley, the earl of Leicester and perhaps the queen's lover. The guard was commanded by Sir Walter Raleigh in his silver armor, who was rivaled by the dashing and reckless young earl of Essex. In retrospect, Elizabeth became "the most glorious sun that ever shined in our firmament of England" (Weldon, I, 313), and Elizabethan England became the good old days, in which the Armada was defeated and red-haired Queen Bess ruled with love and firmness over all Englishmen. Approving jokes were told about the way Elizabeth had kept James dangling for years, grinding his teeth up in the damp rooms of the palace of Holyrood in Edinburgh, waiting to be named her heir. When she was old, it was said, her younger maids, at her urging, would mask themselves to look like her and dance so lustily that spies reported to James that the old queen seemed likely to live forever.

James's court, by contrast with Elizabeth's, was seen as decadent. It was not simply that James and his courtiers were immoral—nothing else was expected—it was that they were corrupt without style. *La Princesse de Clèves*, a novel published anonymously in 1678 and written by Madame de Lafayette, a minor member of the court of Louis XIV, perhaps with the help of such members of her salon as Madame de Sévigné and the duc de La Rochefoucauld, offers a picture of the ideal conception of court culture, wicked but stylish, that was developing. The novel is set a century earlier, in the court of Henri II, where James Stuart's mother, daughter of a French Guise and queen of France for eighteen months as consort to François II, is one of the central characters.

The court is an artificial, claustrophobic place absorbed with the smallest detail of the king's life and searching always for the king's favor. Faction and intrigue are everywhere: the houses of Guise and Montmorency are the leading parties in the novel, similar to the Cecils, Howards, Herberts, Percies, and Villiers of the Stuart court. Love, wealth, religion, rank, and taste are all caught up in palace politics. Gossip never ceases about who is in, who out, who is in love with whom, who takes priority of place at athletic contests, feasts, weddings, and the many other rituals that organize court life. Privacy is difficult to come by, life is lived in public at the king's levée and coucher, visitors are received in ladies' bedrooms, everyone scrupulously observes everyone else, letters are passed around and read aloud.

No one works, of course, and love is the chief interest of the court. Everyone is in love with at least one other person, life is a movement from one lover to another, and the time is passed in the elaborate management of these affairs. Chastity may be praised, but infidelity is institutionalized. The king's mistress,

Diane de Poitiers, who had also been mistress to his father, François I, is at least as powerful a figure as the queen, Catherine de Médicis. Marriages are entirely a matter of convenience, made for wealth and advancement of political ends. The story of the prince de Clèves, who dies of some vague psychosomatic illness when he believes his wife unfaithful, telling her on his deathbed that he has been faithful to her even though he knows that she does not love him, is considered sufficiently bizarre to provide the plot for the novel.

Lies and deceptions are the order of the day in a place where politeness requires the concealment of true feelings. "If you judge from appearance here, you will be often mistaken; what appears is seldom the truth," one of the characters helpfully advises another. To the outer world this may appear hypocrisy, but masking is the dominant mode of the court. Social life is one long effort to suppress what is actually felt, and one of the most critical court activities is trying to discern, in a careless gesture, a misspoken word, or a blush, what is actually being felt by another person at a time of great stress.

In this hothouse atmosphere art flourishes, its rich formalities matching the high style of court manners. Italian painters and architects are highly fashionable. Great nobles and prelates compete for their services, and some appreciation of the arts is required of gentlemen and ladies. Plays were frequent, but provided only backgrounds for flirtations and intrigues. Although Madame de Lafayette's king, Louis XIV, patronized great playwrights (notably Molière and Racine), theatrical performance at the court is treated in an extremely casual way in the *Princesse de Clèves:* "One evening, when there was to be a play at the Louvre, we were all waiting until the King and Madame de Valentinois [the favorite] should come for it to begin, when we were told that Madame de Valentinois was unwell and that the King would not be coming. Everybody guessed that this indisposition of the Duchess was really some squabble with the King. Of course we all knew how dreadfully jealous he had been of M. de Brissac while he was at Court, but it was now several days since he had gone back to Piedmont, so we could not imagine what this was all about" (73). It turns out that while the king and Madame de Valentinois were dressing for the performance the king had noticed that a valuable ring he had given his mistress was missing from her finger and had grown furious at the thought that she must have given it to her most recent lover. They had quarreled bitterly and the king had returned in a miserable state of mind to his apartments. The play, apparently as disposable as a handkerchief at court, was canceled.

The style of courtly life in the English court of James I and in the later and more sophisticated French court of Louis XIV bear no comparison, but Madame de Lafayette's picture of the court of Henri II gives a good sense of the interests of the court of James I as well. There was always, however, even at its best, something noticeably tacky, rough, crude, even sleazy, about the Jacobean court. Even its sins were somehow lumpish. Looking back some years later, one observer remembered James's court as a place of "fools and bawds, mimics and catimites," where debauchery was in fashion and practiced openly (Hutchinson, 84). Another observer, Sir John Harington, by no means a prude, was most distressed at the change from the old queen's court, where he had been, he notes, "sometime an humble presenter and assistant" of plays. But now he reports in 1606 of a visit to James's court:

> I neer did see such lack of good order, discretion, and sobriety, as I have now done. I have passed much time in seeing the royal sports of hunting and hawking, where the manners were such as made me devise the beasts were pursuing the sober creation, and not man in quest of exercise or food. I will now, in good sooth, declare to you, who will not blab, that the gunpowder fright is got out of all our heads, and we are going on, hereabouts, as if the devil was contriving every man shoud blow up himself, by wild riot, excess, and devastation of time and temperance. The great ladies do go well-masked, and indeed it be the only show of their modesty, to conceal their countenance; but, alack, they meet with such countenance to uphold their strange doings, that I marvel not at ought that happens. (I, 352)

In the earliest years of the reign the most powerful man in the court was the dwarfish Robert Cecil—Elizabeth cruelly called him "pigmy"—who ran the kingdom. Cecil was a farsighted and dedicated administrator, one of the few in his time who understood the transition taking place from what we call a feudal kingdom to a modern centralized state, but he was a manipulator, for there was no other way of working. He looked like a villain (see figures 15 and 16), and so everyone thought of him as a deformed and deceitful Machiavel who showed the king "how to enhance his prerogative so above the laws, that he might enslave the nation" (Weldon, I, 324). The gossips of the court whispered that he was a thief of honest men's lands and homes, the seducer of every woman he could lay his hands on. Courted and hated by all, he was attacked by his rival for power Francis Bacon, covertly in "On Cunning" and more openly and cruelly in "On Deformity." A mock epitaph, identifying Cecil with the hunchbacked Richard III, exulted:

> Here lieth Robin Crookback, unjustly reckoned
> A Richard the Third, he was Judas the Second.

The second man of power in the court, Henry Howard, earl of Northampton (see figure 15), did not merely look sinister, he was. Catholic and in Spanish pay, he was a master of the patronage game and of the double or triple cross (Peck, 1982).

The younger courtiers were less astute but no better morally than their seniors. Dress was increasingly ostentatious, banquets became more epicurean, and the stakes at the gaming tables where one had to be seen became ruinous. At the Christmas season of "Golden Play," no one was allowed at the tables without £300 in cash. The king would stand by, allowing one of his favorites, who hoped to receive some of the winnings, to place bets for him. Lawrence Stone speaks of "gambling orgies" in which, for example, Robert Cecil lost £800 on one occasion and £1,000 at dice on another to the earl of Montgomery, who was throwing for the king.

Just how rowdy court life could become appears in a description (quoted in Chapter 4) by Sir John Harington of the feast, followed by a masque, that James gave in 1606 at Theobalds for his brother-in-law, Christian of Denmark. That occasion was particularly revolting, but feasting and entertainment at the Stuart court at any time were not as formal and solemn as performances before heads of state are nowadays. It was, after all, a political occasion and a revel, a feast of release and of pleasure: crowded, noisy, flashy—the setting for competition of haughty aristocrats. But release regularly got out of hand. Thieves were busy during performances of plays, even in court, and there were losses of "chaynes, Jewels, purces and such like loose ware." Dudley Carleton gossips that a number of the ladies in the audience lost their skirts on one occasion, though he does not specify how, or with what consequences. But the suggestion is that things got rough. When the play was over the audience would stand little on the order of their going. It was customary at the end of a performance for elaborate refreshments to be offered to the more favored members of the audience, and the crush to get to the food and drink often turned to riot. What happened after a masque at court on

Twelfth Night 1618 filled the more sophisticated Venetians with horror. After the king departed, they reported,

forthwith the parties concerned pounced upon the prey like so many harpies. The table was covered almost entirely with seasoned pasties and very few sugar confections. There were some large figures, but they were of painted pasteboard for ornament. The repast was served upon glass plates or dishes and at the first assault they upset the table and the crash of glass platters reminded me precisely of a severe hailstorm at Midsummer smashing the window glass. The story ended at half past two in the morning and half disgusted and weary we returned home.

Should your lordships writhe on reading or listening to this tediousness you may imagine the weariness I feel in relating it. (*Calendar of State Papers* [Venetian], XV, 114)

At Whitehall in 1605 there was so great a rush for the exit that "a banquet which was prepared for the king in the great chamber was overturned, table and all, before it was scarce touched" (Carleton, January 7, 1605).

The gossip in the Stuart court which emerges from several Jacobean court memoirs of the "secret-life" variety was as rough as the scene. All were written long afterward, in the 1640s and early 1650s, after the Civil War had made it clear that the writers had lived through momentous times. The authors were themselves courtiers: Francis Osborne, Master of the Horse in the household of Philip Herbert, earl of Pembroke and Montgomery; Sir Anthony Weldon, clerk of the Board of Green Cloth, a financial control office; and Doctor Godfrey Goodman, a court chaplain and later bishop of Gloucester. Considered as reporters of Jacobean court society, these courtiers are considerably less than objective, and their books have in consequence been ignored by responsible historians. Seen from the vantage of the present, Osborne and Weldon especially look like the two courtiers Rosencrantz and Guildenstern in Tom Stoppard's play *Rosencrantz and Guildenstern Are Dead,* who stand largely outside the main line of the action, participating only in odd scenes here and there, interpreting everything in the light of their own interests, never having any real clue to what is going on in the main plot. But the memoirs do preserve for us an unofficial view of day-to-day court living, of what people were saying and feeling. The courtiers are fearful, cynical, mean-spirited, narrow, and desirous of believing the worst of everyone and everything, in the usual manner of fashionable men and women in close competition with one another. As political history these memoirs are suspect; as court gossip they are the thing itself. Interestingly, the Osborne and Weldon memoirs were edited and printed at the beginning of the nineteenth century by the historical novelist and antiquarian Sir Walter Scott, who was anxious to preserve documents of life in the court of a Scottish king.

Although fearing his deviousness—"how perfect the king was in the art of dissimulation, or, to give it his own phrase, king-craft" (Weldon, I, 410)—the English courtiers looked down on the provincial ways of the Scottish king and his Danish queen. James's pedantic and ostentatious learning was sneered at as unworthy a great king, while publishing books was thought a clerkish business avoided by true aristocrats. Admitted to be "a man of great intellectuals," James's bustling intrusion into detailed religious questions, for example, was still treated as vainglorious meddling that gave support to the Puritans by boggling at "surplice, crosier, ring . . . and Common Prayer Book."

These memoirs sometimes bring us surprisingly close to actual life in the Stuart court, as in a little picture of the king amusing himself on an ordinary evening when he

> after supper would come forth to see pastimes and fooleries; in which Sir Ed. Souch, Sir George Goring, and Sir John Finit, were the chiefe and master fools, and surely this fooling got them more then any others wisdome, far above them in desert. Souch his part it was to sing bawdy songs, and tell bawdy tales—Finit to compose these songs; then were a set of fidlers brought up on purpose for this fooling; and Goring was master of the game for fooleries, some time presenting David Droman, and Archie Armstrong, the kings fool, on the back of the other fools, to tilt one at another, till they fell together by the ears; sometimes the property was presented by them in antick dances. But Sir Jo. Millisent, who was never known before, was commended for notable fooling; and so was he indeed the best extemporary fool of them all. (Weldon, I, 398)

Not all amusements in the court circle were so bumptious or so innocent. Symon, servant to Sir Thomas Monson, had, Weldon tells us, "a catzo of an immense length and bigness; with this, being his tabor-stick, his palm of his hand his tabor, and his mouth his pipe, he would so imitate a tabor-pipe, as if it had been so indeed. To this musick would Mrs Turner, the young ladies, and some of that ging, dance ever after supper. The old lady, who loved that musick as well as her daughters, would sit and laugh; she could scarce sit for laughing; and it was believed that some of them danced after that pipe without the tabor" (I, 415). The ingenious and gifted Symon came to an unfortunate end when Sir Thomas "coming to hear of it, turned him away."

In a court where men and women "loved but from the teeth outwards," the competition for favor and position was relentless and brutal. Although cruder, the Stuart court did resemble theatrical portrayals of "Italian" court life by such contemporary playwrights as Marston, Webster, and Middleton. Bribes, pensions, fines, offices, rents, and livings were the stuff of life in Whitehall, and envy of anyone who had anything—wealth, beauty, rank, money, or power—pervaded social life. In this desperate place, lone individuals had no chance, and faction was the means by which people sought to protect themselves from their enemies and further their own interests. Something of the vehemence with which court vendettas were pursued can be heard still in Prince Henry's exclamation about his enemies, the hated Howards, how "if ever he were king, he would not leave one of that family to piss against a wall" (Weldon, I, 394). When Francis Bacon, surely the most subtle intellect at court, tried to strike out on his own, the duke of Buckingham, the king's favorite, made him crawl over and kiss his foot while asking pardon. Watching factions take shape, maneuver against one another, and then break up was one of the prime amusements of the court, and no factional fight in James's time was bloodier than the famous battle by which the Villiers family got rid of the powerful earl of Somerset and the Howards, using every trick in the book, eventually bringing them down by providing James with a new and younger favorite and by convicting their rivals of the murder of Sir Thomas Overbury.

Sex played as crucial a part as money and intrigue in these power struggles. George Villiers was carefully groomed—his breath sweetened, his hair curled, his ribbons carefully tied, his walk coached—to catch the eye of the king. Nothing was more the subject of fascinated court talk than matchmaking, marriage, love affairs, and sexual gossip. The courtiers delighted in hearing that when Buckingham was in Spain he had been tricked with a diseased whore provided by his archenemy, the earl of Bristol, ambassador to Madrid, and they buzzed for years with the story of how the countess of Essex, Frances Howard, got free of her first husband, with the king's help, by advertising the earl's impotence and substituting a veiled young woman for herself in a virginity test conducted by a group of elder women. Fortune-tellers, wizards, and apothecaries, casting spells, preparing charms, and concocting love potions and aphrodisiacs, played an important part in the court's amorous games (see figure 20).

James recognized dynastic necessities and, though he once declared women to be no more than "irritamenta libidinis," during courtship and early married life he played the part of the romantic lover and attentive husband with Anne of Denmark. She had numerous miscarriages but eventually bore him seven children, of whom only three survived. The last pregnancy seems to have been in 1606, so James probably left his marriage bed for good about that time. James's real sexual interest, increasingly so in later life, was in men. Some historians of sexuality argue that the idea of an exclusive homosexual identity did not come into being until the latter part of the nineteenth century, and neither the term nor the strong social antipathy that has gone with it were a part of Renaissance culture. Love between man and man was taken for granted, the argument goes, as one part of a broad range of acceptable erotic behavior in a society that put a high value on male bonding in various forms. Sodomy, mutual masturbation, fellatio, and other practices were not thought of as anything out of the ordinary unless they brought harm to one of the parties involved, a young boy or an apprentice, for instance (Bruce R. Smith; Bray). Christopher Marlowe, Francis Bacon, and Sir Anthony Ashley, by way of a few examples, practiced homoeroticism openly.

James's bisexuality and his ambiguous view of sodomy do fit with this view, but without any question the court and the nation were scandalized by the king's unwillingness to keep his physical love of men in the closet. Perhaps if he had carried it off with more style and grace it would have been less commented on, but, like all things in his court, there was something gross about his constant playing with himself and fondling his favorites in public. His large eyes ever rolled "after any stranger that came into his presence, insomuch, as many for shame have left the roome, as being out of countenance." Then too, there was always something extravagant, some obsessive psychological need, that gave James's masculine affairs an unhealthy air.

Perhaps it was all genetic, or all cultural, but James's homoeroticism would seem to have been deeply entangled in his bizarre childhood background. The stresses of his remarkable earlier years set up an oedipal situation of extraordinary intensity and intricacy. Ernest Jones's famous Freudian analysis of Hamlet's problems (Hamlet delays his revenge because Claudius has acted out the prince's own repressed oedipal desires) is not nearly as strange as the actual

Stuart family romance. The "common theme" in the early life of James Stuart, as in Hamlet's, was the "death of fathers." After the prepartum deaths of his putative biological father, David Riccio, and his legal father, Henry Darnley, James's surrogate fathers—his various guardians—were cut down one after another in terrifying circumstances, sometimes before his eyes. No wonder that in time he became so neurotically fearful of death that he wore his famous stiletto-proof vest, went to pieces at the sight of a naked weapon (though not of one onstage, apparently), and could not bring himself to attend the funerals of Queen Elizabeth, his heir, or his wife.

The plot played out again and again was one in which James's fathers, far from threatening to castrate the son for desiring the mother, were unable to defend themselves. In the Stuart family triangle, James was threatened by a series of strong women: his mother, Mary; the witches of Lothian; Elizabeth; Anne. The block to heterosexual release was, it would seem, a sensational politicized version of the classic Freudian pattern of weak father and dominating mother.

When James was thirteen he found tenderness, likely for the first time, in a substitute father, his cousin Esmé Stuart d'Aubigny, a worldly Frenchman in his thirties (see figure 4), who came to Scotland and became the king's faithful servant, his closest adviser (as duke of Lennox), and in all likelihood his first lover (Bergeron). James wrote passionate, metrically correct love poems to this one man who truly cared for him. But before long Esmé was accused of crimes and driven from Scotland by the magnates who feared his influence over the king. A piece of touching evidence has survived to tell us that Esmé, for all his worldly sophistication, probably genuinely cared for James Stuart. James held long theological discussions with the Catholic Esmé in his pedantic, earnest way and converted him to the strict Calvinism in which the young king had been raised. On the surface this could be simply a politically calculating surrender on the older man's part, humoring a precocious and powerful child. But when Esmé died shortly after he returned to France, he chose to die not a Catholic death with the sacraments but a Protestant one, "unhousel'd, disappointed, unanneal'd."

Although he lost Esmé, James was from that time on close to a number of handsome young men, and when he became king of England he openly made love to a succession of favorites, major and minor, fawning on them in public and private, unable to deny them anything they asked for, neither lands, nor money, gifts, titles. The impudence of a little scene observed by a Venetian secretary, Giovanni Scaramelli, at the coronation in 1603 (how Venetian to notice the sexual byplay at so solemn an occasion!) gives the tone of James's relationship with his handsome young men, and the way in which they flirted with him. "The Earl of Pembroke, a handsome youth, who is always with the King and always joking with him, actually kissed his Majesty's face, whereupon the King laughed and gave him a little cuff" (*Calendar of State Papers* [Venetian], X, 77). Later James took up with Pembroke's younger brother, the even more handsome Philip, who as a result of this intimacy was made earl of Montgomery in 1605. Later, Robert Carr (or Ker), a strikingly beautiful but not strikingly intelligent Scot whom James nursed after he broke his leg at a tournament, became the major favorite and, in time, the all-powerful earl of Somerset (see figure 17). James's need for the open affection of these men was not in his control. He toyed constantly in public with his own codpiece, fondled his lovers openly, nibbled their cheeks, and wrote passionate love letters to them.

Somerset was eventually replaced by George Villiers, duke of Buckingham, the great love of James's life (see figure 18). A letter from Buckingham describes the prince and his minion lying in the same bed, or at least in beds that allowed their heads to touch. Another letter from the king to Buckingham tells us that James saw himself in a sentimental, even mawkish, relationship, both wife and husband, to the handsome young men he loved so dearly, and to whom he wrote such indiscreet letters: "I cannot content myself without sending you this present, praying God that I may have a joyful and comfortable meeting with you and that we may make at this Christmas a new marriage ever to be kept hereafter; for, God so love me, as I desire only to live in this world for your sake, and that I had rather live banished in any part of the earth with you than live a sorrowful widow's life without you. And so God bless you, my sweet child and wife, and grant that ye may ever be a comfort to your dear dad and husband" (Letter 218, December 1623). There is a touch of innocence here still—"dear dad"—as there always was about James, even at his most sinister, but there is no doubt about what is involved. No more doubt than there is in the letter that the king wrote to Carr when he was breaking up with him in 1615 that complained of the earl's "long creeping back and withdrawing yourself from lying in my chamber, notwithstanding my many hundred times earnest soliciting you to the contrary, accounting that but as a point of unkindness" (Letter 159, early 1615).

In spite of his open homoeroticism, James condemned sodomy in *Basilikon*

Doron as heinous and unnatural, and advised his son that it, along with treason and incest, were crimes that should never be pardoned. He was horrified and defended himself violently when the solicitor-general, Sir Henry Yelverton, compared him in the House of Commons to the homosexual Edward II, the subject of Marlowe's earlier, scandalous play of that name. There is something more here than mere hypocrisy, though probably a good deal of that. Some unwillingness or even inability perhaps to connect what he did with the words he and others used. But if the king blanked out the connection between his homoeroticism and the practices he and others regularly attributed with pious horror to the biblical Cities of the Plain, as well as to Catholic Rome and Jesuit seminaries, his subjects did not:

> Now, as no other reason appeared in favour of their choyce [as favorites] but handsomnesse, so the love the king shewed was as amorously con-vayed, as if he had mistaken their sex, and thought them ladies; which I have seene Sommerset [Carr] and Buckingham labour to resemble, in the effeminatenesse of their dressings; though in w[horish] lookes and wanton gestures, they exceeded any part of woman kind my conversation did ever cope withall. Nor was his love, or what else posterity will please to call it, (who must be the judges of all that history shall informe,) carried on with a discretion sufficient to cover a lesse scandalous behaviour; for the kings kissing them after so lascivious a mode in public, and upon the theatre, as it were, of the world, prompted many to imagine some things done in the tyring-house that exceed my expressions no lesse then they do my expe-rience. (Osborne, 274)

Would the connection between the theater and homosexuality taken for granted here, as elsewhere, have stimulated the king's interest in his players?

Although his subjects did not dare say so to the king's face, some of them at least recoiled from sexual activities which Sir Philip Sidney had called the "abhominable filthines" (190) of Plato's Phaedrus and Symposium. Satirists like Marston and Donne named no one, but attacked buggery as one of the more sensational upper-class crimes, particularly at court. Sir John Oglander, a visitor from the Isle of Wight who was unaccustomed to court ways, was, like many another, startled when he visited Whitehall to see that the king "loved young men his favourites, better than women, loving them beyond the love of men to women. I never yet saw any fond husband make so much or so great dalliance

over his beautiful spouse as I have seen King James over his favourites, especially the Duke of Buckingham" (196). The folk were less polite in their
laughter at the practices of this strange king, and a contemporary ballad mocked
two of his greatest weaknesses—with again a glance, perhaps, at the players?

> At Royston and Newmarket
> He'll hunt till he be lean.
> But he hath merry boys
> That with masques and toys
> Can make him fat again.
> (Thomson, 176)

In the time of James Stuart the English court increasingly appeared to sober
people of all ranks a shabby place of epicures, perverts, thieves, beggars, quar-
relers, and sycophants. This was, however, no biblical Sodom or Babylon, or the
scarlet whore of Rome that so exercised Puritan preachers. A doting king playing
with himself and his minions in public, young men of good families prostituting
themselves to get ahead, the peers and great ones of the realm falling down
drunk, rioting, gambling, and whoring their substance away. Sneak thieves stole
fortunes, petty knaves and upscale sluts traded in treason and poison, while
virtue was made a laughingstock. And everywhere there were the quarrelsome,
violent, noisy Scots who had come down with the king from his native land to
suck like an infestation of parasites the life out of the nation.

The players could not improve the morality of the court, but they could
repair its image, and Shakespeare undertook a defense of the king and his court
in 1607 with a play in the popular Roman mode about two of the great sensu-
alists of history: the conquering general Mark Antony and his "Egyptian dish,"
Cleopatra, queen of Egypt. Published first in the 1623 folio of Shakespeare's
plays, *Antony and Cleopatra* cannot be dated with certainty, but scholars have for
good reasons long assigned it to 1607–08. In that Christmas season the King's
Men performed thirteen plays at Whitehall between December 26, 1607, and
February 7, 1608, playing twice on January 6 and once again on January 17.
The plays paid for from the Chamber accounts on those occasions are not
specified, but following their usual practice the players would have taken their
newest plays to the palace for performance on the first nights of the festivities.
One of those plays was probably *Antony and Cleopatra*.

Nothing in her fate seems more obscene to Cleopatra than that after she is conquered she will be staged in Rome by the "quick comedians," who in some hasty piece of sensational theater will bring Antony "drunken forth," while "some squeaking Cleopatra boy[s her] greatness I' th' posture of a whore" (5.2.220). Her long-nosed aristocratic disdain for the public theater and its crude delight in staging scandal in high places is not far from the English court's usual view of plays as entertainments performed by servants. But the players were also what Hamlet calls them: "the abstract and brief chronicles of the time. After your death you were better have a bad epitaph than their ill report while you live" (2.2.524).

Plutarch, from whom Shakespeare drew his plot, contrasted two distinct character types in his story, the sensual Antony and the tightly-controlled Octavius Caesar, later the Emperor Augustus, founder of the Roman empire and author of the worldwide peace known as the *pax Romana*. James I, who liked to present himself as Solomon in his wisdom, also cultivated an ancillary image of himself as Caesar Augustus in his statecraft (Davies). His coronation medal shows him wearing a laurel wreath and bears an inscription hailing him as "Caesar the heir of the Caesars." At the coronation itself, banners proclaimed him "Augustus Novus." Poets and divines throughout the reign expanded on the role of "Our Augustus," and drew parallels between Jacobus Pacificus' peace with Spain and Augustus' pax Romana. James's efforts to unite England, Scotland, and Wales into one country were treated as parallel to Augustus' imperial achievement in ensuring that, as Shakespeare put it, "the three-nooked world Shall bear the olive freely." Shakespeare went a step farther, in his usual way, by giving his character Octavius, on his way to being but not yet become Augustus Caesar, one distinct trait not found in his source, that identified him more firmly with James. The stage Octavius has a weak head for drink, and at the orgy on Pompey's ship enters into the required exchange of toasts only with a well-founded reluctance—"It's a monstrous labor when I wash my brain And it grows fouler" (2.7.98)—for in a moment he has difficulty speaking clearly. Weldon tells us that James drank frequently but "rather out of custom than any delight. [He] seldom drank at any one time above four spoonfulls, many times not above one or two" (II, 3).

In keeping with James's command, Shakespeare did not, however, directly represent the living monarch on the stage. But the audience at Whitehall that Christmas would have been aware that the character of Octavius, representing order and rationality in conflict with anarchy and sensuality, figured James

Stuart in his official position as the governor of the court and the representative of state morality. They might also have observed, as has been interestingly argued by H. Neville Davies, that James's brother-in-law, King Christian of Denmark, had many characteristics in common with Antony. Christian was a soldier, an expert horseman and tilter, and a lover as well, "a man of little sexual restraint," Davies calls him. He was as great a drinker as a whoremaster, drinking thirty to forty glasses in an evening and then setting down in his tables whether he had been carried to bed simply "incapable" or entirely "paralytic." We have already seen Christian in action at the Alexandrian feast at Theobalds, and his departure from Gravesend in August 1606 resembled in many ways—the grandeur of the ships, the exchange of courtesies, and the drunkenness and incapacity of many of the Danes and the English—the drinking scene on Pompey's ship in *Antony*, where the triple pillars of the world get thoroughly plastered and stagger about in a drunken and riotous dance of life. The cup is passed many times, until all, not just Caesar, are drunk enough to be out of themselves.

No doubt the court would have been amused by the parallels between Antony and Christian, and they would have taken as entirely appropriate the familiar identification of James with Octavius. But they could not have thought that the play referred closely and precisely to any contemporary persons or set of political events. James was not, after all, pursuing his hard-drinking Danish brother-in-law to the death for the control of Protestant Europe. Shakespeare's court plays were parables, we might say, not allegories, and the looser form of analogy protected the patronage playwright from charges of lèse majesté by allowing him to press all the "hot buttons" without committing the players to any particular party or ideological stance. Clearly, the issue that most occupied Shakespeare in *Antony* was Stuart court corruption, which was reflected in the excesses of Egypt and the Roman Antony's submersion in them.

The key to fixing the court's image problem was an increase in scale. James and his courtiers looked cheap and vulgar only so long as they were confined to the realistic settings of Whitehall and Windsor. Relocate them to some epic scene and their English vices became Egyptian virtues. London's profligate waste could on the banks of the Nile appear magnificent generosity; carelessness about duties, a refusal to be bound to dull mundanities; lust, energy and fertility. What was required and provided was a vast imperial setting, "Whate'er the ocean pales, or sky inclips." There are forty-two scenes, and the action moves quickly back and forth from Alexandria to Rome, Sicily, Parthia, Athens,

Actium, and Egypt again. The language takes us farther out along the "ranged arch" of a Roman Empire nearly as vast as the British Empire, then at its beginnings, would be. Exotic names stud the play: Cyprus, Lydia, Parthia, Media, Mesopotamia, Sardinia, Scythia, Syria, and Palestine. The vastness of the world exceeds geography and reaches out to include the sky, the sun, the moon, the stars, and the cosmos, the realms of fire and air.

As the world is large, so is it rich and grand, never petty or pinched. The soldier speaks of quartering the world, and fleets move across its oceans "with ships made cities." The vision is cosmic: "Oh sun, Burn the great sphere thou mov'st in! darkling stand The varying shore o' th' world" (4.15.10). As it is vast, so is the world bounteous, fertile, fecund, generous, and throbbing with life, pulsing with vitality. As the Nile spreads its rich mud over the fields, the sower merely drops his seeds and plenty springs up. Where one thing dies, another grows out of the decay. Julius Caesar "ploughed" great Cleopatra and she "cropped," and so does everything else in Egypt, where all "O'erflows the measure," and the earth is heavy with produce, with fish, flesh, and wine.

The commonplace shabbiness of James's court was transformed in this way to a generous Egypt where palace vices like greed or lust, mean in Whitehall, become fecundity, delight in the stuff of the world, and élan vital. Whitehall's bored and restless search for novelty becomes in Egypt participation in the constant and rapid change that is the rhythm of all existence. Nothing here holds its visible shape for more than an instant; whatever is, is only for a moment, and then is gone in a flash, as something new springs up in its place.

The major characters of the play all feel this world of change in which they participate. Pompey knows of the gods, for example, that "Whiles we are suitors to their throne, decays The thing we sue for" (2.1.3). Water, of Nile or of Ocean, is the primary element of a fluid world where everything is in flux. Antony knows, no less than Caesar and Pompey, that "quietness, grown sick of rest, would purge By any desperate change" (1.3.53).

In the cutthroat competition of this ever-turning political and sexual world, the only virtue is to know your moment and seize it. Pompey seeks power and dies because he misses the turning of his fortunes with the tide, when Menas urges him to cut the throats of his shipboard guests. Lepidus is too weak, too friendly, to hold his third of the world, and so Caesar quickly gobbles him up. Left to divide the world between them, Antony and Caesar cannot "stall" together, and are soon at one another's throats. Men and nations move like the

waters of the Nile, spreading "slime and ooze" out of which new crops are bred
and "strange serpents" emerge in the heat of the sun. Like the river, the sky too
brings constant change. With everything lost, his fleet and his army beaten by
Caesar, Antony knows that he must die by his own hand. As he stands preparing
for death he asks his last, significantly named, attendant, "Eros, thou yet
behold'st me?" as if he could not believe that with all his power gone he still
exists, holds his shape, occupies space in the world. Everything else has gone,
why not his person? And then he turns his eyes upward and sees the great bil-
lowing clouds rolling across the sky, constantly changing shape as they go:

> Sometime we see a cloud that's dragonish,
> A vapor sometime like a bear or lion,
> A [tower'd] citadel, a pendant rock,
> A forked mountain, or blue promontory
> With trees upon't that nod unto the world,
> And mock our eyes with air.

For a moment the clouds resemble a horse, but in an instant more they lose all
definition,

> That which is now a horse, even with a thought
> The rack dislimns, and makes it indistinct
> As water is in water.
>   (4.14.2)

Shakespeare worked for his royal master not just a piece of propaganda but a
remarkable transformation, a true piece of theatrical magic. While James-
Octavius coolly controls the world, in the course of the play the shabby deca-
dence of the Stuart court and James's domesticated carnalities—"old dad"
writing to "Steenie" about how he misses him—take on liveliness and erotic
excitement in a world that is big, rich, filled with potential delight, and transient.
Homoeroticism is avoided, except perhaps in the bonding of the Roman soldiers, where it is close to but not on the surface. But Cleopatra and her poly-
morphous sexuality puts onstage the excitement of illicit love of all kinds. Sex in
Egypt takes place in no "dull, stale, tired" matrimonial bed. Marriage is a clog on
pleasure, in Alexandria as in London, and Antony no sooner marries one of his
chaste Roman matrons, the martial Fulvia or the demure Octavia, than he is
bored with her and longs for his "Egyptian dish" again. Hers are all the amorous

arts of the courtesan, guaranteed to keep appetite alive and to make exciting and mysterious the ordinary workings of biology:

> Age cannot wither her, nor custom stale
> Her infinite variety. Other women cloy
> The appetites they feed, but she makes hungry
> Where most she satisfies; for vildest things
> Become themselves in her.
> (2.2.234)

The serpent of old Nile knows every trick to arouse and sustain the sexual interest of her lover and make him feel that "there's sap in't yet." Heavy perfumes and scents. Cross dressing: she puts on his armor and dangles his "sword Phillipan" phallicly in front of her, while he dresses in her robes. Just a touch of sadomasochism: "amorous pinches black," "amorous of their strokes." Constant changes in mood, never remaining the same thing for long, always crossing the lover to annoy and arouse. Cleopatra uses them all. Sex for her is "an art that nature makes," as another play puts it, exploiting and perfecting the natural process of continual change. Even death for Cleopatra is sexual foreplay, as she holds the asp at her bare breast, preparatory to greeting Antony in the next world with kisses and going with him, hand in hand again, to be admired by all the great lovers of antiquity.

If sex was the open scandal of the Jacobean court, money was the root of all evils. The king's financial problems were bottomless and insolvable. Royal expenses were growing at a rapid rate as the household evolved into the executive branch of the government and as the Crown took on responsibilities for organizing and directing new functions in a modern state. Income came mainly from land owned by the king and from various ancient privileges. Additional money had to be voted by Commons, and that body stubbornly refused to levy new taxes unless the Crown gave up certain feudal practices, most notably wardship and purveyance. In wardship, the property and person of all orphaned minors of families of a certain rank were disposed of by the king. These wardships were sold to interested parties, or managed in the interests of the Crown by the leasing of land and the arranging of marriages. Purveyance, the right of the king's agents to set low values on goods commandeered in his name for the support of his household, was much abused in setting below-market rates for a wide variety of goods and services that never reached a palace.

Robert Cecil was one of the few people who understood that the state required more stable fiscal arrangements than those supplied by the ancient rights of a feudal king. He worked throughout his life for a "Great Contract," by which for certain tradeoffs a regular subsidy would be voted by Parliament to the king. But there was too much resistance on both sides, and in the end the deal fell through, leaving James throughout his reign to scramble for money by one device or another to pay his growing expenses.

And they did grow. Instead of Elizabeth's single royal household, James and Anne, and in time the three children, each had an expensive household. The number of court officials increased enormously, and everyone of them was eager for patronage; fees and annuities dispensed from the Exchequer to pay court officials increased from £27,000 in 1603 to £63,000 in 1608. The long-range consequences of all this patronage were that by the 1630s, £350,000 out of a total government income of £618,000 was going to pay officeholders (Aylmer). A close study of Stuart finances has revealed that "amongst the Household charges, fees, pension and annuities almost doubled [in the first year of the Stuart reign], jumping from £27,900.7s.8 3/4 d. to £48,125.19s.3d. By 1614 fees, annuities and pensions had grown to £104,860" (Peck, 1990, 34). Rewards and gifts flowed equally lavishly, rising from £11,741 in the first year of James's reign to almost £79,000 in 1611. The privilege of eating gratis in the royal halls was dispensed so freely that providing food for guests at the king's tables ultimately cost £80,000 annually.

Constant need for money to pay these exploding expenses forced James to a number of unpopular practices. Monopolies were given or sold to suitors who then milked the public of every penny they could extract. Courtiers were supported not with salaries from the Crown but by offices, for which they paid in the first place, and from which they then extracted heavy payment—we would call it graft—for services rendered. Outraged by riotous waste and greedy extortion, people believed that everything was for sale. It was gossiped that there was a "book of rates" setting the value of every position within the gift of the Crown, and this was not far wrong. In 1603 James created a large number of "stay-at-home," or "carpet" knights—46 before breakfast one day; 432 to honor his coronation—gathering in by this device £30,237 in fees in the first six weeks alone of his coming to England. Later, the title of baronet was invented to pay for the Irish wars, and a price of £1,095, payable on the installment plan over a three-year period, set for it. After 1615 baronies also went up for sale, and courtiers were rewarded for various services with rights to sell the patents to various titles. Overall, James doubled the number of English peers and increased the Irish and Scottish titles by even greater percentages.

Under these pressures, what we would call financial corruption was taken for granted, and any attempt at reform was bitterly resisted. Lionel Cranfield, who tried heroically to make sense out of the royal finances by closing some of the drains on the Treasury, inevitably earned the hatred of most of the courtiers, who sneered at him as "a fellow of meane condition" because of his poor beginnings and his bourgeois concern for thrift.

It would be a mistake to think of James as a king who cared much about his financial problems. Although he was often sternly lectured about the lack of money, he seems to have thought the wealth of his new kingdom limitless, spending without caution on honors and gifts to his friends and favorites. There was in him, in addition, some odd compulsion to give and spend, to pour out enormous sums without thought. At times he loathed those who pestered him incessantly for this or that—"You will never leave me alone. I would to God you had first my doublet and then my shirt, and when I were naked, I think you would give me leave to be quiet" (Peck, 1990, 127). But at other times he had a neurotic, obsessive need for an orgiastic giving that amounted to something approaching potlatch. Anything his favorites asked, he gave them, and more. Even people who were not close to him could be, if they only asked, the beneficiaries of his largesse.

Motives are metaphysics, but there was some need in the king for gratitude and love that caused him to give far beyond the requirements of the normal aristocratic carelessness for money and grease for the political wheels. On one occasion, according to story, his desperate Treasurer piled up in actual hard cash the fortune the king had just given away to a begging favorite. (Plutarch relates the same story of Antony, who responds by saying that he had not realized that he had given so little and ordered the sum doubled.) James was said to have been momentarily shocked by the size of his pile of coin, but he was never really able to grasp the reality of money, even though he was regularly short of it in embarrassing ways. Shakespeare found in Plutarch's life of Timon of Athens a model for life as a frenzied giveaway—"We are born to do benefits"—and put it into his play of that name in 1609 or 1610, which showed the bankruptcy and misanthropy that followed once the money ran out and beneficiaries dropped away. *Timon* also contains two artists, a poet and a painter, who live off Timon's patronage. They serve him only by flattery and turn against him when his wealth is gone.

James was generally blamed for the waste, graft, and the profligacy of his court. He was called an "unadvised scatterer" who "fleeced his subjects" in order to fund his endless generosity to the hungry Scots who had followed him south, "by whom nothing was unasked, and to whom nothing was denied" (Osborne, 194). Bishop Goodman describes how on one occasion he sat on the king's bed and tried to talk to him about the inflated rents and the general ruin of the economy, at which James became tremendously agitated and denied that there was any problem. Nothing had any effect, and James gave away over a million pounds' worth of Crown lands and rents—perhaps a quarter of all royal estates—during the course of his reign (Stone, 1967, 225).

James's carelessness with money inevitably set the style for the rest of his court at well. Attendance at court, though necessary if one was to get ahead, became increasingly expensive, and the courtiers found themselves involved in heavy gambling, mandatory gift-giving, and the purchase of elaborate clothing, town houses, coaches, and on and on. Osborne describes these courtiers as pursuing the "glittering splendor of this new star of honour" until they "fall into so deep an ocean of debt, as they are never able to preserve their ancient lands, but are forced to sell [and] dye in a prison or play at bo-peepe all the remainder of their daies with their creditors in London" (258). Some even whispered that it was all a deliberate policy and that James "rejoyced in nothing more than promoting excesse, by which he hoped to ruine nobility and gentry" (226).

From the practical middle-class point of view, this extravagant spending was dangerous and immoral. But there are other ways of looking at it. Norbert Elias, the sociologist of court life, puts the whole matter in an entirely different perspective. He explains that "the 'rationality' of court people is different from that of the professional bourgeoisie. . . . In the bourgeois type of 'rational' behaviour-control, the calculation of financial gains and losses plays a primary role, while in the court aristocratic type the calculation is of gains and losses of prestige. . . . In court circles a gain in prestige was sometimes bought with a financial loss" (92). Luxury and imprudent expenditures were not, in Elias' view, counterproductive but necessary and inevitable in courts where both monarchs like James and the new nobility scrambled for status and power. Spending beyond one's means was a form of social self-assertion, and though it led inevitably to the poorhouse, people who wished to rise in court had no choice except to bankrupt themselves in the relentless pursuit of honor and power.

But few Jacobean Englishmen would have been much taken by this argument. The contrast between courtly and middle-class financial ethos appeared nowhere more sharply than in the expenditures for the court masques. In 1605, a "mere" £3,000 was spent on *The Masque of Blackness*, but by 1634 the cost of the annual masque had inflated to £21,000, much more than £1,000,000 by present values. Protests were widely heard, and even Ben Jonson, who served his patron by writing masques, called them "short braver[ies] of the night," for they were usually shown only on a single occasion—or at most, two—before these vanities melted, as Shakespeare put it, "into air, into thin air." From a practical, middle-class, balance-the-budget perspective this was pure waste, a glittering spectacle mounted at enormous cost to amuse a group of fashionable courtiers for only a few hours. But seen from inside Elias' court world, it was the very extravagance, even the waste, involved in the masques that made them practical. The king's need is to make everyone believe in his riches and power, and a king who could afford such costly, brief amusements must be a very rich and a very powerful man indeed.

The bourgeois Shakespeare had never heard of, let alone practiced, "conspicuous consumption," but he and his age knew too that an impractical generosity and display of luxury were, though risky, the virtues of great princes. And what *Antony and Cleopatra* does for feasting, drinking, and sex in the court, it also does for Whitehall's profligacy and waste, transmuting them into "magnificence," a nobility that expressed itself in public displays of grandness of thought, avoidance of pettiness, and generosity in all things. Magnificence appears when Antony sends a great pearl to Cleopatra, discounting his rich gift as no more than the "treasure of an oyster" and promising "to mend the petty present" in the future by placing kingdoms at the foot of her "opulent throne" (1.5.44). In the same extravagant spirit Cleopatra sends messenger after messenger to Antony at Rome and boasts that he "shall have every day a several greeting, Or I'll unpeople Egypt" (1.5.77).

Enobarbus, the Roman soldier who embodies practicality and good sense, decides, against the tug of his heart, to leave Antony, who seems to have abandoned rational behavior, and desert to Caesar. Upon hearing the news of this loss, Antony is deeply moved and knows that his day is indeed dimming. But there are no recriminations and no whining bookkeeper's complaints along the

lines of "after all I've done for him." Instead, Antony instantly dispatches after
Enobarbus all the treasures that he has collected in Antony's service.

Magnificence as Shakespeare portrays it is a virtue that lays at least as large a
claim on the heart as logic does on the mind. It appears in its full grandeur in the
palace at Alexandria, where Antony sits after he has left the battle of Actium to
follow the sails of the fleeing Cleopatra and her cowardly Egyptians. He knows
with full loathing of himself what he is and what he has done, as well as what
he has lost: half the world. In his despair he is near madness, raging and cursing
himself and his fate, tortured by the thought that he who "with half the bulk o'
th' world play'd as I pleas'd" (3.11.64) must now humble himself before the
"young man" Caesar. Cleopatra is afraid to approach him in this savage mood,
but she gradually moves, step by step, toward him, until she is close enough to
lay her hand upon his shoulder. His response is nothing less than godlike in the
completeness and instantaneity of its generosity

> Fall not a tear, I say, one of them rates
> All that is won and lost. Give me a kiss.
> Even this repays me.
>
> (3.11.69)

After Antony's death, it remains for Cleopatra to fix forever in poetry this
transcendence of all stinginess and pettiness:

> For his bounty,
> There was no winter in't; an [autumn] it was
> That grew the more by reaping. His delights
> Were dolphin-like, they show'd his back above
> The element they liv'd in. In his livery
> Walk'd crowns and crownets; realms and islands were
> As plates dropp'd from his pocket.
>
> (5.2.86)

Cleopatra has the same alchemical power as her lover, transforming vulgar
waste and ostentatious expenditure into beauty and delight. She stages costly
settings for her beauty and power with all the taste and skill that the great
Renaissance masters of the artificial métier contrived for their patrons in spectacle and masque. But what in Whitehall and in many another European court

was often a garish and tasteless display of wealth, in her elegance becomes transcendence:

> The barge she sat in, like a burnish'd throne,
> Burnt on the water. The poop was beaten gold,
> Purple the sails, and so perfumed that
> The winds were love-sick with them; the oars were silver,
> Which to the tune of flutes kept stroke, and made
> The water which they beat to follow faster,
> As amorous of their strokes.
>
> (2.2.191)

Sex, drink, idleness, luxury, waste, and other palace vices are transformed by language like this into something as rich and strange as the beasts that emerge spontaneously in the heat of the sun from Nilus' mud. How James must have enjoyed seeing all those actions about which treasurers and bishops lectured him so tediously and his court sneeringly whispered behind their hands appear on stage before him and his court in the clothing, for once, of vitality and magnificence. That the king of Great Britain would have seen himself in Egypt is unlikely—he was, after all, Augustus—but that he warmed to this soaring portrait of the epicureanism, sensuality, and generosity that were so central to his character is probable.

7

THE MILITARY AND THE

COURT ARISTOCRACIES

CORIOLANUS, WHITEHALL

CHRISTMAS 1608

In Marxist history, early modern Europe was shaped by the class struggle between a feudal landed aristocracy and a rising commercial middle class for the control of the state and the land, which was then the primary means of production. Absolutist Renaissance kings like James I were, in Marx's view, not so much a force in their own right as a temporary buffer between the landed nobility and moneyed capitalists, neither of whom was strong enough to overcome the other conclusively and seize power until 1688 in England and 1789 on the Continent.

Though he knew not the terminology, this transition from the Middle Ages to the modern world is *the* Shakespearean topic. His plays portray the battles between the old and new ways of life in all areas: on the battlefield, in the council chamber, in the public square, and in the bedroom. "Class" may have been an unknown mode of social analysis in his time, but Shakespeare was a member of the rising middle class and unself-consciously participated in its economic practices. His father was a tradesman, who eventually failed in business, and the playwright acquired the money that he later invested in Warwickshire tithes, houses, and land. The English public theater of the sixteenth and seventeenth centuries, in which he worked, was an entertainment industry that grew from a small-scale enterprise to a big business in Shakespeare's lifetime. Entrepreneurs risked money to build large theaters that could hold big audiences. The entertainment product was advertised and made as attractive as possible. The best playwrights and players were hired to draw the public and increase profits (Hill).

Across medieval Europe itinerant playing groups had performed for centuries in churches, on pageant wagons in town streets, on scaffold stages in market squares and the courtyards of inns, and in front of the pantry screen in the halls of colleges and great houses. In England alone by the sixteenth century there were over one hundred troupes, each with a few players and a basket of costumes on a gaunt horse, touring the English provinces and sometimes venturing abroad, especially to the Low Countries and Germany. Then, in the late sixteenth and early seventeenth centuries and at approximately the same time throughout western Europe, buildings specifically designed for performances were erected and groups of professional players—the Italian commedia dell'arte; the Spanish comedia; the French Confrérie de la passion—took up residence and began to produce and sell theater on a regular basis in major European cities: Madrid, Valencia, Paris, Bologna, Venice, and London.

In England the critical step of building professional theaters was taken in the late 1560s and 1570s by a group of entrepreneurs—"projectors" and "adventurers" were contemporary terms—like James Burbage, a carpenter who became a player, and his partner, John Brayne, a grocer; Philip Henslowe, a dyer, slum landlord, and brothel keeper; and Francis Langley, a goldsmith. These Ur-capitalists, looking for investments for their surplus funds, constructed a number of large theaters on the margins of the capital city. The theater always sells illusion, and the new London playhouses were, like the opulent "picture palaces" of the 1920s, grand in appearance: "Urbane mannerism of broken rooflines, conceited parapets, jeweled and strapped enrichments to arcades...on and around the stage" (Rigold, 130). Visitors found these new theaters among the notable sights of London and frequently commented on the "gorgeous playing places" and the "sumptuous theater houses" in a town where "plaiers wexe so riche that they can build such houses."

To attract their audience and keep it coming to the theater, professional playwrights, Shakespeare among them, appeared, and they began to produce plays on a commercial basis. The "star system" also came into being once the professional companies were settled in London, and clowns like Richard Tarleton—who as a PR stunt danced a jig from London to Norwich—and Will Kempe and the tragedians Richard Burbage and Edward Alleyn soon became favorites of the theatergoers.

The workings of capitalistic finance appear directly in the business affairs of the King's Men. Outwardly, the playing company appeared to be a mixture of two ancient social organizations: the medieval guilds of masters, journeymen, and apprentices, and the servants in the household of some great lord. But the players were organized financially as a joint-stock company owned and managed by a few of the senior actors or "sharers." Shares in the company, which by 1630 were worth £100, and by 1640, £200, could be willed, sold, or traded (Bentley, 1984). Sharers were not paid wages but took a percentage of the profits, perhaps three or four shillings a day in good times. The company could contain as many as thirteen or fourteen sharers, several apprentices, and twenty or so hired men—of whom no more than five or six needed to be players—for an approximate total of thirty-five to forty members, cut to fifteen or twenty for tours in the country or to the royal palace.

The assets of the company consisted of a collection of plays that had been bought outright from the playwrights (which were reworked to continue to attract audiences and protected from publication as long as possible); a wardrobe of costumes; properties; and a warrant from the Crown, which constituted a license to perform in the capital—plus whatever reputation and goodwill the company may have built up. Two of the sharers in the King's Men were the managers of the company, John Heminges and Henry Condell, who after Shakespeare's death arranged the publication of his works in folio form in 1623. They took care of the business affairs of the group, hiring additional actors and the many workers needed in a large and active theatrical enterprise: musicians, prompters, scribes, dressers and costumers, money collectors, stagekeepers (an early form of director), and so on. They paid the theater rents, arranged for plays, dealt with court officials and the Master of the Revels, set up court and other private performances, provided transportation for tours, scheduled rehearsals, arranged for playbills to be printed and distributed, and performed all the many other activities needed to keep this busy company going.

In 1599 four of the sharer-players—John Heminge, Cuthbert and Richard Burbage (the sons of the builder of the company's first theater), and William Shakespeare—undertook to use the timbers of Burbage's old playhouse, the Theater, north of the city walls, for the frame of a new and grander house, the Globe, which they built south of the Thames on the Bankside. They rented land from Nicholas Brend, a scrivener and investment broker, for £14.10s. per annum, which rose to £40 by 1635. "Subdu'd To what it works in, like the dyer's hand," as Sonnet 111 describes involvement in the public theater, the Globe was located among other businesses paying rent to Brend—tanners, watermen, brewers, dyers, armorers, bakers, tailors, porters, drapers, saddlers. Since the proprietors of the Globe were also leading shareholders in their acting company, they were, in an early form of the interlocking directorate, in the attractive position of being able to rent a theater to themselves as players at rents favorable to themselves as owners. They may also have had some insurance of another kind, for their landlord was married to Margaret Stalley, whose brother-in-law, Sir John Stanhope, was, after 1596, the Treasurer of the Chamber, the royal household official who authorized payments to players for court performances.

It is possible to find in Shakespeare's works the militant middle-class values that his economic situation would seem to dictate. Like other great Renaissance writers—Rabelais, Cervantes, and Milton, for example—his oeuvre chronicles, with nostalgia but with a sense of inevitability, the death of feudal institutions. But only in *Coriolanus*, whose story he borrowed from one of Plutarch's descriptions of republican Rome, does he portray an open class struggle for control of the state. Here political power determines nothing less than who gets to eat and who goes hungry. Eating is the central image of the play, from a threatening famine in the opening scene and the old politician Menenius' digestive Fable of the Belly, to Volumnia's furious self-cannibalism, "Anger's my meat; I sup upon myself, And so shall starve with feeding" (4.2.50). The topic was timely, for there were shortages of grain in England during 1608—10, the probable date of the play, when the Venetian ambassador reported to the Most Serene Republic that "The weather has been so bad lately that it has been impossible to gather the crop. The corn is suffering and rotting in the fields, just as the drought in the early season caused a poor hay-crop, which is of great importance in this country, because of the number of animals fed on it. All this, joined to the looseness of the money market (*alla larghezza delle valute*) and the great concourse of people at Court, causes a dearth of everything" (*Calendar of State Papers* [Venetian], XI, 326).

Coriolanus opens with riots in the streets by plebians who believe that there is no genuine shortage but that the wealthy have hoarded grain in order to raise prices. The rioters feel that class as well as profit is at the base of the shortage: "We are accounted poor citizens, the patricians good. What authority surfeits [on] would relieve us. If they would yield us but the superfluity while it were wholesome, we might guess they reliev'd us humanely; but they think we are too dear. The leanness that afflicts us, the object of our misery, is as an inventory to particularize their abundance; our sufferance is a gain to them. Let us revenge this with our pikes, ere we become rakes; for the gods know I speak this in hunger for bread, not in thirst for revenge" (1.1.15). No rioters ever spoke in such measured terms, but the language bores into the fact that class hatred goes deeper than hunger and greed. It is rooted in wealth's dislike of poverty—"they think we are too dear"—and in the need of the wealthy for poverty to "particularize their abundance." The patricians deny, however, that there is any grain and coolly recommend prayer since only the gods can provide relief.

All life is political and confrontational in *Coriolanus,* where the scene is primarily the public forum, rarely the private space. Rome's colors are the gray of stone and the red of blood, its sounds those of metal and strident shouts of accusation and fury, triumph and defeat, sword on shield. Only the fittest survive in a place where the strong are ospreys seizing upon fish and eagles among doves. The people, though cursed and brutalized by the nobility, are in their own view the substance of the republic. When one of their tribunes cries out, "What is the city but the people?" they roar their answer, "The people are the city." On the other side, to the Haves, the Have Nots are only

> woollen vassals, things created
> To buy and sell with groats, to show bare heads
> In congregations, to yawn, be still and wonder.
> (3.2.9)

Shakespeare may, by virtue of birth and profession, have felt deeply and given voice to the grinding English antagonism of a threatening middle class to the well-born, but his analysis of the social struggle put more emphasis on the problems of the aristocracy than on those of the tanners, brewers, armorers, porters, and tailors who made up the people of Rome in *Coriolanus* and whose shops stood hard by the Globe Theater. Or, to put it another way, the play does not center so much on the class war as on a broad crisis in the life of the aristocracy of which the struggle with a prototypical middle class was only one, though an important, part.

Demographically, the English aristocracy in early Stuart times comprised a small group. The English peerage, ranging between 70 and 140 dukes, marquises, earls, viscounts, and hereditary barons, made up the core of it. The "political nation" also included a number of Irish and Scottish titles, plus the upper clergy, the baronets and knights, and the higher gentry. In addition there were always a large number of clients of the great: retainers, minor officers, and upwardly mobile dependents. Lawrence Stone, in his *Crisis of the Aristocracy,* estimates that this group in total amounted to only about 2 percent of the population, and only about three-quarters of them, he says, went to court at one time or another.

James Stuart's aristocracy was not for the most part an ancient nobility. "The majority of the Elizabethan and Early Stuart peers and greater gentry were second- or third-generation *nouveaux riches,* who were reaping the fruits of the fierce scramble for power and wealth of 1529–53" (Stone, 86). Nouveaux like Southampton, the third of his family to hold a title, and Robert Cecil, the second of his, were the creations of the Tudor monarchs, ennobled to replace the great independent barons of feudal times and to provide the nucleus of the court bureaucracy needed to govern the new, centralized state the Tudors founded and developed. In the Stuart court these arrivés, their number constantly increasing, mixed uneasily with the remainders of the martial aristocracy, families like Percy and Howard, Vere and Talbot, as ancient, proud, and warlike in their English way as Caius Marcius Coriolanus, of the noble family of the Marcii, was in his Roman fashion. Robert Devereaux, the 2nd earl of Essex, is said to have been the last man to have laid his hand on his sword in the presence of his sovereign when he became angered in a quarrel with Queen Elizabeth. The earl of Northumberland, a Percy, who spent a good deal of time in the Tower, remarked with scorn that if Percy blood and Cecil blood were poured in a bowl together, they would not mix.

Both the old and new aristocracies lived in the country and had their economic power base there. But increasingly they had to spend a part of the year in town and at the court. The London season, except when there was plague, ran from early November through the spring, when the king was in residence at Whitehall and the law courts were in session. In the late spring the courtiers returned to their country estates. Court and country increasingly not only were different places of residence but early political parties, which would eventually develop into Whig and Tory.

In both court and country, seismic shifts rumbled in the seventeenth century through the aristocratic way of life. Clans and extended families were giving way to something approaching the modern nuclear family. As cash replaced blood as the binding power of social life, the courtiers began to move out of the old castles into new types of houses, the "stately homes" of today's National Trust. The households shrank in size, the number of servants was reduced and, as Stone sums up the change, the family "withdrew from the hall to the great chamber and the private dining-room," where there was at least some increase in "privacy and intimacy" (1967, 302). Education now became a necessity for young men destined to provide the officers needed by the new national state, and the upper classes began regularly to find their way to the universities reformed by humanist educators and to the Inns of Court, the London law schools. Literacy, books, languages, knowledge of the classics, and patronage of the arts were increasingly important social furniture for a class whose chief occupations had hitherto been war and hunting.

For people whose identity and continuity were based on inheritance, reproduction was a critical matter. Stone estimates an extinction rate in England of 40 percent each century, so that without new appointments to the ranks of the nobility the peerage would have disappeared in 250 years. Of sixty-three noble families in 1559, twenty-one had failed by 1640 to produce a male heir. Shakespeare's efforts in the first group of his sonnets to persuade the fair young aristocrat to whom they are addressed to marry and produce an heir need to be read in the light of these statistics. A successful marriage was critical to the noble family of this time; it was the key to lands and wealth, a source of future generations, and a defense against the change of fortunes.

Nowhere was the pressure on the aristocracy more painful and unavoidable than in the pocketbook. The latter sixteenth and early seventeenth centuries were hard times for all, brought on by an 800 percent increase in the value of land, an overall inflation of 500 percent, and a fall in real wages by half, all accompanied by a doubling of the population between 1530 and 1660 (Hill). This extended economic depression fell hardest on those like Tom O'Bedlam and the "poor, naked wretches" that King Lear's imagination projects on his conscience in his madness. But though not so vulnerable as the landless laborers and tenant farmers, like Shakespeare's grandfather, the aristocracy too was caught in an economic bind. Their wealth was in land, and theoretically they should have been able to raise rents to keep up with inflation, but although rents doubled between 1590 and 1640, much of the land was tied up in long-term contracts, and there was at the same time a strong tradition against rackrenting. The owners, brought up to think of the land, at least ideally, as a trust held from one generation for the next and used for the benefit of all who lived on it and shared its bounty, found it difficult at first to think of land as capital, to be managed for the maximum return and the production of wealth.

Economic survival, however, required capitalistic practices: new kinds of intensive farming of cash crops, enclosure of the common land, sheep raising, and the driving of inefficient tenants off the land. The landowners learned slowly and painfully what they had to do, but it did not make them any more loved by those who had been their dependents but were now employees. Nor did the hardness of the business improve the landowners' own attitudes toward those they had to exploit. In these circumstances, anger between owners, tenants, and laborers was as endemic as the plague.

No matter what they did, the upper classes were always short of cash, which had not been as critical a part of life earlier. Now they were sometimes forced to go to moneylenders like Shylock, other times to the scriveners and small bankers, who had funds to lend out at 10 to 12 percent a year on mortgages that ran no more than 6 months or a year. To the hard-pressed aristocrat or country gentleman, the court seemed to offer what was so desperately needed, more-or-less ready money in the form of grants, monopolies, and offices that could be made to return a profit on their purchase price.

But if the court offered a way of getting rich and powerful, it also imposed new cash expenses on those who hoped to flourish there: new townhouses, fashionable clothing, money for bribes and gifts, gambling funds, servants, entertainment, perhaps a coach. Once they came to court, there were few courtiers who were not constantly beset by new expenses that required cash outlays. Like the "beautiful people," or the "jet set," or Hollywood actors nowadays, the courtier was expected to spend at a level befitting his importance, not his income, and because making money through trade or business involved a loss of face, the constant requirements of prestige expenditure in time ruined every noble family. To go to court, Norbert Elias asserts, was absolutely to guarantee ruin in either the short or the long run. In Elias' court sociology, what Lawrence Stone treats as a crisis arising in the particular historical circumstances of early seventeenth-century England is but one early instance of the master plot of court life: success followed by overexpenditure and finally ruin.

Changing social circumstances put heavy pressure on the traditional upper-class ethos as well as on their finances and political lives. Elias points out that court life not only required more courtesy and ceremony in relationships with others but by bringing people into close power relationships, it forced more acute observation of others, along with the development of effective modes of nonviolent persuasion and what we now call stroking. People at court and in "good society" were much more closely interdependent and subject to a "chain of compulsions" than a group of widely separated landowners, each a law unto himself. In France interdependence in the court led to the creation of the *monde* (good society): the world of the salon, of manners and ceremony, where it was necessary to observe and deal with other people and to restrain one's own "affect for effect" (Elias). Shakespeare's plays, with their sensitive portrayal of human relationships and close observation of the intricacies of behavior and of interactions on the personal level reflect the new court concerns and instruct the courtiers in the skills needed for success at court.

Under these pressures, the old aristocracy was metamorphosing into a court noblesse of politicians, officeholders, patrons, and clients. The pressures for change on the old aristocracy were numerous and relentless, but adaptation to historical necessity was slow, uneven, and explosive. Henry Howard, earl of Northampton, a member of one of the oldest Roman Catholic families in the kingdom and one of the chief councillors of King James, was a successful politician, a Machiavel, and a master of the patronage game (Peck, 1982). But the ancient attitudes of his class, as uncompromising as those of Coriolanus, can still be heard in a speech he made to Commons in 1607 on the question of the union of England and Scotland. Northampton treated the commons like dirt. Although they were in Parliament, he told them, they had no right whatsoever "to examine or determine secrets of state." His manner was that of superior courtier and a member of the old nobility, haughty and supercilious. Needless to say, his speech persuaded his audience promptly to vote against union.

By way of another example, the old feudal attitudes, extending to something close to droit du seigneur, were still alive in a nasty little episode that John Chamberlain, partly amused, partly scandalized, thought worth recounting. The Lord Mayor of London feasted the Knights of the Bath at Drapers' Hall "with a supper and a play, where some of them were so rude and unruly and caried themselves so insolently divers wayes but specially in putting citizens wives to the squeake, so far foorth that one of the sheriffes brake open a doore upon Sir Edward Sackvile, which gave such occasion of scandall, that they went away without the banket though it were redy and prepared for them. Neither did they forbeare these disorders among themselves, for there were divers picques and quarrells at their severall meetings, but specially at the Miter in Fleetstreet" (II, 35, November 14, 1616).

When the King's Men came up to Whitehall in the Christmas season of 1608—09 to perform twelve plays, titles unknown, *Coriolanus* was probably one of the new offerings. In the Roman aristocrat who was its titular hero Shakespeare found and elaborated an extreme image of an aristocrat of Stuart England unable to adapt to the social pressures that were relentlessly transforming his class. It was not so much the financial pressures that interested Shakespeare as the political, martial, class, family, and sexual changes breaking up the old ways of life at the time.

The action of the play is set in the Roman republic—oligarchy actually—which is described by those who rule it as a commonwealth, a body politic in which all the citizens from the lowest to the highest are expected to contribute to maintaining the community's health and life. As popularized by the Roman politician Menenius in his Fable of the Belly, society is a body, gathering and processing food to stay alive, in ways that require trade-offs, compromises, bargains, and quid pro quos. Although a bit greasy, the Fable of the Belly nonetheless offers an organic conception of the state, in which all people have their duties and responsibilities, and though some, like the head, have a more important function, and others, like the belly, get more to eat, no part exercises tyrannical authority over the others.

In fact, however, the talk of body politic and commonwealth only thinly disguises the hegemony of the upper class. Menenius, like the rest of the patricians, has no great fondness for the people—his fable is a piece of skillful public relations—but he understands the necessity of affability and a public image for the state that includes everyone and assigns them the duties needed to keep things working and maintain the patricians in power. He supplies the supple political skills in the play that the "little beagle," Robert Cecil, brought to the Stuart court.

In Cecil's and Menenius' state, old-style military aristocrats like Essex and Coriolanus were increasingly becoming political liabilities and embarrassments. The world now required smoother manners and more circumspect modes of operation, more soothing voices than that of Coriolanus scorning the people after hearing their contention that there is plenty of corn:

Hang 'em! They say?
They'll sit by th' fire, and presume to know
What's done i' th' Capitol; who's like to rise,
Who thrives, and who declines; side factions, and give out
Conjectural marriages, making parties strong,
And feebling such as stand not in their liking
Below their cobbled shoes. They say there's grain enough?
Would the nobility lay aside their ruth
And let me use my sword, I'd make a quarry [pile]
With thousands of these quarter'd slaves, as high
As I could pick [throw] my lance.
                              (1.1.190, brackets mine)

It has become commonplace nowadays to treat Coriolanus as a fascist, something like Douglas MacArthur or George Patton in twentieth-century American history. Laurence Olivier staged the death of Coriolanus in the manner of
the execution of Mussolini by partisans, who shot him and then strung him up
heels first like a piece of meat. Like our men on horseback, Shakespeare's aristocrat has both a bright and a dark side. If he is honorable, courageous, truthful,
frank, and modest, so is Coriolanus also proud as Satan, disdainful of all others,
hasty and impolitic, bloody-minded, sudden violence personified. There is no
question of his courage in war, for this is the trade his military caste was raised
to. He longs for blood, spilling his own and that of his enemies and friends freely,
with something close to erotic pleasure. On one occasion he emerges from the
gates of a conquered city, bright red, completely covered in battle blood, as if
new born out of his own courage, which is what the feudal aristocrat wanted to
be, the author of himself, beholden for his existence to no person else, and to no
country, Rome or England. His new name, Coriolanus, given him on the occasion, baptizes his self-birth in war.

Although he is necessary to his country in war, as the English aristocracy traditionally was, Coriolanus is a civic disaster in peace, cursing the people for their
complaints, threatening them if they dare oppose him and his senatorial class,
making all compromise or political deals impossible. When the time comes for
him to run for civic office, the ancient custom of the city requires him to put on
"the gown of humility" and go before the people in the marketplace to show
them the scars of the honorable wounds he has received on battlefields in their

defense since he was a young boy. The ritual is designed to bind the nation together, reminding the people of what their leaders have endured for their sakes, reminding the leaders of the necessity of having the voice of the people. Coriolanus grudgingly agrees to go through with the rite, if the people will "wash their faces, And keep their teeth clean," but he performs it in such a churlish manner that although he is elected consul he creates antipathies that soon bring him into conflict with the tribunes of the people. *Tribunes* was a word that had special meaning at the time. The play's argumentative and difficult tribunes, Brutus and Sicinius, need to be interpreted in terms of a scene in the House of Commons in 1606 when Robert Cecil accused the obstreperous John Hare of acting as a "Tribune of the People" (Lockyer). Sir Edwin Sandys, who along with other patriots of the country party (Henry Yelverton, Nicolas Fuller, and Edward Alford) regularly opposed the king, was generally known as "the old Tribune of the House."

Rigid and unyielding Coriolanus remains, and the tribunes must and do contrive to banish him from the city in order to safeguard their own power. Furious and feeling deeply wronged, Coriolanus allows his aristocratic sense of individual honor to triumph over his loyalty as a citizen of the nation. He joins the Volscians, Rome's traditional enemy, to make war on Rome. An exile and a traitor, he remains still a great soldier and soon brings Rome to the point of submission. When his clan, mother, wife, and child come to plead that the city be spared, he is at first relentless, but in time gives way, not for the sake of Rome but before the imperious family claims asserted by his mother, albeit in the name of the state. Having chosen the obsolescent loyalty to family over both states, this proud, isolated man can no longer find any place in the world to live. When he returns to the Volscians, their ministers plot his death and set the mob on to kill him. Aristotle wrote that the man who lives outside the city is a beast, and by Stuart times there was no longer a place in the English nation-state for Coriolanus and his social type—proud, aristocratic individualists oriented toward their personal honor and the clan rather than the national state.

The politics of *Coriolanus* are tragic but clear: modern states require courtiers and politicians, not military barons; without a king to keep the peace between squabbling class interests the nation is in great trouble. The Fable of Coriolanus represented in heroic terms for the nobility sitting in the Great Hall that Christmas of 1608 all the pressures for change, all the conflicts, that were making their lives so difficult on all levels. And, as always, Shakespeare went below the level of politics and family to explore the psychology of his subjects. He, it seems no exaggeration to say, was the first to objectify the modern psyche—Hamlet's depression and alienation from the established social order, Antony and Cleopatra's eroticized imaginations, Lear's disorientation after the boundary markers of his culture disintegrate, Macbeth's deadly anomie after he murders authority. There had been nothing like these psychologized characters before, except in the great religious writers, Augustine earlier, Luther and Calvin nearer Shakespeare's own time, but there were few others who registered the turmoil and complexity of a humanity turned inward on itself. Nowhere does this complex interior life bubble to the surface in the words and actions of the theater more than in *Coriolanus,* where the brutal soldier and proud aristocrat is provided with a tormented and conflicted psyche.

Shakespeare, as has long been recognized, is an oedipal playwright whose plots, musky with sex, regularly track rebellions against patriarchal authority— father, king, law—in a search for freedom, pleasure, power. This oedipal pattern is strikingly obvious in *Coriolanus,* where the old aristocratic ethos is translated into a Freudian neurosis and a failure of socialization. In *Macbeth,* to kill the king is to be mad; in *Coriolanus,* the failure to adapt to the needs of the state is to be sick.

For Freud, the oedipal conflict of the desiring child with the denying father for the gratifying mother is the critical event in life, and on its resolution depends all subsequent happiness—or, more often, unhappiness. In the Freudian view of life as managed neurosis at best, no entirely successful resolution of the opposition between denial and indulgence of the oedipal drive is possible, but there are degrees of adaptation, ranging from a self-defeating denial to some reasonable acceptance of inescapable limitations. Failure to manage the oedipal crisis with modest success leads to serious problems for types like the perpetual rebel, who can accept no control whatsoever and plays out, with predictably disastrous consequences, a series of violent conflicts with authority.

Coriolanus' life is made up of just such a series of personal and political disasters, in which the man who wants to be, as he puts it in the key words of the play, "author of himself" (5.3.36), encounters, violently, various authorities and institutions that attempt to control and shape him to their purpose. And, as in Freud, the central event in the failure to adjust the instincts to social realities is found in the family of the Marcii. What went wrong centers in the mother, Volumnia, the archetypal Roman matron whom Shakespeare found in Plutarch's

Lives of the Noble Grecians and Romans . There is no father in the play, not even the passing reference to the earlier death of one that was given in Plutarch. But the complete absence of the father from the family triangle confers presence upon him, forcing us to wonder who he was and what happened to him. We need not wonder long. Volumnia has preempted the father-husband's role in the family. A stern, denying superego, she sends Coriolanus to the wars as a mere child, offering him no nurturing love, dedicating him to fame and personal achievement.

From a clinical point of view, Coriolanus, like James Stuart, has had no mother, no yielding, no nourishing warmth, no sanctioned release of the pleasure instinct. So total a repression of one large part of his instinctual being has produced a violently angry and destructive man—murderous really—caught in conflicted love-hate relationships with the many father figures who in the name of the state try to control him: Volumnia his mother-father, Cominius his commander, Menenius his political sponsor, Aufidius his rival general, and the patricians (whose name derives from *pater*, "father"), who run the Roman state. Coriolanus' upbringing produces a man who is all father, all self-denial, seeking out hardship and danger, killing the enemies of the state, obedient to a fault, but at the same time he is angry with the fathers—including the internalized father, himself—who deny the erotic instincts pressing for release. He longs for love, but condemns himself for doing so. He can have no pity for the poor, the hungry, or the frightened plebeians whom he leads to death in the wars and despises for their weakness when they petition him for food or care.

So far, so Freud, but Shakespeare goes into still deeper waters in constructing a psychopathology of the old aristocrat as a radically conflicted, elitist, macho personality. Coriolanus' psyche opens up in his language. Shakespeare's plots and his characters would alone make him a great artist, but it is the poetry that, like the music in opera, creates the deep emotions of his characters, makes their lines crackle with psychic energy far exceeding the mere needs of the story, opens up profound depths of feeling and motivation. No better instance of these deeps erupting into sound and image can be found than the words that Coriolanus and his mother use when speaking of and to one another. Her language is at once that of a stern father and a seductive mother, offering and forbidding simultaneously. "If my son were my husband," she tells the wife of his feeble attempt at a new-style marriage based on love, "I should freelier rejoice in that absence wherein he won honor than in the embracements of his bed where he would show most love" (1.3.2). She habitually displaces the erotic to the martial, transforming milk to blood, the vagina to a wound, the penis to the sword, sex to war:

> The breasts of Hecuba,
> When she did suckle Hector, look'd not lovelier
> Than Hector's forehead when it spit forth blood.
> (1.3.41)

Since undisplaced sex and pleasure are identified with weakness, sex can only find release in war, death, pain, and blood.

Coriolanus learns his mother's lesson, and any effort to try to please the citizens of the city with soft words and stroking promises seems to him harlotry: trading favors for pay, with "virgin voice," "schoolboys' tear," and the mountebanking of love. But the pleasure instinct is not entirely suppressed, and it emerges, as it often has in barracks life, in the love of one great soldier for another, a love that can express itself only in war. The love cannot be directly named, of course, but disguised as strife it slides through the crack of dreams and uncontrolled gestures, through the slips of the tongue that constitute Shakespearean metaphor. Aufidius, presumably another product of the same aristocratic training, having been beaten twelve times by Coriolanus, in a characteristic mixture of the amorous and the murderous, dreams nightly

> of encounters 'twixt thyself and me;
> We have been down together in my sleep,
> Unbuckling helms, fisting each other's throat,
> And wak'd half dead with nothing.
> (4.5.123)

The only release he can conceive of is to join with Coriolanus and, as he puts it, pour "war into the bowels of ungrateful Rome." The servants in Aufidius' house see more clearly than the generals what is going on, and they describe it almost explicitly. Of Aufidius they note, "Our general himself makes a mistress of [Coriolanus], sanctifies himself with's hand, and turns up the white o' th' eye to his discourse. But the bottom of the news is, our general is cut i' th' middle, and but one half of what he was yesterday" (4.5.194, brackets mine). It is all carried off, of course, as if it were military discourse, but that is the point: war and sex have melded in a certain type of military aristocratic character.

The climax of the tragedy, both political and psychological, comes in the scene where Coriolanus has conquered Rome, fulfilling on the political level his oedipal desire to master the father-state. His mother comes to him in her double role of forbidder and seducer to plead as a mother and command as a father that he spare his native city and family. Sacking the city is treason, the most heinous of political crimes in the new divine-right state, and psychologically it becomes for Coriolanus the transgression of the most absolute of human taboos, incest. Volumnia's language explicitly identifies the two acts: "Thou shalt no sooner," she tells her son defiantly, "March to assault thy country than to tread on ... thy mother's womb That brought thee to this world" (5.3.122). The word *tread* still carried in Shakespeare's time the meaning of "copulate" as well as "trample."

To sack Rome would resolve on all levels the oedipal tension that has torn Coriolanus apart for so long and so painfully. He could at once kill the city of the fathers, Rome — ripping out its bowels is Volumnia's description — and take the father-mother, Volumnia. But it is not to be, for in Shakespeare, as it was in the Greek tragic writers, men's characters are their fates. Once the personality is fixed in childhood its dynamics constantly play out the same story. And so Coriolanus once more submits to pain and duty, relinquishing pleasure and release. He comes to understand his tragedy only after it is too late and he has spared Rome. Holding his mother "by the hand, silent," for a time, he bursts out,

> O mother, mother!
> What have you done? Behold, the heavens do ope,
> The gods look down, and this unnatural scene
> They laugh at.
>
> (5.3.182)

But the tragic recognition of his fate and its acceptance are only temporary. A moment later he tries to pass the recognition off, as if nothing significant had happened, as if the tragic point of no return had not been passed. But it has. When Coriolanus returns to Antium, Aufidius taunts him with the one word Coriolanus cannot endure, "thou *boy* of tears." Because the charge is true — he has not "grown up" — but cannot be acknowledged, Coriolanus goes wild with rage, threatening Aufidius, reminding him of how many times he has already beaten him, and exclaiming indignantly again and again, "Boy!" "Boy!" "Boy!" Turning away from Rome at his mother's command was as great a political as a psychological failure, and the citizens of Antium, whom he has betrayed, remember the kin that he has killed: "Tear him to pieces! Do it presently!—He kill'd my son!—My daughter!—He kill'd my cousin Marcus!—He kill'd my father!" (5.6.120). Still raging with being called "boy," Coriolanus defies them as they gather around him with words that seem to hang over all existence, "Kill, kill, kill, kill, kill him."

By the time of the Stuart kings, art in the court was a far more sophisticated matter than it had been in Queen Elizabeth's court and earlier, and Shakespeare fulfilled his patronage contract in *Coriolanus* with elegant and highly wrought theater. He offered not some wooden morality play with a debate between Good Counsel and Bad Counsel of the kind that was played in court scarcely fifty years earlier, but an oblique, elaborately wrought treatment of the crisis of the Stuart aristocracy as a complex social struggle for life's necessities.

The king would, like Coriolanus' father, have been noticeably present in this play by his absence from the Roman "republic." We think of it as past, but monarchy was generally held in the Renaissance to be the most advanced type of government. According to James Stuart, it was the "forme of government, as resembling the Divinitie, [which] approacheth nearest to perfection, as all the learned and wise men from the beginning have agreed upon; Unitie being the perfection of all things" (*Trew Law*, 53). As in James's history of Scotland, kings had been the first, the natural, form of government in ancient Rome. The troubles of republican Rome were explained by divine-right theory as the result of having overthrown the city's early kings and what James called "the settled and established State of Crowne and Kingdome." Without a strong king to administer justice and keep the peace, the Haves and the Have-Nots are inevitably at one another's throats, and between them they threaten to destroy the city.

In this class struggle, in a Rome that had banished its kings and in Stuart England where a king was trying to establish absolute authority, nothing threatened the commonwealth more than a class of archaic aristocrats whose traditional warrior role was no longer functional. In Plutarch's biography of an odd and difficult Roman aristocrat, Shakespeare found an uncanny image of the type of noble, warlike and difficult, who was having great difficulty handling the stresses and strains of a new social and political order in Stuart England.

But Shakespeare's history is always psychohistory, in which political problems take their shape from the dynamics of inner life and the cross currents of the family. How modern *Coriolanus* is, the social scene as a stage on which the instinctual, particularly the sexual, patterns of childhood—its failures and its successes, or, more often, its barely workable compromises—are acted out as politics. It seems unlikely that the Whitehall audience would have made much of this, particularly since the psychological themes are carried in large part by the poetry, whose fine details, available on the printed page, are difficult to catch in oral performance. But in *Coriolanus,* Shakespeare's patronage art once again transcends its immediate social function, going beyond an oblique defense of strong monarchy and an attack on aristocrats who considered themselves superior to the state, to a demonstration that such an attitude is mentally deviant and self-defeating behavior.

If the pride, destructiveness, radical individualism, and intransigence of members of the upper class are the consequence of a common failure in socialization, then they are no longer merely inconvenient traits, counterproductive in a "state of settled Kings and Monarches," but self-destructive psychic disorders. It was one of Shakespeare's great gifts to his patron to weld his political theories to a normative psychology.

When James Stuart on March 21, 1609, addressed Parliament at Whitehall, he spoke of "the Philosophers wish, That every man's breast were a Christall, where through his heart might be seene"—*Cor Regis in oculis populi*—and went on to declare that he now intended to expose his own true beliefs and intentions (McIlwaine, 306). But politics never achieves this end, and certainly James did not at Whitehall that day. Art can come closer to revealing the human heart, and the crystal that Shakespeare looked through in *Coriolanus* revealed a place where so fragile and natural a thing as a butterfly has no chance once it has been spied by a boy raised with the traditional aristocratic values, without respect for his country and its people: "H'as such a confirm'd countenance. I saw him run after a gilded butterfly, and when he caught it, he let go again, and after it again, and over and over he comes, and up again; catch'd it again: or whether his fall enrag'd him, or how 'twas, he did so set his teeth and tear it. O, I warrant, how he mammock'd it!" (1.3.59).

"'Tis a noble child," an observer wisely concludes.

8

THE KING AND THE POET

THE TEMPEST, WHITEHALL

WINTER 1613

The fall and winter of 1612—13, probably the last of Shake-speare's tenure as resident playwright with the King's Men, were disturbed times at Whitehall. Robert Cecil, the real power behind the throne and the most farsighted politician in England, had died on May 24, 1612, aged forty-nine. The court, mean as ever, buzzed with the news that he had died of syphilis. Arbella Stuart, melancholy and with a streak of willfulness, was also gone from the court, having tried the king's patience too far at last. Her story is pure Shakespearean romance from beginning to end. She had a claim to the throne, as good in law as that of James, who kept her at court like Hamlet in Claudius' Elsinore, so that he could keep an eye on her and prevent her marriage, which might have pro-duced a dangerous heir. Life at court kept Arbella broke, as it did most courtiers, and she played the marriage card, her only trump, more than once, in order to extract money and gifts from James. In 1610 she seems to have been carried away by her own game and fell in love with William Seymour, the second son of Lord Beauchamp, descended through Catherine Grey from Henry VII, and the one man whom James could not allow her to marry. Sey-mour's claim to the throne combined with Arbella's held the pos-sibility of political mischief, if anyone cared to make it—as someone always did. Nervous about the legitimacy of his own claim to the throne, and brokering every court marriage to pre-vent rivals, James questioned the lovers, separately and together, about their relationship.

The scene intrigued the Venetian ambassador for its undercurrents, and his report is worth repeating for what it tells us about the way in which the king interacted with his courtiers, particularly about marriage:

As we reported, the King is anxious that the marriage of the lady Arabella [*sic*] with the nephew of the Earl of Hertford should not go forward, so as to avoid the union of the claims of these two houses, who are the nearest to the Crown. After examination separately they were both summoned before the King, the Prince and the Council and ordered to give up all negotiations for marriage. Lady Arabella spoke at length, denying her guilt and insisting on her unhappy plight. She complained again that her patrimony had been conceded by the King to others. She had sold two rings he had given her. She was then required to beg the King's pardon, but replied that seeing herself deserted she had imagined that she could not be accused if she sought a husband of her own rank. All the same, if error she had made she humbly begged pardon. This did not satisfy the King; he demanded an absolute confession of wrong and an unconditional request for forgiveness. That she complied with, and received fresh promises of money and leave to marry provided the King approved. (*Calendar of State Papers* [Venetian], XI, 439)

Money was the king's usual way of patching up quarrels, and Arbella took it, but she went on to marry Seymour secretly in the spring of 1610. The king was furious when he heard, exclaiming that a woman with royal blood had no right to live or marry as she wished. James then played the role of the villainous king of romance, like Leontes in *The Winter's Tale* (which, with its obvious connections to Arbella, was performed in court on November 5, 1611), confining Seymour to the tower and trying to send Arbella to Durham in 1611, although he got her no farther than Highgate. Arbella dressed as a man, in black wig, long cape, and rapier—just like Portia or Rosalind—and fled to France, whither William also went. At the last moment Arbella's ship was captured, and she was returned to England and the Tower, where, still like some heroine of romance— Hermione, say—imprisoned by a cruel tyrant, she lingered until 1614 and then died. James remained unrelenting to her pleas to be reunited with William, responding only with a stern Calvinist message, "Ye had eaten of the forbidden tree" (Durant, 184).

In a better world, 1613 would be best remembered as the year in which the last heretic was burned in England, when the wretched Bartholomew Legate died at Smithfield on March 18 and a few days later Edward Wightman suffered the same fate at Lichfield for no better reason than to affirm the authority of an ecclesiastical court to inflict capital punishment. But no one cared much for the suffering of these unknowns in the crowded time when over the course of a year the scandalous divorce of Frances Howard from the earl of Essex was pushed by the king, Cecil died, Arbella went to the Tower, the princess Elizabeth was betrothed, and Henry, prince of Wales (see figure 9), died after a long and mysterious illness in the fall of 1612, leaving his brother, the unpromising Charles, the successor to the throne.

There was always bad blood between the prince and his father, and the court had been scandalized years earlier when James hit his son with a tennis racket for some minor irritation. In a scene that sounds like something out of *Lear*, the king's fool, Archie Armstrong, "was after every night they could meet him tossed like a dog in a blanket" (Osborne, 269) by Prince Henry's men, simply for pointing out to King James that his son was becoming more popular and had a larger retinue than he. This fool, despite accumulating a fortune by selling his influence in the court, seems in the end to have been entirely fool, for he later, in Charles' time, had "his coat pulled over his head" and was banished from the court for some unhelpful remarks to the archbishop of Canterbury about high church policy. Henry's death was inevitably viewed by many at court as highly suspicious. Historians have concluded that Henry died of typhoid, but during his long, painful, and undiagnosed sickness, some of the court gossips, according to Sir Simond D'Ewes, recalled Tacitus' description of the poisoning of Germanicus. Others saw in the prince's death a Catholic plot linked with the assassination in 1610 of the prince's model, Henri IV. It was even said that if James had not poisoned his son, nonetheless the physicians feared to treat the disease lest they "might possibly offend no lesse by his recovery then death" (Osborne, 269). Chief Justice Coke, by then on the outs with the king, was less circumspect, voicing the suspicions of many when he said darkly, "God knows what became of that sweet babe, Prince Henry, (but I know somewhat)" (Weldon, I, 427).

The prince was dead, but arrangements were already forward for the marriage of his sister Elizabeth to Frederick of Heidelberg, Elector of the Rhineland Palatinate, and it was decided not to allow mourning to interrupt this state marriage. James intended to play a hand in Continental religious politics, which were then working up to the Thirty Years' War, and the marriage would establish an English base on the Continent. A formal betrothal was celebrated on

December 27, 1612, and the wedding took place, prettily, on Valentine's Day 1613. In the period between the engagement and the wedding, the palace was busy with various festivities, and the King's Men, one of four royal companies providing plays, were paid for twenty performances, the largest number they had yet given in a single season, from Christmas through May 20. The royal pair passed their days before the wedding riding, boating, playing cards, hunting, and attending plays and other court entertainments. Frederick was made a member of the Order of the Garter in St. George's Chapel at Windsor. Rich gifts were exchanged as expressions of esteem and worth—spurs set with diamonds, a bottle cut out of a single agate, a chain of diamonds and a tiara (Akrigg, 1962).

The court buzzed about James's "desire to be rid of [the Princess Elizabeth] with least expense" and said maliciously that the match was made only "to render himselfe the umpire of all Christian differences" (Osborne, 282). The queen was snippy. Jealous of her daughter's being the center of attention, she referred to her as "Goodwife Palsgrave," to make certain that no one missed the fact that the princess was marrying down. But whatever the family may have felt privately, James spared no expense publicly, spending £50,000, which he could ill afford, on the festivities and £40,000 more on his daughter's dower. The Thames opposite Whitehall was packed with boats of all kinds, and a model of Algiers was built on the south bank, while a display of fireworks was loosed from barges, showing Saint George battling the dragon in a setting of castles, rocks, bowers, and forests. Oohs and ahs greeted squibs ignited to create a pack of hounds chasing a deer through the air, "making many rebounds and turns with much strangeness, skipping upon the air as if it had been a usual hunting upon land" (Akrigg, 1962, 237). The coup was a naval battle in which an English fleet flying the red cross of Saint George attacked a Turkish fleet, with much mock cannon fire—and many real accidents—until the Turks surrendered and were brought by the English admiral to the Whitehall stairs, where they submitted to the royalty assembled there to watch the fete.

After these festivities, the great show of the marriage itself began. The procession took the long way to the royal chapel in Whitehall in order that as many as possible might see the bride, with her golden hair hanging loose to her waist—a sign of her virginity—and interwoven with "a roll or list of gold-spangles, pearls, right stones and diamonds" (Akrigg, 1962, 242). Her coronet alone was said, by her father, who had commissioned it, to be worth a million crowns. On a stage in the royal chapel, Elizabeth, wearing a white satin gown and jewels valued at £400,000, was joined by her mother and took a seat opposite Frederick and her father, the latter covered with rich gems said to be worth £600,000. An anthem was sung and then the dean of the Chapel preached a sermon on the wedding at Cana in Galilee. The ceremony itself was performed by the archbishop of Canterbury, attended by a bishop, both in splendid vestments. The Elector mumbled his vows in broken English. Benediction was pronounced, and another anthem, composed by Dr. John Bull especially for the occasion, was sung, after which the Garter King of Arms proclaimed to the audience the new titles of the royal couple. The royal party took communion before they withdrew from the chapel.

A state dinner was followed by Thomas Campion's *Lord's Masque,* set by Inigo Jones on a stage with two levels, the first for the anti-masque danced by twelve "franticks" representing various kinds of unsocial behavior. This was followed on the second stage by Prometheus fixed against a background of stars, along with eight dancing lords attended by sixteen pages. Amid "pilasters all of gold, set with Rubies, Saphyrs, Emeralds, Opals and such like," the lords moved toward silver statues that turned into living ladies. When the masque ended and the revels began, from the audience Frederick and Elizabeth were taken out to dance by the masquers first, and as the dancing began, golden statues of the bridegroom and bride flanking a silver obelisk were revealed on stage.

John Donne, long seeking a place at court but destined to dangle for a time longer, composed an *Epithalamion* describing the extended day and the sexual climax toward which it slowly moved:

> And why doe you two walke,
> So slowly pac'd in this procession?
> Is all your care but to be look'd upon,
> And to be others spectacle, and talke?
> The feast, with gluttonous delaies,
> Is eaten, and too long their meat they praise,
> The masquers come too late, and'I thinke, will stay,
> Like Fairies, till the Cock crow them away. . . .
> But now she is laid; What though shee bee?
> Yet there are more delayes, For, where is he?
> He comes, and passes through Spheare after Spheare,
> First her sheetes, then her Armes, then any where.
>
> (l. 61)

Donne's witty freedom with the royal privy parts was matched by the interest of the king, who, with his usual frank curiosity about such matters, called on the couple after their first night and, bouncing up and down on the bridal bed, asked for explicit details of the consummation. He need not have worried, for it was a love match between the sixteen-year-olds from the start, and before its tragic end it would produce thirteen children, including Prince Rupert of the Rhine and the Princess Sophia, the progenitress of the Hanoverian kings of England.

The celebration was by no means over with the ceremonies and royal bedding, for on the next night the gentlemen of the Middle Temple and Lincoln's Inn marched by torchlight down the Strand to Whitehall to present a masque by George Chapman, the dead Prince Henry's playwright. Small boys were dressed as baboons, musicians rode in cars, the masquers were costumed like the Indians of Virginia, accompanied by Moors and followed by floats and two hundred halberdiers. The next night still another masque, prepared this time by the gentlemen of Grey's Inn and the Inner Temple with Sir Francis Bacon serving as producer and master of ceremonies, arrived by water in illuminated boats. Never did Bacon experience more painfully the truth of his mot "rising into place is laborious." Nothing went well from the beginning. The masquers had trouble getting ashore at Whitehall because of the tide, and when all was ready the king was so exhausted and out of sorts that he put off the performance until another time. The masquers were despondent, feeling that, as John Chamberlain wrote, "the grace of theyre maske is quite gon when theyre apparele hath ben alredy shewed and theyre devises vented so that how yt will fall out God knowes, for they are much discouraged, and out of countenance, and the world sayes yt comes to passe after the old proverb, the properer men, the worse luck" (I, February 18, 1613). Bacon's essay "Of Masques and Triumphs" takes the high philosophic view that "these things are but toyes," but when his own reputation was involved, he was unable to take them so lightly. He pleaded with the king, begged really, and even the king's promise to watch the masque four nights later could not repair the shattering loss of face he suffered, no matter what the reason, in having his entertainment publicly refused after such extensive and expensive preparations and, as Chamberlain understood, in having all the surprise of the masque's devices lost.

Few weddings can have been celebrated by so much artistic talent as this— Campion, Donne, Shakespeare, Bull, Chapman, Jones, Bacon, Beaumont, and Fletcher—a master demonstration of art in the service of the prince. The King's

Men had to reach deep into their repertory for some of their older plays to fulfill the needs of the festivities, performing *Much Ado about Nothing* twice, if *Benedick and Betteris* is, as seems likely, *Much Ado*. With its war between the sexes and multiple marriages it would have been an obvious repeat during the celebration of a wedding. Altogether the plays for which they were paid were: *Philaster, Knot of Fools, Much Ado about Nothing, The Maid's Tragedy, The Merry Devil of Edmonton, The Tempest, A King and No King, The Twins' Tragedy, The Winter's Tale, Falstaff, The Moor of Venice, The Nobleman, Caesars Tragedy, Love Lies a Bleeding, A Bad Beginning Makes a Good Ending, The Captain, The Alchemist, Cardenio, Hotspur, Benedick and Betteris*. The Beaumont and Fletcher team was taking Shakespeare's place by now as the resident playwrights of the King's Men, and their recent plays, *A King and No King* and *Philaster*, were the newest offerings of the season.

Still, Shakespeare remained the staple when his company played at court, and six of his plays, possibly seven, if *Caesars Tragedy* be taken for his *Julius Caesar*, were performed. So great was the need for plays that Shakespeare's recent pieces, *The Winter's Tale* and *The Tempest*, which had been performed at court the year before at Hallowmas, were performed again. Bacon may not have been the only disappointed producer at these celebrations, for it is likely that an unnamed "stage play to be acted in the Great Hall by the King's players," which aroused "much expectation" on February 16, the second night after the wedding, but was then dropped because "greater pleasures [a masque] were preparing" (Chambers, 1923, II, 213), was Shakespeare's new play of the season, *Henry VIII*, possibly written in collaboration with John Fletcher. The play was designed as a tribute to Elizabeth Stuart, climaxing in the triumphant birth of the great queen after whom she had been so hopefully named. It is impossible to understand why *Henry VIII*, so suitable for the occasion, was not put on in place of one of the older plays in the spring of 1613. Something must have gone badly wrong, for the first known performance was downtown, and in June 1613 the Globe burned down during a performance of the play when cannons, fired to announce the birth of Elizabeth Tudor, ignited the thatch roof of the theater.

But the older plays served, and by the spring of 1613 Shakespeare's *Tempest*, perhaps reworked, some have said, to add the betrothal masque that Prospero provides for Ferdinand and Miranda, suited the occasion on which it was performed somewhat more shrewdly than could have been anticipated when it was first played at court about a year and a half earlier. Prospero instructing his daughter and her prospective husband in the duties of marriage, and providing a magnificent betrothal masque for them, fit very nicely with the Solomonic James lecturing his children, spending a fortune displaying them to the public eye, and providing numerous amusements.

Claribel, daughter of Alonso, the play's king of Naples, in sailing to her wedding in Tunis journeyed no farther than did Elizabeth when she sailed out of the Thames shortly after her own wedding. The beautiful and prolific Winter Queen went first to Heidelberg and then to Bohemia, where she was crowned queen (see figure 10). She and her husband were deposed in 1620, after which she remained in exile, not to return to England for fifty years. And then only after her beloved brother Charles, although defended by her remarkable sons, Prince Rupert of the Rhine and Prince Maurice his faithful companion, had been executed, and her nephew Charles II had at last been restored to the English throne. The Stuarts, by no means excluding the stodgy but still quirkily interesting James I, are surely the most romantic of the European royal families. The Romanovs cannot match them. From Mary, queen of Scots, and the martyr king, Charles I, to the Old Pretender and Bonny Prince Charlie, the Stuart family underwent a journey from Holyrood Palace to the back street in Rome where the dissolute Young Pretender died and suffered a "sea change" no less total than those sung of in *The Tempest*, where the skeletons of drowned men turn to coral and their eye sockets fill with pearls.

Before so sea-changed a family, *The Tempest* opened appropriately, though ominously, with a spectacular scene of falling yardarms, wildfire, a great storm, and a ship striking rocks, which much resembled a recently printed description of a wreck in the Bermudas of ships on their way to the new Virginia colony. The survivors in the play are cast up on a desert island, similar to the brave new worlds that Englishmen on the eve of empire were at that time encountering in Asia, Africa, and America. The courtiers were naturally curious about what went on in these far places, and especially what the natives were like—were they cannibals or noble savages? There was money involved as well, for the court was investing heavily in these new ventures. The earl of Northampton, who after Cecil's death had become the real power in the government, invested a good deal in the Irish plantation in Ulster—the native Irish being thought of as aliens at least as strange as the Indians of North America—in the Hudson Venturers in 1610, in the Northwest Passage Company of two years later, and in a

Newfoundland plantation intended to trade fish with the Mediterranean. Salisbury, Pembroke, Shakespeare's old patron Southampton, and 650 other members of the highest levels of society had put large sums into the Virginia project.

The Tempest projected the freshness and excitement of the newfound lands where the courtiers were investing their surplus capital. Springs and brine pits, berries and trees, fish and birds, pignuts and filberts, untrodden beaches where the "printless foot" flies across the yellow sand and the flats of oozy tidal mud, a sky "full of noises, Sounds and sweet airs, that give delight and hurt not." The courtiers' conflicting expectations of the natives—hard and soft primitivism at once—were confirmed by the aborigines who appeared on the stage. Caliban (an anagram of *cannibal*), repellent and fishlike, all earth and water, is the savage of hard primitivism, lusting to rape white women, good only for menial work, controlled by superior intelligence and force. Ariel is the more delicate and playful side of uncivilized life, a fanciful and obedient noble savage, treading "the ooze Of the salt deep," running "upon the sharp wind of the North," doing his master's "business in the veins o' th' earth When it is bak'd with frost" (1.2.255). The emerging image of the white man's burden was loaded on Prospero, the patriarchal ruler of the island, whose magical knowledge and stern moral sense give him absolute power over the untrustworthy aborigines, as well as over the female of his own family, his daughter Miranda.

Humanist artist that he always was, Shakespeare once again stooped to truth and moralized his song, dramatizing for the court not only the wonders of the brave new world of overseas colonies, but the various ways that their European discoverers could and did conceive of their new possessions and subjects. For the old courtier Gonzalo, as for those who would later settle the many utopian communities of America, the new world offers the opportunity to recover the lost Eden where, freed of the weight of European society, human nature will be purified and the sins of the old world left behind:

> All things in common nature should produce
> Without sweat or endeavor: treason, felony,
> Sword, pike, knife, gun, or need of any engine,
> Would I not have; but nature should bring forth,
> Of its own kind, all foison, all abundance,
> To feed my innocent people.
>
> (2.1.160)

If for some the new world is potentially John Winthrop's "City on a Hill," to others it is imperialism's city of gold, Cortez's Mexico, Pizarro's Peru, a fountain of eternal youth, to be taken by those bold enough to seize and hold it. The drunken servingmen Trinculo and Stephano find on the island an opportunity to plunder and rape; they enslave the one native they encounter and treat him as a monster to be taken home and displayed in a sideshow. To the courtiers Antonio and Sebastian the island is the heart of darkness, with no policeman around the corner, a place to kill their king, Alonso, and seize power for themselves.

To others, the encounters with the vastnesses of an untouched nature bring profound psychological changes. Loss, and his helplessness within it, engender in the king of Naples remembrance and repentance for old wrongs he has done. His son, the youthful Ferdinand, finds the wonder of love in his new condition of freedom. Prospero, who preceded all these visitors to the island, has found in his exile a close encounter with his own person, body, and appetite in the form of Caliban, his imagination and creation in Ariel, and he has developed as a result a new sense of self and his magical powers over the world.

The primary work of the Renaissance artist was to create the lavish displays of wealth and grandeur required by noble patrons to spectacularize their authority, wealth, and power. This was as true for Shakespeare as it was for other artists who worked in the palace, the church, and the great houses. *The Tempest* supplied his noble audience with images of the expansion of empire: into the religious politics of the Continent and into the conquest of the new world. But from time to time the artist took a place in his art, along with his patrons and their interests.

Even some workaday Renaissance painters and sculptors began to think of themselves in time as artists rather than simple craftsmen and servants of their patrons. They asserted their improved social status by cultivating good manners, stressing their intellectual attainments, and, in Italy, organizing painting fraternities like the Academia di Santa Luca. Concepts of "the artist" and "the work of art," especially in Italy and even more especially in the fine arts, began to take rough shape, usually in connection with the greatest artists. Giorgio Vasari wrote stories of their lives in the 1550s and 1560s, and by the 1600s a mythology of the artist had already taken shape. The Holy Roman Emperor, Charles V, was said to have handed brushes to Titian as he painted and, in a different version of the same story, Cardinal Barberini was described as holding the mirror for Bernini as he chiseled his self-portrait in the face of David. Although only the statues of Moses and of the two slaves were completed, the myth of Art created a pretty picture of Michelangelo and Pope Julius II, artist and patron together, sitting in a marble quarry planning for the pope a tomb of such previously unknown beauty that it would realize the human dream of perfection in art. The paintings by towering figures like Titian were sought without regard for subject or size, and as early as around 1520 works were commissioned "for no other reason than the desire of the patron to have, for example, a *Michelangelo*: that is to say, an example of his unique *virtù*, or his *art;* the subject, size or even medium do not matter" (Shearman, 44).

The success of art increasingly "led to two results in the mind of the artist, ... the concept of the work of art as an enduring virtuoso performance ('something stupendous') and the concept of the 'absolute' work of art" (Shearman, 44). More and more, artists asserted their social dignity and the importance of the artist and his work in cultural life. By the mid-seventeenth century the painter Salvator Rosa could boast to a would-be patron in a high romantic fashion that "I do not paint to enrich myself, but purely for my own satisfaction. I must allow myself to be carried away by the transports of enthusiasm and use my brushes only when I feel myself rapt" (Haskell, 22). Rosa refused to set a price for his pictures beforehand on the grounds that he did not know how his work was going to turn out. "I can see," said an agent, "that he would rather starve to death than let the quality of his produce fall in reputation" (23).

This elevated status and increased sense of dignity registered itself in various ways—self-portraits of the artist, for example, which were becoming commonplace; or the inclusion of art within the artwork, like the play within the play. Artist figures moved among their social superiors inside the work, like the poet in Shakespeare's sonnets and the painter in Velázquez's *Las Meninas* (see figure 30). Michelangelo painted an image in *The Last Judgment* of himself sitting woefully holding his skin as the flayed Marsyas, who contested with the god of art, Apollo, on oboe against the flute and lost.

Nowhere does Renaissance art speak of its powers with more confidence than in *The Tempest*, where its greatest dramatic poet, figured as an exiled duke-magician instructing kings and their heirs on a desert island, proudly catalogues the accomplishments of his theatrical magic in a list that invokes with eerie memories the entire Shakespearean oeuvre:

> I have bedimm'd
> The noontide sun, call'd forth the mutinous winds,
> And 'twixt the green sea and the azur'd vault
> Set roaring war; to the dread rattling thunder
> Have I given fire, and rifted Jove's stout oak
> With his own bolt; the strong-bas'd promontory
> Have I made shake, and by the spurs pluck'd up
> The pine and cedar. Graves at my command
> Have wak'd their sleepers, op'd, and let 'em forth
> By my so potent art.
>
> (5.1.41)

In the play, Prospero's magic is the magic of the theater, his power the theatrical one of staging illusions that deeply move and teach his audience. Compared to the rough actualities of production and performance on the Bankside and even in Whitehall, the circumstances on the island stage of *The Tempest* are ideal for the exercise of Prospero's art. Whatever the playwright-magician conceives is performed instantly by Ariel and his "meaner fellows." The skill of Ariel's spirit-actors transfixes his noble audiences, renders them "spellbound," totally absorbed in the tableaux put before them, something a court dramatist must have dreamed of more often than he achieved it. And though the theatrical experiences are intensely real to the stage audiences, they are never in physical danger. The clothes which the travelers wear in the shipwreck are not stained by seawater and lose no color. The great storm and the destruction of the ship that seem catastrophic to them are only illusions, done and undone with the wave of a wand.

After experiencing wreck and immersion, the travelers straggle ashore in three groups at different points of the island, each thinking the others dead. Ferdinand, the young prince of Naples, comes out of the waves first, alone and utterly despairing, "Sitting on a bank, Weeping again the King my father's wrack." But then Prospero's art begins to work on him positively, as it already has negatively by stripping him of his social identity, and the music of Ariel's song creeps by him upon the waters, "Allaying both their fury and my passion With its sweet air" (1.2.393). The strange promise of the song means nothing to Ferdinand, but it is intriguing enough to get him up on his feet and moving off the beach toward the center of the island. Life is renewed at once by the sight of Prospero's daughter, Miranda (whose name means "wonder"), already in love with him, as he is with her, at first sight. But Prospero's and Shakespeare's art is moral as well as erotically stimulating, and Prospero freezes Ferdinand when he advances with sword uplifted—like the "hellish Pyrrhus" in *Hamlet*—and then puts him to the hard Calibanish work necessary to keep the world going.

Miranda has previously been instructed by her father, who recounted for her how they came to the island and what they experienced there. The engaged couple is later instructed in the necessity of premarital chastity, after which they are treated to a celebratory masque, "a most majestic vision," written by Prospero and executed by Ariel and his actors. The ballet is danced by country nymphs and swains, while the goddesses Juno and Ceres invoke the fertility of a bursting world of plenty to bless the plighted pair:

> Honor, riches, marriage-blessing,
> Long continuance, and increasing,
> Hourly joys be still upon you!
> (4.1.106)

At the play's end Ferdinand and Miranda are at the center of the island and are there revealed by the drawing of a theatrical curtain, engaged in a game of chess, a play within a play, life and marriage as an intricate artwork. At every stage of their journey the young lovers have been instructed and controlled by Prospero's art, arriving at a point where social life becomes an art form, a combination of game and theater.

If art in the Ferdinand and Miranda plot shows "virtue her feature," the Trinculo-Stephano plot shows "scorn her own image." These servants come to the island like some group of Conrad's thugs—say, Mr. Brown and his gang in *Victory*—debarking in paradise to pollute it. Intoxication is their passage into the illusion of the island, and they ride ashore on a cask of wine, which they begin to imbibe at once. They see not the wedding masque but Caliban's Hollywood adventure of killing Prospero, taking over the island, and raping Miranda. "O brave monster," says Stephano, "lead the way," as he introduces the monster to liquor and to the possibility of an anarchic freedom: " 'Ban, 'Ban, Ca-Caliban, Has a new master, get a new man."

Prospero's art controls these comic conquistadors, and as they move on his cell planning gory mayhem, he has Ariel put in their way a heap of colorful theatrical costumes and gilded props. Much to Caliban's disgust, Stephano and Trinculo immediately begin looting these tinsel fineries, losing sight of their plan. These are children, capable of viciousness but easily diverted and amused by any kind of gaudy spectacle and by fantasies of dressing up as great nobles and bold heroes. Theater is crude and its audiences often vulgar, and the playwright manages the appetites he encourages by fear, as well as pleasure. As the servants root around among the bright clothes, putting on a colorful coat, belting on a sword, trying on a plumed hat, Prospero calls up a pack of dogs. They come yelping and roaring through the woods, like some obligatory ending of a cheap crime movie, to chase Stephano, Trinculo, and Caliban through brambles and briars, driving them at last into a foul pond where they stand mired up to their chins in mud and rotting matter.

Prospero's art does not address these groundlings—"capable of nothing but inexplicable dumb shows and noise"—through their reason, but deters them from mischief by amusing them at times and frightening them at others. The groundlings are, however, apparently capable of learning something, for after he gets out of the pond Stephano mumbles, "Every man shift for all the rest, and let no man take care for himself" (5.1.256). But no real regeneration takes place, and Stephano and Trinculo are sent back, along with Caliban, to menial work once more, which they are glad to accept to escape the freedom which has been so disappointing and painful.

Theater shows the very age and body of the time his form and pressure to the court group gathered around Alonso: his counselor Gonzalo; Antonio, who usurped Prospero's dukedom; and Sebastian, brother to the king of Naples. The habits of life in all these older men are deeply ingrained, not easily changed, and the men are, with the exception of Gonzalo who is incurably innocent, inured to their guilt. The journey to the center of the island, which represents geographically the change of heart that Prospero's art works toward, is therefore more lengthy and painful for them, and their transformation less complete, than it is for Ferdinand. Alonso's immersion in the ocean of an indifferent and violent nature in the opening shipwreck, and the loss of his son, Ferdinand, overwhelm the king with despair, but Sebastian and Antonio are unmoved by the storm. The island is for them an opportunity to seize power. When Prospero's art produces before the famished wanderers a rich banquet and then causes it to disappear to remind them of their sins and to show them the necessity of "heart's sorrow," the effect is less than complete. Sebastian and Antonio refuse to acknowledge any guilt, and, drawing their swords, they race through the island striking at the air, like the passion-mad lovers pursuing one another in the forest of *A Midsummer Night's Dream*. Alonso, however, is more deeply touched, and the banquet tableau opens up a buried memory of the old wrong that he had done Prospero. But the beginnings of repentance at first drive him only deeper into despair and thoughts of suicide.

In their different ways these older courtiers are "spell-stopped," locked in their reactions to the knowledge of guilt that the island and Ariel's production has made them know and unable on their own to take the next step. In this condition they are brought to Prospero's cell at the center of the island where, in the words of the original stage direction, "all enter the circle which Prospero has made, and there stand charm'd" (5.1.56). In the "O" of this ultimate magical theater, Prospero makes himself known, forgives those who set him adrift so long ago, draws the curtain to reveal Miranda and Ferdinand, and reunites the royal family. Ariel's song symbolically foreshadows the transformation that is the central plot of all the Shakespearean comedies and tragedies and is the ultimate form of the sea change that Prospero's art works on the visitors to his theatrical island:

> Full fadom five thy father lies,
>   Of his bones are coral made:
> Those are pearls that were his eyes:
>   Nothing of him that doth fade,
> But doth suffer a sea-change
> Into something rich and strange.
>
> (1.2.397)

As usual in Shakespeare, not everyone shares in the regeneration and community that the end of the play brings. Antonio and Sebastian refuse the feast of life, speaking no word in the last scene until the end, when they recover their bravado enough to snarl at the offered forgiveness. The "thing of darkness," Caliban, remains unregenerate (to become the darling of late twentieth-century anticolonialists), and Prospero has to acknowledge his inescapable involvement with him. The art of theater can work its magic on some but not all, change some things but not everything. But for those who open themselves to its spell and allow their feelings to flow with it, it provides a renewal after all seems lost, a feeling of union with the rest of being, "a sea-change Into something rich and strange." Even the sailors on the king's ship who sleep out the time of the action are brought to the stage at the center of the island to share in the general reunion and forgiveness with which the play ends.

The artist-magician of *The Tempest* is the leading character in a sketchy version of "The Growth of a Poet's Mind," in which the artist is very much made, not born. Once Prospero was the great duke of Milan—non sanz droit?—athirst with a desire for knowledge, who avoided the practical responsibilities of life to bury himself in his study with his books. His magic is founded on the lore preserved in arcane volumes like the work of Paracelsus or "thrice-great Hermes," but the written word cannot alone give him the power to work his will upon the world by means of art. Experience finally gives him that power. Only after having been betrayed and deposed by his brother and set adrift in the open sea in a leaking boat with his infant daughter, Miranda, and only after living long years in exile on a desert island, working with Ariel and Caliban, does the scholar develop the magical skills of the artist. Only, that is, after going through the standard journey of Shakespearean tragedy, like that of Lear in his movement from the castle to the heath, is the artist able to work his magic. Theatrical magic is not, in the Shakespearean art myth, some supernatural gift but wisdom about life acquired only after long study and painful experience.

Prospero's art is not finally perfected until he encounters and masters those mirrors of the division in his own nature, the physical Caliban (body) and the delicate Ariel (fancy). But Prospero's ego-control of these two components of his art, sensual appetite and playful inventiveness, is never complete. In an artistic psychomachia, both body and spirit continue throughout the play to long for the freedom to live their own lives exempt from work in one case, confinement or limitation in the other. The education of the Shakespearean artist is no Wordsworthian election by higher powers, as in *The Prelude*—"I made no vows, but vows Were then made for me"—but a much more realistic and painful training involving hard study, disillusionment, isolation, and a painful process of learning how to master the basic powers out of which the creating reason, or the romantic imagination, makes art.

The purpose of art is never so unambiguous for Prospero as it would be for the romantic Wordsworth. In the first exercise of his art, the illusion of a shipwreck with which the play opens, the powers of the artist are used for the intensely personal end of revenge against those on board, Prospero's brother, Antonio, and Alonso, king of Naples, who set him and his daughter adrift in the open sea to die. And as Prospero uses his art to manipulate the feelings and manage the wanderings of the castaways throughout the play, his heart remains hard toward them. But when at the end of the play Ariel reveals the suffering of his old enemies, he is, like Lear in similar circumstances, made pregnant to good pity:

> Hast thou, which art but air, a touch, a feeling
> Of their afflictions, and shall not myself,
> One of their kind, that relish all as sharply
> Passion as they, be kindlier mov'd than thou art?
> Though with their high wrongs I am strook to th' quick,
> Yet, with my nobler reason, 'gainst my fury
> Do I take part. The rarer action is
> In virtue than in vengeance.
>
> (5.1.21)

Art, as Shakespeare depicts it, begins as a satiric art to hurt and instruct enemies, but ends in comic identification and sympathy with the audiences it manipulates.

If there is some piece of Shakespearean biography in this, the key is unfortunately lost forever, though it would be easy enough to contrive parallels. But art is longer than life, and in the Shakespearean view it apparently transforms its practitioners as well as its audiences, moving them from narrow purposes to larger understanding, and from self-serving interests to broadly shared humanitarian concerns.

The Tempest makes the proud humanistic claims of pleasing and instructing that were standard for the Renaissance. But immediately after boasting of the magical powers of his theater to work sea changes without risk to its audience, the magician-dramatist Prospero, like some medieval poet—Petrarch or Chaucer—writing his palinode, abjures his "rough magic," breaks and buries his staff, and "drowns" his book "deeper than did ever plummet sound" (5.1.56). Shakespeare, soon to leave the theater and return to Stratford, had made no arrangements to publish *his* book. More than half his plays remained unprinted until the 1623 folio published after his death. He had a mixed attitude toward theater, partly a proud insistence on its ability to get at the truth of things and partly a feeling of shame about the crudities and deceits of its methods. Whenever players appear as characters on his stage they are bumbling, like Bottom and company in *A Midsummer Night's Dream*, or lower-class and hammy, like the Wittenberg troupe in *Hamlet*. The limitations of theater are discussed openly in *Henry V,* written about 1599, where, at the height of Shakespeare's powers, the Chorus apologizes for a "bending author" and the "flat unraised spirits" who "force a play," "in a little room confining mighty men," on the "unworthy scaffold" of a "wooden O," where "time ... numbers, and due course of things, ... cannot in their huge and proper life Be ... presented." The references here are to the public theater on the Bankside, but the concerns about the limitations of theatrical pretense would apply as well to theater at court, if not to the masques, then surely to the plays performed there on the temporary trestle stages erected at the end of the hall.

These uneasy feelings about the inadequacy of theatrical spectacles are still present in *The Tempest,* where even the great masque of Juno and Ceres is spoken of slightingly by its creator as no more than "some vanity of mine art," its characters only "spirits" who when the performance is over "are melted into air, into thin air." The play's flimsy pretense is easily destroyed by the appearance of the drunken servants, who lack the imagination to comprehend it. In the end, having held the stage for only a brief moment and then disappeared into the nothingness where all plays go after the performance is over, "the baseless fabric of this vision" becomes no more than an "insubstantial pageant faded," leaving not even a wisp of cloud behind to mark where and what it once was.

The greatest of the world's playwrights was apparently unable to shake off his knowledge that the theater even at its best was only greasepaint trumpery, magic in its most trifling sense of prestidigitation, a few words, some stock jokes, a couple of costumes, a prop or two, music, and a dance. Here for an illusory moment, then gone forever. But then, Prospero reminds us, the great world itself is in the long run little more substantial and enduring than the brief tinseled moment of the play:

> The cloud-capp'd tow'rs, the gorgeous palaces,
> The solemn temples, the great globe itself,
> Yea, all which it inherit, shall dissolve,
> And like this insubstantial pageant faded,
> Leave not a rack behind.
> (4.1.152)

Whitehall and Westminster endured longer than *The Tempest*'s two hours' traffic on the stage that evening in the palace in the late winter of 1613, when King James and his court watched the play as part of the wedding celebrations of Princess Elizabeth. But now these, too, have gone, leaving perhaps fewer traces behind—an empty banqueting hall, gossip about the king's sex life—than *The Tempest*. Our playwright was right: the transitoriness of the theater is its final comment upon the great globe itself and all that is in it. "All the world's a stage" was a familiar trope, and one that Shakespeare used often in his long career, and now he used it one last time to justify an art that had its force not in its permanence, as he had once boasted in Sonnet 55—"Not marble nor the gilded [monuments] Of princes shall outlast this pow'rful rhyme"—but in its evanescence.

As Prospero sailed away for Milan after breaking his staff and drowning his book, so Shakespeare about the time of *The Tempest* left a stage where he had performed for his royal patron for years and went back to the country town from which he came. It must have been one of the great moments of English theater when Prospero turned that night to the king and queen sitting in their State, their two remaining children beside them, and to the glittering court watching the performance, to speak one last time for the bending author and ask his royal patron for his release from service. Whatever transcendent claims his play may have made for his art, Shakespeare, like the professional court playwright he had become, deferentially asserted at the end no more than that during all these years he had sought only to amuse his royal patron and his court:

> Let me not,
> Since I have my dukedom got,
> And pardon'd the deceiver, dwell
> In this bare island by your spell,
> But release me from my bands
> With the help of your good hands.
> Gentle breath of yours my sails
> Must fill, or else my project fails,
> Which was to please.

COURT ART AND THEATER

Under the patronage of kings and their nobility, the arts flourished in the Renaissance, not as "art-for-art's-sake," but as a part of the process of legitimating the state and its monarchs. Architects built great palaces, artists painted portraits of the aristocracy, sculptors made equestrian statues, historians narrated the story of the nation, poets sang the praises of the kings in epic poetry, and theatrical designers and dramatists created spectacular performance settings for divine-right ideology. Although England lagged behind the Continent in fostering the arts, the Stuarts were extraordinarily sensitive to the uses of art for the purposes of the state, and after their arrival in England, the cultural budget increased many fold. Inigo Jones worked for King James as an architect and theatrical designer, while Shakespeare enjoyed the patronage of the earl of Southampton and in time became the king's official playwright. His sonnets offer an in-depth picture of the patronage relationship.

The Stuart court was in advance of the rest of Europe in its theatrical resources, and the public theaters of London provided the court with actors and playwrights of unparalleled ability. The skills of the architect-designer Inigo Jones transformed the Great Halls of the Stuart palaces into theaters of miraculous illusion. Shakespeare's Stuart plays are one of the great patronage oeuvres of the Age of Kings, comparable to such masterworks as Michelangelo's Medici Chapel at San Lorenzo in Florence, and the court paintings of Velázquez for the Spanish ruler, Philip IV.

21 Henry Wriothsley, 3rd earl of
Southampton, by Nicholas Hilliard,
ca. 1594 (Enlarged; courtesy
Fitzwilliam Museum, Cambridge)

22 William Shakespeare, ca. 1610,
exact date and artist unknown,
perhaps John Taylor (Courtesy
National Portrait Gallery)

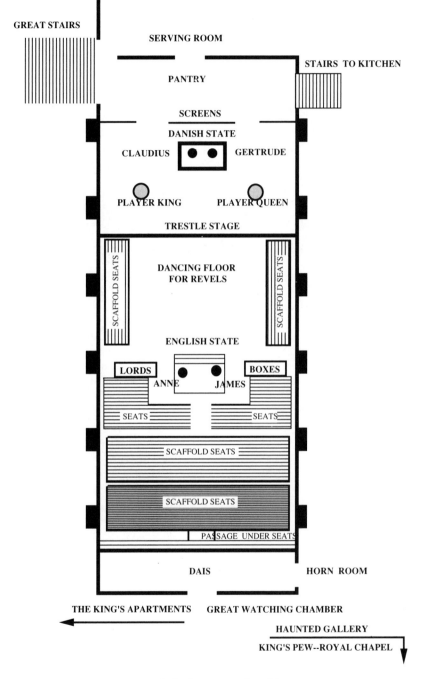

23 Author's reconstruction of the
Great Hall, Hampton Court, set up
at Christmas 1603: play within the
play, *Hamlet*, 3.2

24 Inigo Jones, self-portrait (Devonshire Collection, Chatsworth.
Reproduced by permission of the Chatsworth Settlement
Trustees)

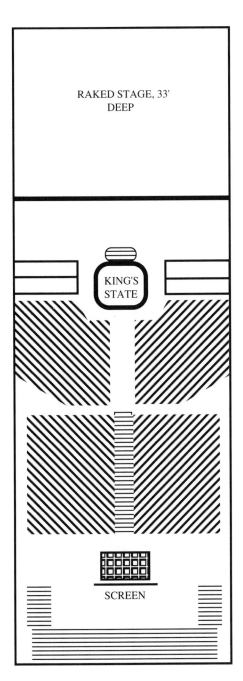

RAKED STAGE, 33'
DEEP

PIAZZA, 12' DEEP

LORDS OF THE COUNCIL
BOXES

KING'S
STATE

7 ROWS OF 2' SEATS
"WILL CONTEYNE 200
PERSONS TO SITT AT EASE."

ACCESS PASSAGE 2.5'

13 ROWS OF SEATS,
18" WIDE
FOR 350 PERSONS

PASSAGE UNDER
SEATS

RAILS FOR 130
LOOKING UNDER

LIGHTS AND SEATS FOR
LADIES AND SERVANTS

SCREEN

STAIRS FROM LOBBY

SCAFFOLDS FOR 130

25 Author's reconstruction of Christ Church Hall, Oxford
(40' x 115'), arranged for a royal performance, probably by
Inigo Jones, August 27, 1605

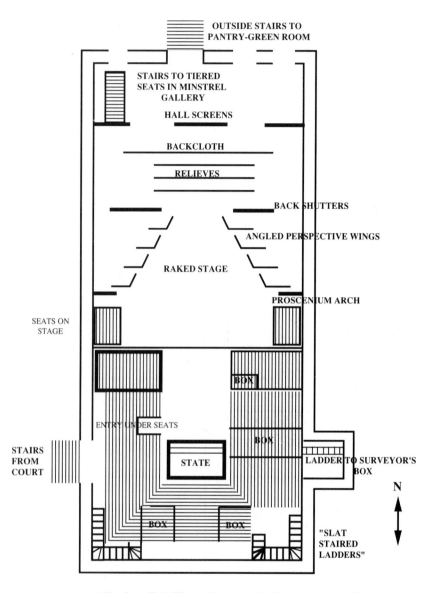

OUTSIDE STAIRS TO
PANTRY-GREEN ROOM

STAIRS TO TIERED
SEATS IN MINSTREL
GALLERY

HALL SCREENS

BACKCLOTH

RELIEVES

BACK SHUTTERS

ANGLED PERSPECTIVE WINGS

RAKED STAGE

PROSCENIUM ARCH

SEATS ON
STAGE

BOX

ENTRY UNDER SEATS

STAIRS
FROM
COURT

BOX

STATE

LADDER TO SURVEYOR'S
BOX

N

BOX

BOX

"SLAT
STAIRED
LADDERS"

26 The Great Hall, Whitehall, 1635, author's schematization of
Inigo Jones's plan: *Florimène* (From British Museum,
Landsdowne MS. 1171)

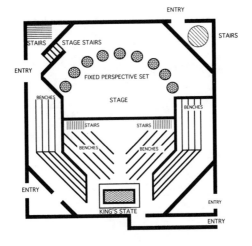

27 Author's reconstruction of the
Cockpit in the Court, Whitehall,
Jones and Webb, 1635

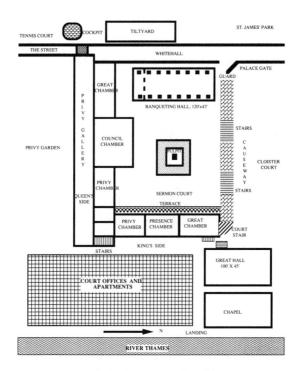

28 Author's reconstruction of the
ground plan of Whitehall

29 The Medici Tomb, San Lorenzo, Florence, Michelangelo,
1520–34 (Alinari/Art Resource, N.Y.)

30 *Las Meninas*, Velázquez, 1656 (Courtesy Museo del Prado)

9

SHAKESPEARE'S SONNETS AND

PATRONAGE ART

In spite of postmodernist skepticism, we conceive, in our still romantic way, of all art of any worth as being the privileged expression of the unlimited creative imagination of the individual artist. We think of patronage, therefore, even as we call for government art subsidies, as a condition of servitude against which the true artist by nature rebels, and one which inevitably produces bad art.

But in the Renaissance, art was—as it still largely is to this day in costly public arts like opera and architecture—designed in the first instance to satisfy a rich patron. To display their wealth and power, prelates competed for the most fashionable artists to plan and decorate the churches they had chosen as their monuments. Secular princes required not only palaces but heroic portraits of themselves and their families, or depictions of biblical and mythological scenes in which they appeared. (Erotic scenes from mythology were sometimes specified by the German princelings.) Dimensions were sometimes written into contracts for artwork intended to fit into a particular place and blend with other works in the increasingly fashionable fine-art collections, like those Charles I and the earl of Arundel assembled in the seventeenth century. Samples—*modelli*—patterns, and sketches were sometimes required, particularly if the painter was not well known. Artists and patrons usually made agreements beforehand not only for subject and fee but for the amounts to be paid for stretchers, canvas, colors, scaffolding—if it was required for frescoes and the like—and even for meals, if the painter would be working away from home (Haskell).

On the Continent, particularly in Italy, relationships between

patrons and artists, particularly painters, were often as warm and mutually sus-
taining as the arrangement

> frequently described by seventeenth-century writers as *servitù particolare*.
> The artist was regularly employed by a particular patron and often main-
> tained in his palace. He was given a monthly allowance as well as being
> paid a normal market price for the work he produced. If it was thought that
> his painting would benefit from a visit to Parma to see Correggio's frescoes
> or to Venice to improve his colour, his patron would pay the expenses of
> the journey. The artist was in fact treated as a member of the prince's
> "famiglia," along with courtiers and officials of all kinds. The degree to
> which he held an official post varied with the patron; . . . some princes
> might create an artist *nostro pittore,* "with all the honours, authority, pre-
> rogatives, immunities, advantages, rights, rewards, emoluments, exemp-
> tions and other benefit accruing to the post." (Haskell, 6)

If, as we saw in the last chapter, an autonomous aesthetic was beginning to
appear in Renaissance Italy—in Benvenuto Cellini's fanciful memoirs, for
example—patronage remained for most artists a well-defined and smooth-
working social arrangement for the production of art. When Pietro da Cortona
"refused to choose his own subjects and claimed that he had never done so in his
whole life" (Haskell, 11), his indignation reveals how completely most artists in
the patronage situation accepted the priority of the interests of the patron as the
normal artistic situation.

But if patronage worked well for the visual arts on the Continent, it did not
meet the needs of the talented young men who appeared in England in the late
sixteenth century to try to make their way in the world as professional writers.
The aristocratic Sir Philip Sidney, who, seeking advancement in court, used
poetry as one tactic in the patronage game, constructed in his life and writings
a mythology of the poet. According to Sidney in his *Apologie for Poetrie* (ca.
1584, published 1595), the poet was the first thinker and bringer of light in all
societies, an Orpheus, or a David, Homer, Dante, Chaucer. Etymology, as well
as history, established the poet as *vates* or maker. Where history and other forms
of discourse merely imitate nature, the poet, said Sidney, transcends all limits,
political or natural, to create beyond the existing world a more perfect imaginary reality: Nature's world "is brasen, the Poets only deliver a golden." The
poet teaches and delights by showing not what is but only "what may and

should be." Sidney's poet inhabits a world where poetry plays not only a metaphysical but a social role as well, whether it be Hungarian songs of one's ancestors' valor, the border ballads of the Percy and the Douglas, or even the more humble Irish satires that rhyme rats to death. But in all noble societies the poet commands respect with his ability to lift the mind "from the dungeon of the body to the enjoying of [its] own divine essence" (161).

In his noble life and death Sidney came close to his ideal, but other writers who tried, like Shakespeare, to make a living by their art found the going rough. There was as yet no reading public and no open market that could support an independent author. In all of England 45 books had been published in 1500, and only 460 were published in 1630. Printings were legally limited to 500 copies, and 250 was more usual. There was no author's copyright to protect a writer's work. A manuscript belonged to whoever had a license to print it, not to the person who wrote it. Thomas Churchyard, who put together 60 books during a fifty-year career, was a rare, and unsuccessful, writer who tried to live by the sale of his work, and the poet George Wither (Pope's "wretched Withers") was a lonely voice far ahead of his time, obsessively insisting that writing was property and that the person who wrote a book owned it.

In these limited economic circumstances, the relationship with patrons necessarily was the central fact of literary life for professional writers. Ninety percent of all published books appeared with a dedication to an actual or a prospective patron (Franklin B. Williams). In late Tudor times about 250 works were dedicated to Elizabeth I alone and similar numbers to her favorite, the earl of Leicester, and her secretary William Cecil, Lord Burleigh. Over a twenty-year period at the end of the sixteenth and the beginning of the seventeenth centuries there were 80 dedications to the Sidney and Herbert families, the most generous literary patrons of their age. In a time when there were too many writers and too few patrons, the search for patrons never ceased. Robert Greene addressed 16 different great ones in his 17 published books, while Thomas Lodge tried 12 patrons in the period 1584—96. "What need hast thou of me? or of my *Muse?*" Ben Jonson plaintively asked the most powerful man in the realm in the early seventeenth century, Robert Cecil, "Tofore, great men were glad of *Poets*. Now, I, not the worst, am covetous of thee" ("To Robert, Earl of Salisbury," VIII).

An ideal patronage contract of mutual support and respect—what writers offered the patron and what they hoped for in return—is to be found in the dedication to Leicester of *The Five Bookes of the Famous, learned, and eloquent man, Hieronimus Osorius* (1576): "Neither Princes maye live cleare and knowen to posteritie wythoute the penne and helping hande of learned Arte, neyther men excelling in learning, woulde be either in lyfe reputed or spoken of after death, withoute the countenaunce, defence, and patronage of noble Peeres" (sig. a3). The words already sounded old-fashioned in Stuart times, when the reality of letters had become something far different from Osorius' utopian view. Flattery of person, praise of land and house, condolence and congratulation, masques, exercises of wit, and celebrations of visits, progresses, processions, and marriages were the day-to-day writings a patron required. A glance at the table of contents of the collected writings of even the greatest poets of the time, Donne or Jonson, say, shows how regularly they engaged in some form of service writing. Their skill lies in the way they develop their art of words inside these patronage genres, not outside them.

The relationship of the English writers with their patrons was always difficult, and professional writing in Tudor and Stuart England was a stressful business. Edmund Spenser, coached by his Cambridge tutor Gabriel Harvey, used his poetry quite deliberately to advance his career, and he succeeded far better than most, becoming secretary to a bishop and a clerk in the earl of Leicester's household. With Leicester's support, Spenser later held a secretary-ship in Ireland, became a landholder and Sheriff of Cork, and eventually received a modest pension, which he considered inadequate, from Queen Elizabeth. Spenser was one of the first in the new class of educated professional writers who attached himself to a political circle of the great men of his world — Sidney, Leicester, and Raleigh — and proved his worth to the state with such professional writing as his national epic, *The Faerie Queene,* which identified England's legendary king, Arthur, with its reigning queen, Gloriana-Elizabeth. The poem was designed primarily to please her majesty, but it opened with an address to Sir Walter Raleigh, followed by seventeen dedicatory sonnets to different courtiers. Spenser's poetry was patronage poetry from start to finish, but he was unable entirely to suppress outrage at what life at the feet of the mighty meant for the artist:

> Most miserable man, whom wicked fate
> Hath brought to court, to sue for [that] ywist,
> That few have found, and manie one hath mist!

Full little knowest thou that hast not tride,
What hell it is, in suing long to bide:
To loose good dayes, that might be better spent;
To wast long nights in pensive discontent;
To speed to day, to be put back to morrow;
To feed on hope, to pine with feare and sorrow;
To have thy Princes grace, yet want her Peeres;
To have thy asking, yet waite manie yeeres;
To fret thy soule with crosses and with cares;
To eate thy heart through comfortlesse dispaires;
To fawne, to crowche, to waite, to ride, to ronne,
To spend, to give, to want, to be undonne.
          (*Mother Hubberd's Tale*, l. 892)

John Donne did little better. An early mistake of marrying above his station without his patron's (or his powerful father-in-law's) permission removed him for years from the usual paths of advancement at court. He sought patronage all his life, often with flattery that sounds sycophantic to modern ears, and finally got it, but in a way he did not want, by taking orders and becoming the king's chaplain and dean of Saint Paul's. King James stubbornly refused to favor him, though he admired him greatly, except in the church. But though Donne sought patronage ceaselessly and obsequiously, he, like Spenser, did not conceal his disgust with what went on at a court where everyone, including himself, smiled and watched all that happened with reptilian intensity and a precise calculation of their own advantage "When the Queene frown'd, or smil'd." Hoping to advance their suits, the court hangers-on idled and gossiped about "who loves; whom; and who by poyson Hasts to an Offices reversion." Eyeing their rivals nervously, they gossiped about "who' hath sold his land, and now doth beg A licence, old iron, bootes, shooes, and egge-shels." Breathlessly, they speculated on the sex lives of the great, "who loves whores, who boyes, and who goats" (Satire IV, l. 99).

The arrival of the Stuarts, with their heightened appreciation of the usefulness of art to the state, offered artists new patronage opportunities, of which they were not slow to take advantage. The coterie poet and author of *Cleopatra,* Samuel Daniel ("well-languaged Daniel"), a tutor and member of the countess of Pembroke's early-Bloomsbury, high-culture circle at Wilton, galloped north posthaste, along with every other office seeker, to greet the new king on his journey south in 1603. Daniel caught up with him at the house of Lucy, countess of Bedford, where James refused to sit still for *all* of the 72 ottava-rima stanzas of Daniel's *Panegyrick*. But he listened for a while, and this was all that was necessary. The countess of Bedford had herself earlier hastened to Edinburgh on the news of Elizabeth's death and immediately gotten the trust of the new queen, who needed gossips familiar with the English court. The two, along with the countess of Pembroke, who also became a confidant of Queen Anne, contrived to procure for Daniel the patronage plum of writing the Twelfth Night masque that, as we have seen, allowed the queen to display her legs on her first Christmas season in England. The role he created for her as Athena so pleased her majesty that she made him the licenser of a company of child actor-singers she controlled, the Children of the Queen's Chapel.

Encouraged by his rapid rise, Daniel finished a Senecan tragedy, *Philotas,* written according to the most advanced neoclassical principles—unities, decorum, and those sorts of things—and used his new authority to get it performed by his troupe of boy players. *Cleopatra* had been a closet drama, designed only for reading to the highly cultured ears of the Wilton art circle, and Daniel found himself wishing that he had left *Philotas* in the closet as well when he was called before the Privy Council in early 1605 to explain it.

Philotas, an officer of Alexander the Great, learns of a plot against the king, but since he is already troubled by Alexander's claim to godhead, he fails to tell Alexander of it, and for this he is informed on by two unscrupulous councillors, tortured, and put to death. The story seems to point directly to James's claims of divine right and to Sir Walter Raleigh's failure in 1603 to let the authorities know about the Bye plot. And Wilton had, as we saw earlier, been involved in trying to help Raleigh. But it was now charged that the two vicious councillors in *Philotas* were portraits of Cecil and Howard, pursuing not Raleigh but Essex to his death (Michel).

Under heavy pressure, Daniel sweated and denied any political purpose. The first three acts had been written before Essex's rebellion, he protested; the play had been passed by the censor; he had read parts of it to the duke of Devonshire, who found no objections; need alone had forced him to print the play and to have it performed. Above all, he wrote to Cecil, my lord must realize that the play was not history but art, a universal story about political activities that occur in all ages: "I p[ro]test I have taken no other forme in personating the Actors yt p[er]formd it, then the very Idea of those tymes, as they appeared unto mee both by the cast of the storie and the universall notions of the affayres of men, w[hi]c[h] in all ages beare the same resemblances, and are measured by one and the same foote of understanding. No tyme but brought forth the like concurrencies, the like interstriving for place and dignitie, the like supplantations, rysings & overthrowes, so yt there is nothing new under the Sunne, nothing theas tymes yt is not in bookes, nor in bookes that is not in theas tymes. And therefore good my lord let no misapplying wronge my innocent writing" (Michel, 37). Daniel squeaked through, just barely, without the loss of his freedom or his ears, but only after learning how dangerous writing that played too forward a part in the affairs of great men and their courts could be.

The stresses and rewards of writing for the court stand out even more sharply in Ben Jonson's career, with its continuous involvement in patronage. Coming from humble circumstances—he was a bricklayer—and, like Shakespeare, lacking a university education, although he went to Westminster school, Jonson made himself the voice of classical correctness in letters and prospered socially and financially in the reigns of James and Charles I beyond any other writer. From the time of James's arrival in England, Jonson was at home in the court, living with Lord d'Aubigny, writing most of his poetry in praise of the important people of the realm, attacking enemies and rivals (Evans), and collaborating in the annual masque. He was equally at home with patrons like the earls of Newcastle and Pembroke and after 1616, he drew an annual pension from the king of a hundred marks and, later, an annual butt of wine. Jonson justified the poet's right to such support by identifying his writing with that of the classical authors. Along with many other advertisements for himself, he published his "Workes" in a sumptuous folio volume, composed learned commentaries on the art of writing, and insisted always that the poet is not merely an adornment but an index to the greatness of a kingdom.

Adept at attacking enemies and flattering the nobility in distinguished poetry, most notably in his praise for the Sidneys' style of life at their great house in "To Penshurst," Jonson's masques provided the court with theater that gave brilliant reality to divine-right ideology. Setting his pieces in front of the spectacles and ingenious machinery of Inigo Jones, Jonson invented a theatrical form in which a grotesque anti-masque first presented various kinds of disorder that were identified with the king's enemies, only to be displaced and controlled in the masque proper, where divine right and hierarchical order triumphed over chaos in poetry, music, and dance. The triumph of order over anarchy emblematized the benign power of the chief spectator, the king, in language sufficiently elevated and symbols sufficiently arcane to give stage life to the divine authority which James Stuart claimed for himself. Year after year, Jonson's masques glanced at the court's affairs of the moment—the success of the new favorite, Buckingham, in *The Gypsies Metamorphosed* or the successful return from Spain of Prince Charles in *Neptune's Triumph*—but always Jonson's baroque art blazed the triumph of hierarchy and the mystical authority of kings (Riggs).

Jonson had the greatest success of all the English professional writers working in patronage circumstances, and yet this contrarious and aggressive man never fitted entirely comfortably into the court where he did so well. In his first Christmas there in 1603 he was asked by the Lord Chamberlain to leave the Hall for obstreperous behavior. His manner afterward improved somewhat with his fortunes, though he remained a roughneck, but he always had trouble with the authority and hierarchy of the court that he praised so brilliantly. He was frequently in trouble with the censor, and while making his reputation and living at court, he continued, though less and less frequently, to write plays for the public theater—where he had begun years before as a combative actor—that bring authority of all kinds into question. This tendency climaxed in *Bartholomew Fair*, a play performed downtown in the Hope Theater in 1614 by Princess Elizabeth's Men. The Puritan Zeal-of-the-Land Busy, the tutor Humphrey Wasp, and the magistrate Adam Overdo constitute a range of religious and civil authority figures who futilely attempt to control the carnival life of the fair—eating, cheating, fornicating, fighting, drinking, playing, and voiding—that gathers around the booth of Ursula the pig woman, who is the basic, unregenerate, carnal stuff of human nature itself. Jonson's personality and his art were at once authoritarian and antiauthoritarian, obsequious at court and rebellious in the town. In his troubled life, as well as in his criticism and poetry, he acted out, without ever resolving, a contradiction between art and authority that was appearing increasingly in the patronage art of England and the Continent.

Shakespeare was incomparably the greatest writer of his time, and those of his plays written for and performed at the court of James I constitute one of the summits not only of English but of all European patronage art. But he too, like his writing fellows, never fitted entirely comfortably into the artistic and social arrangements of patronage. On the one occasion when he included patronage artists, a poet and a painter, in a play, *Timon of Athens,* they are portrayed as parasites who feed on their patron when he is wealthy and drop off him when his riches are gone. But Shakespeare was himself involved in patronage, as well as public, theater from his earliest professional days. As an actor he may once have served the Stanley family, as he later served the Hunsdons, and he looked for a personal patron when he first came to London in the late 1580s. He found one in the 3rd earl of Southampton, the young Henry Wriothsley (see figure 21), to whom his early erotic poems, *The Rape of Lucrece* and *Venus and Adonis,* were fulsomely dedicated: "Right Honourable, I know not how I shall offend in dedicating my unpolisht lines to your Lordship, nor how the worlde will censure mee for choosing so strong a proppe to support so weak a burthen." We know little of the details of this relationship, but Shakespeare's sonnets, written over time and published in 1609, portray a poet in a patronage situation that throws light, however indirectly, on the Southampton-Shakespeare connection. Even more important, the sonnets portray the tensions in patronage relationships everywhere in the late Renaissance. Cellini's *Life,* Rousseau's *Confessions,* and Goethe's play *Torquato Tasso* are perhaps the only other familiar writings that probe as deeply the condition of patronage as do these sonnets.

Shakespeare's sonnets are the supreme love poems of the English language, and attention has long focused almost exclusively on their exquisite language and subtle feelings. But though there are large gaps in the narrative, each of the poems is also an abbreviated, often cryptic, incident in a loose framing story concerning an older, socially inferior poet and an aristocratic young patron of "beauty, birth, wealth . . . wit," the scion of a noble house. The narcissistic young man is reluctant to marry, enjoying his pleasures too much to undertake the family responsibility of getting an heir. Serious about the social function of his art, the poet, who is the speaking voice in the sequence, opens by urging upon the unidentified patron this most necessary business for the nouveau nobility like the Wriothsleys. The poet also offers the young lord those patronage staples praise and fame, claiming for his art an ability to preserve the patron's fame better than rival sculptors and architects: "Not marble, nor the gilded monuments Of princes, shall outlive this pow'rful rhyme" (Sonnet 55). The obscurity of time and death may insult "o'er dull and speechless tribes," but "So long as men can breathe or eyes can see, So long lives this, and this gives life to thee" (Sonnet 18).

Appropriately for his inferior social background, the poet is deferential, modest about his art, and self-deprecating. After all, in this kind of patronage art, the patron and his interests, not the poet or the poem, are the things. The poet tacitly accepts the primary condition of the patronage contract by acknowledging that any value in his verse comes not from the poet's skill but from the power and the beauty of its subject, the patron:

> How can my Muse want subject to invent
> Whilst thou dost breathe, that pour'st into my verse
> Thine own sweet argument, too excellent
> For every vulgar paper to rehearse?
> (Sonnet 38)

"Be thou the tenth Muse," the poet says, bowing deeply to his benefactor and acknowledging his person as the source that gives all "invention light."

The patron is young, rich, noble, and beautiful. His hopeful poet is old (forty winters), tanned, and chapped (see figure 22). He comes from a plebeian background—"public means which public manners breeds"—feels limited in his abilities—"desiring this man's art, and that man's scope"—and is worn down by troubles—"tired with all these, for restful death I cry." We hear only the voice of the speaker-poet, never the voice of the upper-class patron, who is always distanced by the lyric point of view, bustling in and out, saying nothing, seemingly indifferent to the intense feelings of the poet.

As the sonnets proceed, however, social protocol and the established poet and patron roles begin to break down under the pressures of actual life and feeling. Love, of many kinds, is the disintegrating force. The poet is soon taken with the young aristocrat, and deferential observations of the young man's chastity and praise of his beauty heat up to an unexpected intensity—"A woman's face with Nature's own hand painted Hast thou, the master mistress of my passion" (Sonnet 20)—but the sexual passion is, at least on the surface, immediately relinquished, since nature "prick'd thee out for women's pleasure." Nonetheless, the relationship has become and remains hotter in other respects than is prudent or comfortable. The sensitive poet puts too much into and expects too much from what should strictly be a standard business exchange of art for favor, while the patron remains distant and coolly reserved—"Who, moving others, are themselves of stone." Inevitably there are disappointments—"Farewell, thou art too dear for my possessing"—followed by what the poet feels as mutual sexual betrayals. The interests of the poet wander. The young man seduces the poet's mistress, and is in turn seduced by the poet's amorata, the Dark Lady, who brings such further erotic complications into the poem as guilt, enticement, satiety, and postcoital tristesse.

Within the sonnets may well lie a lost chapter of Shakespeare's life, and many books have been written to ferret it out. A homoerotic attraction, perhaps unreciprocated, to the rich and beautiful earl of Southampton, who, some surmise, gave the poet the money that made it possible for him to invest in the rebuilt Globe Theater in 1599. Who probably got the Stuart government to make Shakespeare's company the King's Men for their help during Essex's rebellion in 1601. Patron and poet may even have shared a dark-complexioned mistress, Emilia Lanier, the daughter of a court musician, who broke up their own relationship (Rowse, 1965; Akrigg, 1968). But Shakespeare was not an autobiographical writer, not at least in any simple, direct sense. Anything but. He remains, in fact, the most anonymous of our great writers—we seem always to glimpse only the back of his head just as he slips around the corner—a professional artist who worked in the formal, impersonal style of High Renaissance and baroque art.

And it is art that is finally the primary subject of the sonnets, gradually usurping the center of the sequence. In the earliest sonnets, centered on the patron, the style belongs not so much to the poet as to the social world for which he writes. The sweet lyric line of Petrarch, Ronsard, Wyatt, and Spenser—the golden style that had developed historically in conjunction with the interests of noble patrons and royal courts—plays its fashionable games with little or no irony: "Shall I compare thee to a summer's day?" This courtly style, like the neoclassic poetics of which it is a part, enacts verbally the ethos of aristocratic life. *Grazia,* a grace and ease of manner: quiet, understated, genial. *Sprezzatura,* an easy manner that makes the difficult seem effortless. *Mediocrità,* an avoidance of too didactic and absolute a position, rejecting Puritanical earnestness by holding opposites in balance and choosing indirectness, never entirely open but always oblique, its interests gracefully masked (Javitch).

As the sonnets proceed, however, and the patronage relationship gets more tangled, the poet begins to doubt the ability of the Golden Age style of which he is the flawless master to portray the realities of his relationships, first with the young man and then with the Dark Lady. Dissatisfied with his style's inadequacies, he becomes increasingly self-conscious about his art, more preoccupied with the problems of poetry than of patrons. Why should he repeat things that have been said so many times before? Why should his verse, unlike the new and fashionable metaphysical poetry of John Donne, or the subtly offbeat classical lines of Ben Jonson, always sound the same, "so far from variation and quick change?" He worries particularly about a rival poet like George Chapman and his epic line—"the proud full sail of his great verse, Bound for the prize of all-too-precious you" (Sonnet 86). His own style has become so repetitive that "every word doth almost tell my name." In the end he specifically renounces the Petrarchan courtly tradition, in the famous Sonnet 130—"My mistress' eyes are nothing like the sun"—in favor of a style that renders more accurately an uneidealized female reality: hairs that are black wires, breasts that are dun, voices that are shrill, breath that reeks.

One way of describing the plot of the sonnets is to speak of a movement from the lyric to the dramatic mode (Crutwell). There are hints throughout that the poet is involved with the theater—"made myself a motley to the view, Gor'd mine own thoughts, sold cheap what is most dear" (Sonnet 110)—and as the sequence proceeds, his language becomes increasingly dramatic—tense, ironic, contradictory, difficult, and many-voiced—as he tries to capture in words the more and more complex reality he is encountering. Take, for extreme example of the dramatic style, the elaborately tangled mutual deceits that the poet and the Dark Lady knowingly practice on each other, like two old actors or like Shakespeare's Antony and Cleopatra, trying to convince each other, and themselves, that they are, in fact, in love:

> When my love swears that she is made of truth,
> I do believe her, though I know she lies,
> That she might think me some untutor'd youth,
> Unlearned in the world's false subtilties.
> Thus vainly thinking that she thinks me young,
> Although she knows my days are past the best,
> Simply I credit her false-speaking tongue.
>   (Sonnet 138)

The movement of the poet's affections from the young man—"The better angel is a man right fair"—to the Dark Lady—"The worser spirit a woman color'd ill"—is both a love story and a description of a failed patronage relationship. But at the same time it is also a coolly calculated poetics, developed through a series of exact formal polarities that structure the story: young man-dark lady, male-female, homosexual-heterosexual, fair-black, aristocratic-common, young-old, innocent-experienced, chaste-promiscuous, beautiful-ugly, constant-change-able, simple-complex, lyric-dramatic. The autonomous aesthetic that John Shearman sees in *quattrocento* Italian art emerges in Shakespeare's sonnets from the artist's need for a style that renders not the ideals of patrons but the realities of human beings.

The famous picture *Las Meninas* (1656, see figure 30), by Velázquez, court painter to King Philip IV of Spain, visualizes perfectly the artistic status that patronage artists, like Shakespeare in his sonnets, were increasingly claiming, perhaps half unknowingly, for themselves and their work in the Renaissance. In Velázquez's painting, the central pictorial space that would normally have been filled by his royal patrons, the king and queen of Spain, is occupied largely by the painter Velázquez, facing outward toward the viewer, and by the back of the canvas he is working on. Like the patron of the sonnets, who is always in the distance, the royal pair having their picture painted are reflected only dimly in a mirror on the back wall. There are other observers in the center of the picture, alongside the artist—children, servants, the court dwarf, a dog, a nun and friar, and a mysterious figure against the light of a rear doorway—a strange collection of those who, like the artist, look at the world from the perspectives of marginal power. The artist, who dominates the scene, faces us, and his sightline reverses normal pictorial perspective, looking outward toward a widening space occupied by the king and queen—and by the spectator looking at the picture. Art, the picture implies, is now at least as interesting as the political power it is paid to serve. This is exactly the point at which Shakespeare's sonnets also arrive, moving from a lyric art that serves an aristocratic patron to a dramatic style that centers on the poet and his art. That the Spanish king favored *Las Meninas* and hung it in his private apartment, and that Velázquez was of all the great Renaissance artists the most domesticated to the palace and serviceable to its business, only shows once again how seldom those who are involved in history consciously perceive the direction in which they are moving.

That Shakespeare thought deeply about patronage, and that he had grave doubts about it on both social and poetic grounds, the sonnets clearly show. We shall see in the next chapter that he had similar reservations about the aristocratic audiences who watched performances of theater in the court. Despite his own uneasiness about patronage, however, Shakespeare, very like Velázquez, was no artist rebel. He continued to work without audible demur, though presumably with silent reservations, for his theatrical patron, the king of England—what real alternative was there?—putting on the white gloves protocol required when the King's Men played at court. At Whitehall and Hampton Court his plays were court events, which, however slightly regarded, not only reflected but participated in political and social life during the early years of the seventeenth century. Whatever King James may have written as a young man in his *Short Treatise* about the necessity for poets avoiding matters of state, year after year his official playwright offered the king and his court not mere entertainment but plays dealing obliquely and tactfully, but nonetheless palpably, with the issues that most seriously engaged the court: the law (*Measure for Measure*), primogeniture and witchcraft (*Macbeth*), kingship (*King Lear*), court corruption (*Antony and Cleopatra*), unrestrained generosity (*Timon of Athens*), the crisis of a martial aristocracy being transformed to a court noblesse (*Coriolanus*), empire and the uses of art (*The Tempest*).

In performance, these plays had to have been unexceptionable. Certainly, they caused no scandal in their time. Shakespeare prospered as the king's playwright. The king remained the patron of Shakespeare's acting troupe, giving the company gifts to help them in times of plague when the public theaters were closed, attending their performances at court whenever they played. Chamberlain wrote no letters to Carleton about scandalous court productions of Shakespeare's plays, and the ambassadors and chaplains at the Venetian embassies did not mention them by name in detailed reports to a state that was greatly interested in the arts. Except for the unfortunate, and quickly shut down, *Gowrie* and Jonson's *Sejanus*, the plays of the King's Men in Shakespeare's time fitted smoothly into court life, fulfilling the unwritten patronage contract by providing entertainment for foreign dignitaries, celebrating a royal wedding, defending divine-right kingship, putting the royal patron's family tree onstage.

Not all dramatists managed so well. As we have seen, Shakespeare's fellow playwright Ben Jonson was always in trouble. Besides being charged early in his unruly career with the murder of another actor, for which he got off, barely, by reading his neck-verse, "he was imprisoned for his share in *The Isle of Dogs*, 1597; cited before Lord Chief Justice Popham for *Poetaster*, 1601; summoned before the Privy Council . . . for *Sejanus*, 1603; imprisoned for his share in *Eastward Ho*, 1605; 'accused' for *The Devil Is an Ass*, 1616; examined by the Privy Council for alleged verses of his on Buckingham's death; and cited before the

Court of High Commission for *The Magnetic Lady,* 1632" (Jonson, XI, 253). But in the 577 cases of *Scandalum Magnatum* prosecuted in Star Chamber during James's reign, William Shakespeare's name nowhere appears (Patterson). Even in the trouble over *Gowrie,* there is no record that anyone threatened to brand him, cut off his ears, slit his nose, or punish him in the other barbarous ways sometimes used on those who outraged mighty princes.

He got along, but he was not, however, a sycophant or state propagandist. George Peele's *Arraignment of Paris,* performed at court for Elizabeth in the 1580s, gives us an idea of what prince-pleasing in the theater could be at its most charming. Pastoral, graceful in style, and adroit in its choice of the story of Paris, the play is as delightful as entertainment as it is effective as royal compliment. Its picture of a social and moral hierarchy built on mythic and metaphysical correspondences, all culminating in the queen, is serenely untroubled. Dramatic suspense requires Paris to struggle with the question of which goddess should receive his golden apple, but his dilemma is solved once the stage opens out at the end, as in the revels that brought masques to a conclusion, to include the Virgin Queen, who has been sitting under the State in the Great Hall, the chief spectator and participant, all along. Diana, Venus, and Juno, joined by the Fates, immediately agree that the golden orb should be given to Elizabeth, and, appropriately, Diana, the goddess of chastity, "delivereth the ball of gold to the Queenes owne hands."

Delightful as this is, it was not Shakespeare's patronage style. His plays were not flattery, nor were they light-hearted get-pennies, mere amusements stuffed with "such conceits as clownage keeps in pay." Neither were they overt Stuart propaganda, like the court masques, which used the most advanced theater technology and poetry to dramatize, almost without a touch of irony, the cult of hierarchical authority and the ideology of divine-right monarchy. Shakespeare's plays were—as generations of readers and audiences since have perceived— deep, searching portrayals of the most serious political and social issues, conservative in their premises but daring in their implications.

In the late twentieth century critics have shown a tendency to make Shakespeare into a crypto-revolutionary, a deliberately subversive writer whose plays are an "inscription of opposition" (Belsey), a carnivalesque "agon between authority and release" (Bristol), the "circulation of subversion" (Greenblatt, 1985), and a chapter in the Marxist history of class warfare (Dollimore). I share with these New Historicists the view that Shakespeare's Stuart plays are not fixed mirrors but active participants in the shaping of perceived reality. But the fundamental, and romantic, assumption of the New Historicists—that artists are necessarily and always revolutionaries by virtue of being artists—can be applied to Shakespeare only by using a methodology that finds meaning not in the center of the plays and the mainstream of their plots but in small, barely noticeable details in nooks and crannies on the perimeter of the artwork and on the edges of the society with which it interacts. New Historicism, like psychoanalysis, employs a methodology of the arcane, assuming that meaning never stares you in the face but is always hidden, obscure, and discoverable, therefore, only by the special insights of the interpreter.

In the specific court setting I have described, where the players quite obviously had to please their patron and dramatize acceptable political and social values in an interesting but unthreatening way, it is obvious on the face of it that Shakespeare could not have been a rebellious romantic artist like Shelley or Brecht, using his art in some dramatic "belief war" to attack authority and undermine traditional social views. But at no stage do the plays merely dramatize state ideology. They served their royal patron by legitimating official values in new ways, locating them in some unfamiliar scene, grounding them in some human and natural bedrock. Nothing radical there. But as they did so, their art carried them not into crypto-subversive political attitudes, but into the kind of radical realism recommended by the great Venetian painter Titian, at the time he was working on the portraits of Emperor Charles V and his son, Philip II of Spain: "The painter ought, in his works, to seek out the peculiar properties of a thing, forming the idea of his subjects so as to represent their distinct qualities and the affections of the mind, which wonderfully please the spectator" (Jay Williams, 123).

Nothing could describe better the leading characteristic of the great Shakespearean patronage plays than this kind of searching, probing realism. And as the plays sought out the "peculiar properties" of things and represented the "distinct qualities and the affections of the mind," they created the concentric, expanding ironies which attract the attention of modern directors and interpreters. The plays are, as one critic brilliantly puts it, "radical in comprehensiveness" (Mullaney, 129). A flood of words stirs up an infinity of possibilities. Imagery opens up motives that are deeper and more doubtful than the dramatic situation strictly requires. More characters than are needed by the plot introduce moral counterpoints. Plots extend to a *longue durée* in which life changes so slowly that it seems doubtful whether it is affected by events at all.

In keeping with its morality-play structure—a willful king who goes mad paired with a sensual aristocrat who is blinded; two evil daughters and one good, one good son and one bad; a faithful servant and an opportunist—*King Lear* finally justifies kingship and the kingdom. In the humanist manner of art advising princes, Shakespeare's play shows the too-willful king making terrible mistakes, for which the kingdom suffers, but at the end, the monarchy, however diminished, is still in place, while its enemies are dead. In its broad outlines, then, *Lear* conforms roughly to the views of the king who told his son of the strengths and dangers of kingship in *Basilikon Doron* and the *Trew Law of Free Monarchies*. But in its exploration of kings and kingdoms, *Lear* goes into areas James had not. James's arguments that kings were built into God's order were based on the truisms of his culture: histories in which kings were prior to the law, books of the Bible in which Yahweh gave kings to Israel, and Great-Chain-of-Being science, which showed hierarchy to be the inevitable way of nature. Shakespeare grants the king his premises—the king is the law and prior to the state—but he tests these time-worn orthodoxies against the hard realities of life: the indifference of nature, cruelty, lust, ambition, poverty, madness, ignorance, and despair. Shakespeare's true king endures not because God restores him to his throne, but because he looks unblinking into the face of nothingness and learns to be capable of pity for his poor subjects, who are ground up by the world's iron workings; because he forgives and seeks forgiveness; because he identifies himself with the human community—"as I am a man I think this lady To be my child Cordelia" (4.7.68). Shakespeare's monarchical state endures not because of some mysterious hierarchy-seeking force in nature but from the basic, absolute human need for social order. The kingdom is there at the end because a dog-eat-dog world is too grim to be endured. In the face of chaos at least some men and women do somehow feel sympathy for one another in their deepest distress, and "the art of their necessities" sets them on the path of rebuilding a humane culture and an ordered state.

Shakespeare's patronage theater never contradicted the views of his royal patron but always transcended his immediate commission. His work in the court was legitimation, not revolution, and in his service to the king, he grounded his patron's history and politics in the materialistic view of nature and the depth psychology that were becoming a part of consciousness in the seventeenth century. In Shakespeare's Stuart plays, to kill a king is to be mad, and to live without a king in a state of nature is to be no more than a "poor, bare, fork'd animal."

Michelangelo's Medici Chapel in Florence served the later Medici popes, Leo X and his brother Clement VII, in much the same way that Shakespeare's plays served James Stuart. The Medicis hired Michelangelo in 1519 to design and execute a tomb in the church of San Lorenzo for their great father, Lorenzo the Magnificent, and his brother Giuliano de' Medici. The chapel remains unfinished, but the patrons got the monument to Medici grandeur they commissioned, if not quite in the way either they or the artist planned. From the beginning the Medici chapel exceeded strict patronage requirements. Outside, it was a living organism of a building so original that Giorgio Vasari credited it with freeing architects from the tradition of the past. Inside, two brooding figures in the niches above the two opposing tombs dominate, and two great statues recline on the edges of each tomb. Night and Day rest uneasily on one sarcophagus, while the mirror figures of Dawn and Dusk recline, overwhelmed by sorrow, on the other. The figures are sad but highly charged erotically (see figure 29).

The artist is reported to have said that a thousand years later the question of what the owners of the tomb had looked like would be of no importance to anyone, and the features of the statues in the central niche above the crypts are not those of their intended or even of their actual inhabitants, but serene representations, one active and one meditative, of the mutability of living creatures. (Indeed, even the sex of the figures is ambiguous—male models were used for the two female figures.) Accident placed unintended bodies in the tombs. Lorenzo and Giuliano, whom the chapel was intended to feature, are memorialized simply by modest inscriptions to one side. Giuliano's tomb actually contains a later duke of the same name, and Lorenzo's crypt contains only a minor descendant of his, plus the unrecorded body of the tyrannical Duke Alessandro the Moor, whose rise to power forced Michelangelo to flee Florence for good and abandon work on the tomb in 1534.

Out of this concatenation of patronage, art, and purposes mistook in time emerged a monument whose very unfinished and accidental quality contributes to its power. It does indeed serve the purpose the patrons intended of preserving forever the name of Medici and its greatness. But it goes beyond this honorable social function. In this eerie enchanted house of the dead, the unfinished quality and the mix-up in the occupants make the visitor feel how ultimately transitory are even the most powerful of men and families.

The Medici tomb is not a case of a divine artist transcending the vulgar interests of his patrons, the story the romantic myth usually tells about patronage art, but rather of a fully social art that catches art's involvement with human existence in the flow of time. The Medici Chapel puts on the same stage, with great poignancy, the unchanging human hopes of achieving meaning by great actions and great wealth and the eternity in which, without art, they would disappear altogether, as if they had never been. Here, the visitor feels less vital than the images, and art looks through the flimsy veil of life into the eternity in which time mingles and consumes all things.

10

WHAT THE KING SAW,

WHAT THE POET WROTE

Probably we shall never have a contemporary description of James and his court watching a Shakespeare play performed in the palace. But we do have a number of accounts of the first Stuart king of England sitting at a play. Dudley Carleton tells us that during the first holidays the king spent in England there was "every night a public play in the great hall, at which the King was ever present." The Venetian almoner, Orazio Busino, zooms in on the scene as the king arrives at a performance at court:

> At about the 6th hour of the night [10 o'clock] the king appeared with his court, having passed through the apartments where the ambassadors were in waiting. . . . On entering the house, the cornets and trumpets to the number of fifteen or twenty began to play very well a sort of recitative, and then after his Majesty had seated himself under the canopy alone, the Queen not being present on account of a slight indisposition, he caused the ambassadors to sit below him on two stools, while the great officers of the crown and courts of law sat upon benches. The Lord Chamberlain then had the way cleared and in the middle of the theatre there appeared a fine and spacious area carpeted all over with green cloth. In an instant a large curtain dropped, painted to represent a tent of gold cloth with a broad fringe; the background was of canvas painted blue, powdered all over with golden stars. *(Calendar of State Papers* [Venetian], XV, 112)

James went to the plays at court and made his views of them known, but he was not exactly stagestruck. He "liked or disliked as he saw cause," Carleton said, "but it seems he takes no extraordinary pleasure in [plays]. The queen and prince [Henry] were more the players' friends" (January 15, 1604). Still, we can tell from the amount of the payments to the King's Men that whenever they played at court the king was present.

With his distaste for and fear of crowds, James was never very relaxed or comfortable on the occasions when plays were performed in overheated halls ablaze with candles and crammed with people. Plays were put on after protracted feasting, tense dealings with courtiers, and the entertainment of foreign ambassadors. Much wine and heavy food would have been consumed. Under these pressures James often became touchy and sometimes did not conceal his annoyance with the dull, pretentious stuff he frequently had to watch. At a performance of a Latin play, *Ajax Flagellifer,* in Christ Church Hall, Oxford, on the evening of August 28, 1605, "The King was very weary before he came thither, but much more wearied by it, and spoke many words of dislike" (Nichols, I, 550). Things got even worse the next night, after another long day of elaborate ceremonies: "That night, after supper, about nine, began their Comedy called *Vertumnus,* very well and learnedly penned by Dr. Gwynn. It was acted much better than either of the other [plays the king had seen] and chiefly by St. John's men, yet the King was so over-wearied at St. Marie's, that after a while he distasted it, and fell asleep; when he awaked, he would have bin gone, saying, 'I marvel what they think me to be,' with such other like speeches shewing his dislike thereof, yet he did tarry till they had ended it, which was after one of the clock. The Queen was not there that night" (552).

On the occasion of the masque, described in Chapter 8, that was arranged by Bacon and performed by the gentlemen of the Inns of Court celebrating the marriage of Princess Elizabeth, the king became so exhausted and testy that, as we have seen, he postponed the performance. The hall was stifling, and John Chamberlain wrote Alice Carleton that "the King was so wearied and sleepie with sitting up almost two whole nights before, that he had no edge to it." Bacon, who was the producer of the masque, was understandably devastated by the loss of face involved in the king's refusal to see his masque, and entreated "his Majestie, that by this disgrace he wold not as it were bury them quicke." But, Chamberlain goes on, "I heare the King shold aunswer, that then they must burie him quicke for he could last no longer, but withall gave them very goode wordes and appointed them to come again on Saterday" (February 18, 1613).

As the king grew older and more impatient with all ceremony, the outbursts at theater in the Great Hall got louder and more crusty. One of the spectators

records such an explosion, and the wonderful piece of courtiership that followed:

> We were so crowded and ill at ease that had it not been for our curiosity we
> must certainly have given in or expired. . . . [The dancers] performed every
> sort of ballet and dance of every country whatsoever such as passamezzi,
> corants, canaries. . . . Last of all they danced the Spanish dance, one at a
> time, each with his lady, and being well nigh tired they began to lag,
> whereupon the king, who is naturally choleric, got impatient and shouted
> aloud, Why don't they dance? What did they make me come here for?
> Devil take you all, dance. Upon this, the Marquis of Buckingham, his
> Majesty's favourite, immediately sprang forward, cutting a score of lofty
> and very minute capers, with so much grace and agility that he not only
> appeased the ire of his angry lord, but rendered himself the admiration and
> delight of everybody. (*Calendar of State Papers* [Venetian], XV, 111)

Things could get much worse at the theater when James was present, as they did
at the drunken theatricals provided for Christian of Denmark at Theobalds.

Such anecdotes of theater in the court as these suggest that at performances
no one, including the king, paid much attention to the play. The argument
described in Chapter 1 between court officials and college dignitaries at Christ's
Church in 1604 about the placement of the State to ensure that James, not the
play, was the cynosure establishes that the official court view, but not that of the
academics, was that the king, not the play, was the thing.

Clearly, the great halls on the occasion of theatrical performance in the court
were most uncomfortable places. But it would be a mistake to think that James
paid no attention whatsoever to the meaning of the plays that he watched. He
sat through a college play at Cambridge twice, and he ordered a repeat performance of *The Merchant of Venice* at the Christmas festivities of 1604–05. One
can only speculate about his reason for the latter, but the legal and religious
courtroom debate between Portia and Shylock was just the kind of intellectual
give-and-take he liked best when sparring with witches and Jesuits.

He liked other kinds of theater as well. "The King made his entrie [to Cam-
bridge] the 7th of this present [March 1615] with as much solemnitie and concourse of gallants and great men as the hard weather and extreme fowle wayes
wold permit. The Prince came along with him, but not the Quene." The university wined and dined the court with no expense spared and amused them

with a series of plays, plus a number of "acts and disputations" in Divinity, Law, and Physic. Chamberlain was in the party and describes the festivities to Carleton in the letter from London of March 16 quoted above, which gives a good picture of university theatricals staged for royal visits. How crowded, "2000 persons," they were:

The Kinge and Prince lay at Trinitie College where the playes were represented, and the hall so well ordered for roome that above 2000 persons were conveniently placed. The first nights entertainment was a comedie [Sir Edward Cecil's lost *Aemilia*] made and acted by St. Johns men, the chiefe part consisting of a counterfait Sir Edward Ratcliffe, a foolish doctor of phisicke, which proved but a leane argument, and though yt were larded with pretty shewes at the beginning and end, and with somwhat too brode speach for such a presence, yet yt was still drie. The second night was a comedie [George Ruggle's *Ignoramus*] of Clare Hall with the helpe of two or three goode actors from other houses, wherein David Drommond in a hobby-horse, and Brakin, the recorder of the towne under the name of Ignoramus a common lawier bare great parts: the thing was full of mirth and varietie, with many excellent actors . . . but more than halfe marred with extreme length. The third night was an English comedie called Albumazer, of Trinite Colleges action and invention, but there was no great matter in yt more than one goode clownes part. The last night was a Latin pastorall of the same houses excellently written and as well acted, which gave great contentment as well to the King as to all the rest. (Letter 225)

Chamberlain obviously enjoyed the shows, and was favored with a place near enough the king that he "had the hap to be for the most time within hearing, and often at his heales." From this position, where he could see and hear the king, like Horatio at *The Murder of Gonzago*, Chamberlain could tell that James was "exceedingly pleased many times both at the playes and the disputations." It was a Latin play in the manner of Plautus, called *Ignoramus*, that was the hit of the visit. The extant play is a five-hours-long traffic of the stage, and an incredibly complicated romance. Inserted into the romance plot is a satire on "common lawyers": those who argued for the priority of the common law, a position with which the university, as well as the king, had long been at odds because of the university's interest in preserving the rights of ecclesiastical courts to render judgments in jurisdictions increasingly being claimed by the common law. *Ignoramus* ("we know of no such crime") was at that time the legal term used by grand juries to indicate that they could find no grounds for an indictment.

Ignoramus was intended as a caricature of the Cambridge town recorder, but the audience immediately identified the stage character as Sir Edward Coke, who had done the king's bidding as prosecutor at the Raleigh and Gunpowder trials (Bowen). But now, as Lord Chief Justice of the King's Bench, he was engaged in a bitter struggle with his monarch. James roared with laughter, clapped frequently, and called out "Plaudite" as Ignoramus-Coke, spouting pig Latin and legalese, strutted the stage, attacked bishops and laymen, and courted a young girl with bawdy macaronic verses: "*Et dabo* fee simple, *si monstras* love's pretty dimple."

James could not stop laughing, and he tried to have the play brought to London. When that proved impossible, he returned to the university two months later, after a hunting trip, to see *Ignoramus* again. The play was put on for him a second time, according to James Tabor, registrar of the university: "About 8 of the clock the play began and ended about one: his majesty was much delighted with the play, and laughed exceedingly; and oftentimes with his hands and by words applauded it" (Mullinger, II, 544). Coke, who was a graduate of Trinity, was not amused, and he made a quarrel of it, attacking scholars from the bench but wincing visibly from that time on whenever the term *ignoramus* was heard in Westminster Hall. Chamberlain reported that the play had "so netled the Lawiers that they are almost out of all patience, and the Lord Chief Justice both openly at the Kings Bench and divers other places hath galled and glaunced at schollers with much bitternes." Chamberlain thought, however, that "yt was a scandal taken rather than geven" (Letter 229, June 13, 1615).

On another occasion, when James was himself mocked in a stage satire, he was not so amused. The French ambassador, Monsieur de la Broderie, wrote on April 8, 1608, to the Marquis de Sillery that the Children of Blackfriars had in March attacked James's Scottish followers and presented his majesty as having been drunk for a month and cursing heaven over the way a hawk flew and beating one of his gentlemen for injuring a hunting hound. The king was so enraged by the play that he swore that the players would have to beg their bread in the future and ordered all London theaters closed on March 29, with a threat of permanent closure (Chambers, 1923, II, 53; III, 257).

Matters could get even more dangerous when the king felt seriously threatened by what was staged for him. Girolamo Lando, a Venetian ambassador, would almost seem to have had *Hamlet* in mind in his description of a performance at the court in January 1620 of an unidentified play. He thought the story worth recounting to the Venetian serenities "owing to the mystery it involves": "The Comedians of the prince, [Charles] in the presence of the king his father, played a drama the other day in which a king with his two sons has one of them put to death, simply upon suspicion that he wished to deprive him of his crown, and the other son actually did deprive him of it afterwards. This moved the king in an extraordinary manner, both inwardly and outwardly." Lando then goes on to make the surprising statement that "in this country however the comedians have absolute liberty to say whatever they wish against any one soever, so the only demonstration against them will be the words spoken by the king" (*Calendar of State Papers* [Venetian], XVI, 111). It would be fascinating to know at what point in the play King James decided that Prince Charles, Hamlet fashion, was using his players to link his father to the death of his elder brother and to taunt him with the suggestion that Charles might himself prove more dangerous in the end than the warlike Henry. It would be equally interesting to know what were the words spoken by the king when he was moved "in an extraordinary manner, both inwardly and outwardly." The Venetians who reported back to the Most Serene Republic seem sometimes to have preferred to amuse those at home with the sensational rather than the strictly factual, but there must have been a startling scene of some sort, although James may not have exactly risen Claudius-like and called for lights.

The unidentified play sounds as if it might have been Fulke Greville's *Mustapha,* although in that play Zanger avenges himself on his father, Soliman, for the murder of his brother, Mustapha, by killing himself rather than the sultan. But the point is similar, or might well seem so to someone whose attention drifted away before the long-delayed conclusion. Greville, out of favor in 1604 when the play was first written, became the Chancellor of the Exchequer in 1614, but even then *Mustapha,* though revised many times, was not licensed for printing by the Master of the Revels, Henry Herbert, until 1632.

James Stuart was not an unlettered man: quite the contrary. His education at the hands of George Buchanan had been thorough, extensive, and bookish. Even if a French ambassador could refer to him wittily, but with some justice, as "the wisest fool in Christendom," James was in fact a considerable linguist, a competent poet, and a scholar who actually published books on poetics, politics, witchcraft, and tobacco. He was, that is to say, a Gutenberg man whose consciousness had been formed in large part by and who worked out his ideas in print. With a book in his hand—the Bible by way of conspicuous example—he was a close reader and a scrupulous, even casuistical, interpreter of difficult meanings. But in the oral situation of the theater, as our examples show, his attention flagged easily, he soon grew tired and bored, he came to be seen rather than to see and listen, he understood what was going on in the most obvious way, and his full attention was captured only when events on stage bore directly on his own interests.

None of this would surprise a director or an actor, long inured to the inevitable lack of close attention or sophisticated interpretation by theater audiences. But the king's playwright, for all his theatrical skills as an actor and his long success on the boards as a dramatist, was also a man of the written word, who, along with a number of other playwrights, was revolutionizing the theater by using his oral-visual medium to carry the subtle and complex meanings of the printed page. The drama "from antiquity had been controlled by writing. Euripides' tragedies were texts composed in writing and then memorized verbatim to be presented orally" (Ong, 133). But the theatrical text, with the exception of the works of a few playwrights with a dense literary style like Aeschylus, remained until Shakespeare's time little more than an outline for performance, not a great deal more complicated than the written plot outlines that the commedia dell'arte players in Shakespeare's time still tacked up on the wing of the stage. The English Renaissance playwrights changed all this by creating a poetic drama of extraordinary intensity and complexity.

George Puttenham in his *Arte of English Poesie* speaks with scorn of the rude language of people "in any uplandish village or corner of a Realme, where is no resort but of poore rusticall or uncivill people" (150). From such a place did the Shakespeares come, and if we can judge by their use of marks for signatures, both the merchant father and tenant-farmer grandfather were illiterate. The better-born mother may have been able to read, although female education in even the best families often did not extend to reading and writing. But the son, though not a university man, amassed an astounding, even a miraculous, written vocabulary. As counted in the *Harvard Concordance* the Shakespearean oeuvre, a total of 884,647 words (680,755 in verse, 203,892 in prose), uses 29,066 different words. A use vocabulary of 29,000 words, along with the elegant intricacies of phrasing and complex grammatical turns characteristic of Shakespeare, are the marks of a *writer* rather than of a *speaker*, who has no use for such an extensive vocabulary and must speak fairly directly. Although he published only half his plays (but all his poems), Shakespeare is still very much a Gutenberg man, with assumptions about the complex and subtle meanings of words that have been locked in place on the printed page.

The richness of this "great feast of language," to use Shakespeare's own words from his language play, *Love's Labour's Lost*, can be fully appreciated only in comparison with other great founding poets of the Renaissance. Dante's *Commedia* contains 101,499 words, made up from a vocabulary of 14,822 words. Petrarch in the *Canzoniere* has 57,635 words, with a small total vocabulary of 4,491, of which 3,284 words are used more than once. Shakespeare's contemporary, the playwright and poet Christopher Marlowe, himself a "mighty man of words" like his heroes, wrote 148,337 words, using a total vocabulary of 11,448, of which, startlingly, 5,074 appear only once. Marlowe, of course, wrote far less than Shakespeare, but a comparison made possible by the computerized Marlowe (Ule) and Shakespeare (Spevack) concordances shows that had Shakespeare written only the same number of words as Marlowe, he would, based on the frequency with which different words appeared in his own work, have shown a total vocabulary of 12,744, which makes him a mightier man of words than the "dead shepherd" whom he remembered in *As You Like It* for his "saw of might."

If we would like to know what the king and his courtiers thought of the Shakespeare plays performed before them, it would be still more fascinating to know what the poet-playwright expected from his audience when his plays were taken up to court. The evidence is indirect and comes from the Elizabethan period, but the playwright has left us a number of dramatic comments on playing in the palace, all of which show characteristic print anxiety about the audience. Several of his plays contain brief theatrical performances, set always in a court or some noble house. When Shakespeare portrayed a theater, he did not, except for the choruses in *Henry V*, imagine a public theater. And in each of his plays within the play the players are as base as the audience is noble, and they are as awkward and out of date as the audience is fashionable and inattentive.

There are internal plays of this type in *The Taming of the Shrew* and *Love's Labour's Lost*, but the full Shakespearean scheme of playing in the court does not appear until *A Midsummer Night's Dream*, where a courtly stage audience made up of the duke of Athens, Theseus, and his bride, the Amazon queen Hippolyta, along with two other just-married aristocratic couples, sit in the palace at a wedding celebration watching a company of artisans turned players. These amateurs, hoping to please the duke and gain a pension of sixpence a day for life, put on the "tedious brief scene" and the "very tragical mirth" of a playlet on the love and deaths of Pyramus and Thisbe. The play is as bad as can be, "not one word apt, one player fitted," but Theseus, having been present at many an awkward public performance given by the common people in his honor, has learned the importance of what he calls "noble respect," the necessity of giving "thanks for nothing," and taking "what poor duty cannot do . . . in might, not merit" (5.1.91). Noble respect substitutes the generosity of the aristocratic audience for the deficiencies of the players, recognizing that "the best in this kind are but shadows; and the worst are no worse, if imagination amend them" (5.1.211).

But despite Theseus' intentions, he and the other members of the court audience are more than a little deficient in the needed imagination. Theseus has already recorded his view that imagination is idle—"the lunatic, the lover and the poet"—and at the performance the court chatters away, exchanges witticisms about the ineptitude of the players, and preens itself on its own sense of social and intellectual superiority. For the Athenian courtiers, plays are only a source of amusement, not to be taken seriously, a way of passing the time until they go to bed and beget heirs for their noble houses.

It is, however, in *Hamlet* that Shakespeare offers his most extended comments on the gap between players and audience at court. The play was written, probably in 1601, while Shakespeare's experience of playing at the court was for Elizabeth, but the playing situation it shows would scarcely have changed when James Stuart sat in the State. The players in *Hamlet* are a professional troupe, from the city of Wittenberg, not London, cut down to six players in order to travel. They have lost their audience to troupes of boy comedians performing bitter satires of the kind which had become the rage in London in the early seventeenth century, and have come to Elsinore to perform before the Danish court with a repertory that includes a play on Dido and Aeneas and another on a sensational murder in Vienna, *The Murder of Gonzago*. Once arrived at the Danish palace, the players are servants and are so treated by the king's principal secretary, Polonius. When he is commanded by Hamlet to see them "well bestow'd" and "well us'd," he remarks testily that he "will use them according to their desert," implying that their status entitles them to very little.

The heir apparent, who has visited the company many times in their theater in the city, coming to know the actors and their repertory (even getting many lines from their plays by heart), greets them warmly: "You are welcome, masters, welcome all. I am glad to see thee well. Welcome good friends" (2.2.421). He jokes familiarly with the boy who plays female parts about his voice breaking, and twits one of the younger players about his new beard, "O, old friend! why, thy face is valanc'd since I saw thee last; com'st thou to beard me in Denmark?" (2.2.422). Hamlet is a theater buff, like one of the young lords or lawyers from the Inns of Court who sat on the stage, or in the gallery boxes above the stage, in the London theaters and commented learnedly and wittily on the action. Like them, too, he professes the latest neoclassical aesthetic standards and looks down on the popular theater's crudity, its ranting tragedians, melodramatic acting styles—parts "to tear a cat in"—bombastic blank verse, "inexplicable dumb shows," vulgar clowns, and the crude audience of groundlings who stand in the pit.

In spite of the familiarity of the prince, the actors know their place. Hamlet jokes with them, but not they with him. The players are deferential and quietly agreeable to the courtiers, though likely to mock them behind their backs. Hamlet has to warn the leading player not to ape Polonius as he follows him. The players say little, but listen attentively—though they change nothing—when the prince lectures them about his sophisticated views of acting: "Suit the action to the word, the word to the action, . . . o'erstep not the modesty of nature" (3.2.17), and of play construction: "well digested in the scenes, set down with as much modesty as cunning" (2.2.439). They humor him, however, and when he recites some lines from a speech in a play about Dido and Aeneas that he has particularly liked, the players tactfully applaud his delivery. When Hamlet asks for a performance the next evening—"We'll ha't tomorrow night"—of *The Murder of Gonzago*, they are ready to perform and can easily manage—"Ay, my lord"—the dozen or sixteen lines which Hamlet "would set down and insert in't."

But the players, however deferential to the prince, are still popular entertainers. Their Dido play may be "caviary to the general," but by 1601 it was old-fashioned rhetorical bombast, and *The Murder of Gonzago* is a primitive Elizabethan tragedy, complete with a Vice, morality-play structure, dumb show, and stiff formal speeches. Their plays are sharply at odds with Hamlet's courtly, humanistic, neoclassical "idea of a theater" that prevailed in the palace and places of high culture like the countess of Pembroke's closet-drama circle at Wilton.

This neoclassical aesthetic gets a mechanical application in the pedantic, "inkhorn" views of Polonius, whose attitudes toward the theater were shaped by his humanist education at Wittenberg, where he played the part of Julius Caesar in a classical play. His systematic run-through of all possible combinations of the major genres, "tragedy, comedy, history, pastoral, pastoral-comical, historical-pastoral" (2.2.396), smells with the odor of the lamp. He is conventional in his views of theater: duly, and dully, repeating by rote that Seneca is the model for tragedy, Plautus for comedy; that the Aristotelian rules require observance of the unity of place, the "scene individable," while the "law of writ and the liberty" allows free play with time and space. Unusual diction such as "mobled queen" is for him the highest mark of invention.

It is in the instructions that Hamlet gives, at considerable length, to the players, however, that we hear neoclassical criticism applied to the theater in a far more serious manner. It was long thought that Hamlet's advice to the players represented Shakespeare's own dramatic theories, but more surely they bespeak the intellectual, upper-class aesthetic views that took shape in Italy in the sixteenth century and found expression in England in the work of writers like Sir Philip Sidney, "well-languaged" Samuel Daniel, Fulke Greville, and others like the intellectual Hamlet. King James in his youthful book of poetics, *Ane Schort Treatise*, espoused these same neoclassical principles, and he too had connections with Wilton. Sidney's *Apologie*, which is the source for many of the details of Hamlet's attack on the popular theater (Ringler), was the bible of English neoclassical poetics. When Hamlet instructs the players that the purpose of theatrical art is "to hold as 'twere the mirror up to nature: to show virtue her feature, scorn her own image, and the very age and body of the time his form and pressure" (3.2.21), he raises the central issue in neoclassical poetics: whether art was mimetic or creative, realistic or fantastic, and he comes down, as neoclassicism most frequently did, on the side of imitation. In other key respects he is equally neoclassical, particularly in his emphasis on the whole rather than the parts, on subordination, restraint, and shapeliness.

Clearly the Wittenberg company, despite their goodwill, fails to meet Hamlet's neoclassical standards in both their acting style and their plays. But in the end they do "tell all," and *The Murder of Gonʒago,* for all its artistic crudity and its "inexplicable dumb show," holds the mirror up to and reveals the hidden crime, the murder of the old king by his brother, that is poisoning the Danish state. The Elsinore play thus fulfills the Horatian moral requirements of humanist theater, to please and to instruct, but the audience does not respond, as the theorists had predicted, like

> guilty creatures sitting at a play [who]
> Have by the very cunning of the scene
> Been strook so to the soul, that presently
> They have proclaim'd their malefactions.
> (2.2.589)

Sir Philip Sidney, using the ulcer imagery so prominent in *Hamlet,* had argued a similar view in the best neoclassical manner, that tragedy "openeth the greatest wounds, and sheweth forth the ulcers that are covered with Tissue; [it] maketh Kinges feare to be Tyrants, and Tyrants manifest their tirannicall humors; that, with sturring the affects of admiration and commiseration, teacheth the uncertainety of this world, and upon how weake foundations guilden roofes are builded" (177). He offers the example of a Greek tyrant so overwhelmed with a production of Euripides' *Trojan Women* ("What's Hecuba to him?") that he immediately repented and changed his wicked ways. Shakespeare is not so sure. Claudius sees his murder staged, and his conscience is wrung—"O, my offense is rank." He retreats to the chapel to pray. But there he quickly finds that he really cannot bear to give up his ill-gotten gains, either Gertrude or Denmark—"My words fly up, my thoughts remain below" (3.3.97). Far from repenting his crime, he decides to commit another murder by sending Hamlet, now too dangerous to keep in Denmark, to England for execution.

The other members of the courtly audience, though the play speaks almost as directly to their situations as it does to that of Claudius, are less perceptive than the king. Ophelia knows so little of theater, or anything else, that she cannot puzzle out the obvious meaning of the dumb show. Gertrude, who may or may not have known about the murder of her first husband by her second, fails to see, or ignores, the mirror of her own unfaithfulness held up to her by the player queen: "the lady doth protest too much, methinks." Even Hamlet, the theater expert, is a bad audience. He makes vulgar and loud remarks to other members of the audience, baits the actors, and criticizes the play while it is going forward. These actions, as always in Shakespeare's plays within the play, are signs of a deeper failure in understanding the play.

The prince treats the play as if its only purpose were the political one of catching the conscience of the king. In this it succeeds brilliantly, if momentarily; although ironically, given Hamlet's condemnation of inexplicable dumb shows, it is the mime rather than the main play that has the greatest effect. But Hamlet, like the others in the audience, misses entirely the point of the long and formal rhetorical exchange between the Player King and Queen that constitutes the major portion of *The Murder of Gonzago*. It is this part of the internal play, however, that really shows "the very age and body of the time his form and pressure." The Player Queen vociferously assures the Player King that she will never wed again if he should die, and he solemnly tells her in sonorous, lofty tones that although people intend what they swear, human passions change and human purposes weaken in time. Life goes on, and as it does, it carries people to places they never intended or expected:

> Our wills and fates do so contrary run
> That our devices still are overthrown,
> Our thoughts are ours, their ends none of our own.
> (3.2.211)

When the dialogue between the Player King and Queen is given full weight—as it never is in performance, where it is regularly cut—the internal play focuses on the helplessness of the human will in the undertow of fate that is the lot of everyone in Elsinore. But no one there, including Hamlet, sees the applicability of the play to their conditions. Only after his actual experience of death on his sea voyage and in the graveyard where Ophelia is being buried can Hamlet conclude that "If it be [now], 'tis not to come; if it be not to come, it will be now; if it be not now, yet it [will] come—the readiness is all" (5.2.220). This is pretty much what the Player King said, but the meaning becomes real not when it is spoken on the stage, but only when it is directly experienced.

On the night of performance before the assembled court at Elsinore, the Wittenberg players, despite interruptions, do their work like the professionals they are, until the play is broken off by the rising of the agitated king and his call for lights. We hear no more of them and may assume that, like Shakespeare's company so many times at the palace, they packed their costumes in their hampers and went off to play elsewhere. Their play had told all, but it was understood by no one and changed nothing. In spite of the lower-class quality of the Wittenberg troupe—"public means which public manners breeds"—and the crudeness of their old-fashioned play, they had useful things to say to the court. Their play revealed the concealed facts of murder and adultery in Elsinore, and offered, in addition, an image that goes to the very bottom of life, in Elsinore or in Whitehall, an image of the human condition as one of players in a play not in their own control. "There's a divinity that shapes our ends, Rough-hew them how we will" (5.2.10).

In *Hamlet*, as in his sonnets, Shakespeare claims a value for his theatrical art, however rough it may be, and assigns it a place of dignity, however minor and subservient to other offices, in the life of the court. Francis Fergusson long ago said that *Hamlet* was *the* Renaissance play, existing "at the heart of the society," set in all the symbolic places of the palace on which the kingdom centered. Opening on the battlements, where the guard encounters and tries to question a ghost from beyond, the action moves on to the king's Presence Chamber, where affairs of state are dealt with, through various private chambers and public areas, on to the Great Hall, set up for a theatrical performance, and thence to the prie-dieu in the royal chapel, to the queen's bedroom, and on out of the palace at last to a field where a great army passes on the way to battle, to the burial ground, and back into the palace to the Presence Chamber, where the rest becomes silence. In these settings, the primary rituals of the Renaissance court are performed. The mounting of the guard, the dispatch of ambassadors, the disposal of children, councils, funerals, duels, treaties, marriages, coronations, and, among these other court rituals, theater. Yet even as Shakespeare, somewhat boldly, locates theater among the major institutions of the state, he unblinkingly acknowledges that his art, no matter how potentially useful he makes it out to be, is not fully understood even by aristocratic intellectuals like Hamlet, and it is altogether a blank to the other self-centered courtiers who watch it. The play may be the thing, but it seldom, if ever, catches the conscience of a king who was often "very weary before he came [to the theater] but much more wearied by it, and spoke many words of dislike."

APPENDIX A

THEATRICAL CALENDAR OF

THE KING'S MEN AT COURT

1603–14

1603

FEBRUARY 2 (Candlemas)	Last performance before Queen Elizabeth, at Richmond
MARCH 19	Playing banned because of Elizabeth's illness; ban continues through the year because of the plague
MARCH 24	Death of Elizabeth
MAY 19	Warrant issued that makes the company the King's Men
SPRING AND FALL	On tour sporadically, playing at Bath, Shrewsbury, Coventry, Ipswich(?), Mortlake. *Hamlet* probably played at Oxford and Cambridge.
JULY 25	Coronation of James and Anne

1603–04 Season

DECEMBER 2	Play given at Wilton before king and court (*As You Like It?*)
DECEMBER 26 (St. Stephen's Night)	At Hampton Court (*Hamlet?*)
DECEMBER 27	At Hampton Court; play unknown
DECEMBER 28 (Innocents' Night)	At Hampton Court; play unknown
DECEMBER 30	At Hampton Court before Prince Henry; play unknown
JANUARY 1	At Hampton Court before Prince

	Henry; *A Midsummer Night's Dream.* Second performance at Hampton Court of unknown play.
JANUARY 6 (Twelfth Night)	Public performance at Maldon
FEBRUARY 2 (Candlemas)	At Hampton Court before Florentine ambassador; play unknown
FEBRUARY 8	Granted "free gift" from king of £30 because plague keeps theaters closed
FEBRUARY 19 (Shrove Sunday)	At Whitehall. Perhaps give Ben Jonson's *Sejanus,* which, along with the anonymous *Fair Maid of Bristow,* was among the plays performed by the company during the season at court.
MARCH 4	Delayed coronation procession from the Tower to Westminster. Each of the King's Men, designated Grooms of the Outer Chamber, issued four and a half yards of red cloth to make clothing for procession.
APRIL 9	Public theaters open again at end of Lent; plague abates
MAY 7 – JUNE 16	At some time during this period company performs at Oxford
AUGUST 9 – 27	Paid £21.12s. for attendance on Spanish notables who have come to London to sign peace treaty

1604—05 Season

BEFORE DECEMBER 18	At the Globe; give two performances of the anonymous *Gowrie* before being forbidden to perform this play
NOVEMBER 1 (Hallowmas)	At Whitehall, Banqueting House; *Othello*
NOVEMBER 4	At Whitehall, Great Hall; *Merry Wives of Windsor*

DECEMBER 26 (St. Stephen's Night)	At Whitehall, Great Hall; *Measure for Measure*, by "Shaxberd"
DECEMBER 28 (Innocents' Night)	At Whitehall; *The Comedy of Errors*
JANUARY 1–6	At Whitehall; *Love's Labour's Lost*
EARLY JANUARY	*Love's Labour's Lost* performed before the queen, who has already seen all the "new plays," at Cecil's house or at Southampton's house, perhaps both
JANUARY 7	At Whitehall; *Henry V*
JANUARY 8	At Whitehall; *Every Man Out of His Humour* (Ben Jonson)
FEBRUARY 2 (Candlemas)	At Whitehall; *Every Man In His Humour* (Ben Jonson)
FEBRUARY 3	At Whitehall; a play is ready but not shown. Payment made.
FEBRUARY 10 (Shrove Sunday)	At Whitehall; *Merchant of Venice*
FEBRUARY 11	At Whitehall; *Tragedy of the Spanish Maze* (anonymous)
FEBRUARY 12 (Shrove Tuesday)	At Whitehall; *Merchant of Venice* repeated by king's command

1605–06 Season

OCTOBER 5	Plague closes public theaters
OCTOBER 9	At Oxford; other times at Barnstaple and Saffron Walden
DECEMBER 15	Theaters open again
DECEMBER 26 (St. Stephen's Night)	At Whitehall, Banqueting House; play unknown. Ten plays, exact dates and titles unknown, given this winter season. Payment made March 24.
JULY 7–8	At Greenwich; two plays, titles unknown, performed at festivities connected with visit of King Christian IV of Denmark
JULY	Plague breaks out again

JULY 28 – 31	At Oxford
AUGUST 7	At Hampton Court; a play, probably *Macbeth*, performed as part of farewell for the Danish king
AUGUST	At Leicester
SEPTEMBER	At Marlborough and Dover
NOVEMBER 2	At Maidstone

1606 – 07 Season

DECEMBER 26 (St. Stephen's Night)	At Whitehall; *King Lear*
DECEMBER 29	At Whitehall; play unknown. Nine plays, seven with titles and dates unknown, played between December 26 and February 27.
FEBRUARY 2 (Candlemas)	At Whitehall; *The Devil's Charter* (Barnabe Barnes)

1607 – 08 Season

DECEMBER 26 – FEBRUARY 7	At Whitehall; thirteen plays, exact dates and titles unknown. Two plays performed on both January 6 and 17.

1608 – 09 Season

CHRISTMAS SEASON	At Whitehall; twelve plays, titles unknown

1609 – 10 Season

CHRISTMAS SEASON	At Whitehall; thirteen plays, titles unknown

1610—11 Season

CHRISTMAS SEASON	At Whitehall; fifteen plays, titles unknown

1611—12 Season

OCTOBER 31	At Whitehall; play unknown. Twenty-four plays performed between this date and June 8, eight titles known.
NOVEMBER 1 (Hallowmas)	At Whitehall; *The Tempest*
NOVEMBER 5	At Whitehall; *The Winter's Tale*
NOVEMBER 9	At Whitehall; play unknown
NOVEMBER 19	At Whitehall; play unknown
DECEMBER 16	At Whitehall; play unknown
DECEMBER 26 (St. Stephen's Night)	At Whitehall; *A King and No King* (Francis Beaumont and John Fletcher)
DECEMBER 31	At Whitehall; play unknown
JANUARY 1	At Whitehall; *The Twins' Tragedy* ([Richard?] Niccolls)
JANUARY 5	At Whitehall; play unknown
JANUARY 7	At Whitehall; play unknown
JANUARY 12	At Greenwich, with the Queen's Players; *The Silver Aeidg* (Thomas Heywood)
JANUARY 13	At Greenwich, with the Queen's Players; *The Rape of Lucrece* (Thomas Heywood)
JANUARY 15 —APRIL 26	At Whitehall; eleven performances, titles unknown
FEBRUARY 20	At Whitehall; *The Nobleman* (Cyril Tourneur)
JUNE 8	At Whitehall, before the ambassador of the duke of Savoy; *Cardenio* (Shakespeare and John Fletcher?)

1612—13 Season

CHRISTMAS THROUGH MAY 20

At Whitehall; payment for twenty plays (seven, possibly eight, by Shakespeare, in connection with festivities celebrating the betrothal and marriage of Princess Elizabeth; *Much Ado about Nothing* probably performed twice). Dates not given, but titles specified: *Philaster* (Francis Beaumont and John Fletcher), *Knot of Fools* (Thomas Brewer), *Much Ado about Nothing, The Maid's Tragedy* (Francis Beaumont and John Fletcher), *The Merry Devil of Edmonton* (anonymous), *The Tempest, A King and No King* (Francis Beaumont and John Fletcher), *The Twins' Tragedy* ([Richard?] Niccolls), *The Winter's Tale, Falstaff, The Moor of Venice, The Nobleman* (Cyril Tourneur), *Caesars Tragedy (Julius Caesar?), Love Lies a Bleeding* (alternate title for *Philaster*), *A Bad Beginning Makes a Good Ending* (anonymous), *The Captain* (John Fletcher), *The Alchemist* (Ben Jonson), *Cardenio* (Shakespeare and John Fletcher?), *Hotspur, Benedick and Betteris.*

1613—14 Season

NOVEMBER 4—MARCH 8

At Whitehall; fourteen plays, no titles

Appendix B

The Great Hall at Christ Church,

Oxford, August 1605

An anonymous drawing of an unidentified hall that had been set up as a royal theater was identified by John Orrell in 1983 as a design of the hall at Christ Church College, Oxford, for theatrical performances before King James on the occasion of his visit in August 1605. A schematized version of this plan appears as figure 25. Orrell, a leading expert on Renaissance English theaters, argues (1983, 1988), convincingly to my mind, that the design of the hall-theater is the work of Inigo Jones and that the description accompanying it was written by Simon Basil, then Comptroller of the King's Works, in order to guide the carpenters of the Works in setting up the hall for royal performance. Jones was duplicating as best he could in the circumstances a classic theater design of Sebastiano Serlio printed in *Il secondo libro di perspettiva* (Paris, 1545).

Orrell bases his identification of the anonymous plan with the Christ Church Hall on the fact that the dimensions of the hall given in the plan and those of Christ Church Hall are the same, 115 feet by 40 feet: "To my knowledge there is only one hall in England that is commonly stated to be 115 feet by 40 feet, and that is at Christ Church, Oxford" (1983, 131). It has often been reported, however, that the Great Hall at Hampton Court (see figure 23) is also 115 feet by 40 feet, but Orrell rejects this measurement as incorrect: "E. K. Chambers, *The Elizabethan Stage* (Oxford, 1923), I, 15, unaccountably gives the length of the hall at Hampton Court as 115 ft. In fact it is 97 ft. long, and well known for being smaller than its contemporary at Christ Church. See Nikolaus Pevsner, *Middlesex*, The Buildings of England (Harmondsworth, 1951), p. 80" (Orrell, 1983, 180). Orrell is partly correct: the hall at Hampton Court is not 115 feet by 40 feet; but he introduces another error by giving the length as 97 feet. The Hampton Court Great Hall, as measured at my request in 1993 by the Historic Royal Palaces, is said by the Head Office (Chief Executive, David Beeton) to be 40 feet in width, 92 feet 9 inches in length, not including the screen passage. Including the screen passage it is 105 feet 6 inches. These dimensions are used in the sketch, in figure 23, of the Hampton Court Hall set up for the performance of *Hamlet*.

Orrell's basic point still holds, however, and his identification of the anonymous plan with Christ Church Hall, and not with Hampton Court, made it possible to connect the plan with two other documents describing the 1605 royal visit to Oxford. One, a Latin description of the performance of *Rex Platonicus* (1607), was written by Isaac Wake; the other, a document (Additional MS.34) in the Cambridge University Library by a visitor named Philip Stringer, describes the argument between the university authorities and the king's courtiers, discussed in Chapter 1, about the placement of the State, which the courtiers wanted raised higher and removed farther from the stage than the 12 feet specified in the plan (shown in figure 25). With this brilliant piece of detective work, Orrell put together the most complete description to date of the set-up of a Great Hall for court performance.

BIBLIOGRAPHY

First rather than inclusive page numbers are given.

Akrigg, G. P. V. *Jacobean Pageant, or The Court of King James I.* Cambridge, Mass., 1962.

———. *Shakespeare and the Earl of Southampton.* Cambridge, Mass., 1968.

Allde, Edward. *The King of Denmarkes welcome Containing his arrivall, abode, entertainement, both in the Citie and other places.* London, 1606.

Allen, E. Quist. "Lord Darnley's Skull and Femur." Hunterian Museum, Royal College of Surgeons of England, Information Sheet No. 24, n.d.

Andrewes, Lancelot. *Ninety-Six Sermons.* 5 vols. Oxford, 1843.

Anglo, Sydney. "The Courtier, the Renaissance, and Changing Ideas." In Dickens.

———. *Spectacle, Pageantry, and Early Tudor Policy.* Oxford, 1969.

Asch, Ronald G., and Adolf M. Birke, eds. *Princes, Patronage, and the Nobility: The Court at the Beginning of the Modern Age, c. 1450–1650.* Oxford, 1991.

Ashton, Robert, ed. *James I and His Contemporaries.* London, 1969.

Aylmer, G. E. *The King's Servants.* London, 1961.

Bacon, Francis. *Essays.* World's Classics. London, 1902.

Barber, C. L. *Shakespeare's Festive Comedies: A Study of Dramatic Form and Its Relation to Social Custom.* Princeton, 1959.

Barroll, J. Leeds. "A New History for Shakespeare and His Time." *Shakespeare Quarterly* 39 (1988): 441.

———. *Politics, Plague, and Shakespeare's Theater: The Stuart Years.* Ithaca, 1991.

Beckerman, Bernard. *Shakespeare at the Globe, 1599–1609.* New York, 1962.

Belsey, Carol. *The Subject of Tragedy: Identity and Difference in Renaissance Drama.* London, 1985.

Bender, John. "The Day of *The Tempest.*" *ELH* 47 (1980): 235.

Bentley, Gerald E. *The Profession of Dramatist in Shakespeare's Time, 1590–1642.* Princeton, 1971.

———. *The Profession of Player in Shakespeare's Time, 1590–1642.* Princeton, 1984.

Bergeron, David. *Royal Family, Royal Lovers, King James.* Columbia, Mo., 1991.

———. *Shakespeare's Romances and the Royal Family.* Lawrence, Kans., 1985.

Bernthal, Craig A. "Staging Justice: James I and the Trial Scenes of *Measure for Measure.*" *SEL* 32 (1992): 247.

Bianconi, Lorenzo. *Music in the Seventeenth Century.* Trans. J. B. Robinson. Cambridge, 1987.

Bianconi, Lorenzo, and Thomas Walker. "Production, Consumption, and Political Function of Seventeenth-Century Opera." *Early Music History* 4 (1984): 209.

Bingham, Caroline. *James VI of Scotland.* London, 1979.

———. *James I of England.* London, 1981.

Bland, Olivia. *The Royal Way of Death.* London, 1986.

Bodin, Jean. *The Six Books of a Commonweal*. 1576. Trans. Richard Knolles, 1606. Ed. Kenneth D. McRae. Cambridge, Mass., 1962.

Bold, John. *John Webb: Architectural Theory and Practice in the Seventeenth Century*. Oxford, 1989.

Boswell, John. *Christianity, Social Tolerance, and Homosexuality*. Chicago, 1980.

Bowen, Catherine Drinker. *The Lion and the Throne: The Life and Times of Sir Edward Coke (1552–1634)*. Boston, 1956.

Bowes, Robert. *The Correspondence of Robert Bowes*. Ed. Joseph Stevenson. London, 1842.

Bradley, E. T. *The Life of Lady Arabella Stuart*. 2 vols. London, 1889.

Bray, Alan. *Homosexuality in Renaissance England*. Boston, 1988.

Brennan, Michael. *Literary Patronage in the English Renaissance: The Pembroke Family*. London, 1988.

Bristol, Michael D. *Carnival and Theater: Plebeian Culture and the Structure of Authority in Renaissance England*. New York, 1985.

Brown, Keith M. *Bloodfeud in Scotland, 1573–1625: Violence, Justice and Politics in an Early Modern Society*. Edinburgh, 1989.

Buchanan, George. *The History of Scotland*. 4 vols. Trans. and ed. James Aikman. Glasgow, 1827.

Burke, Peter. *The Historical Anthropology of Early Modern Europe*. Cambridge, 1987.

———. *The Renaissance Sense of the Past*. New York, 1969.

Burnet, Gilbert. *The History of My Own Times*. 6 vols. Oxford, 1833.

Butler, Martin. *Theater and Crisis, 1632–1642*. Cambridge, 1984.

Caldwell, John. *The Oxford History of English Music*, Volume I: *From the Beginnings to c. 1715*. Oxford, 1992.

Calendar of State Papers and Manuscripts Relating to English Affairs, Existing in the Archives and Collections of Venice and in other Libraries of North Italy. 37 vols. Ed. R. L. Brown et al. London, 1864–1947.

Calendar of State Papers, Domestic Series, of the Reigns of Edward VI, Mary, Elizabeth, and James I (1547–1625). 12 vols. Ed. Robert Lemon and M. A. E. Green. London, 1856–72.

Caraman, Philip. *Henry Garnet, 1555–1606, and the Gunpowder Plot*. London, 1964.

Carleton, Dudley. *Dudley Carleton to John Chamberlain (1603–1624): Jacobean Letters*. Ed. Maurice Lee, Jr. New Brunswick, N. J., 1972.

Castiglione, Baldesar. *The Book of the Courtier*. Trans. Charles S. Singleton. New York, 1959.

Cecil, Robert. *Calendar of the Manuscripts of the Most Hon. The Marquess of Salisbury Preserved at Hatfield House, Hertfordshire*. Ed. M. S. Giuseppi. London, 1930, 1933, parts XV and XVI.

Chamberlain, John. *The Letters of John Chamberlain*. 2 vols. Ed. N. E. McClure. Philadelphia, 1939.

Chambers, Edmund K. *The Elizabethan Stage*. 4 vols. Oxford, 1923.

———. *William Shakespeare: A Study of Facts and Problems*. 2 vols. Oxford, 1930.

Clubb, Louise George. *Italian Drama in Shakespeare's Time.* New Haven, 1989.

Cohen, Walter. *Drama of a Nation: Public Theater in Renaissance England and Spain.* Ithaca, 1985.

Cook, Ann Jennalie. *The Privileged Playgoers of Shakespeare's London, 1576–1642.* Princeton, 1981.

Cook, David, ed. *Dramatic Records in the Declared Accounts of the Treasurer of the Chamber, 1588–1642.* The Malone Society, 1961, Collections, vol. VI. Oxford, 1962.

Crutwell, Patrick. *The Shakespearean Moment and Its Place in the Poetry of the Seventeenth Century.* New York, 1960.

Danby, John. *Elizabethan and Jacobean Poets: Studies in Sidney, Shakespeare, Beaumont & Fletcher.* London, 1964.

Daniel, Samuel. *Philotas.* In Michel.

———. *Royal Masque Presented at Hampton Court (The Vision of the Twelve Goddesses).* 1604. In *The Complete Works in Verse and Prose of Samuel Daniel.* 5 vols. Ed. A. B. Grosart. Reprint. New York, 1963, vol. I.

Davies, H. Neville. "Jacobean *Antony and Cleopatra.*" *Shakespeare Studies* 17 (1985): 123.

D'Ewes, Simond. *Autobiography and Correspondence.* 2 vols. Ed. J. O. Haliwell. London, 1845.

Dickens, A. G., ed. *The Courts of Europe: Politics, Patronage and Royalty, 1400–1800.* London, 1977.

Dollimore, Jonathan. *Radical Tragedy.* Chicago, 1984.

Donne, John. *The Poems of John Donne.* Ed. Herbert Grierson. Oxford, 1933.

Durant, David N. *Arbella Stuart, a Rival to the Queen.* London, 1978.

Edmond, M. *Hilliard and Oliver: The Lives and Works of Two Great Miniaturists.* London, 1983.

Elias, Norbert. *The Court Society.* Trans. Edmund Jephcott. Oxford, 1983.

Evans, Robert. *Poetry and Power: Ben Jonson and the Poetics of Patronage.* Lewisburg, Penn., 1984.

Fergusson, Francis. *The Idea of a Theater.* Princeton, 1949.

Finkelpearl, Philip J. "'The Comedians' Liberty': Censorship of the Jacobean Stage Reconsidered." *English Literary Renaissance* 16 (1986): 123.

———. "The Role of the Court in the Development of Jacobean Drama." *Criticism* 24 (1982): 138.

Finnet, John. *Finetti Philoxensis.* London, 1656.

Franklin, Julian. *Jean Bodin and the Rise of Absolutist Theory.* London, 1973.

Fraser, Antonia. *Mary Queen of Scots.* London, 1969.

Fritz, Paul S. "From 'Public' to 'Private': The Royal Funerals in England, 1500–1830." In *Mirrors of Mortality: Studies in the Social History of Death.* Ed. Joachim Whaley. London, 1981.

Frye, Roland Mushat. *The Renaissance Hamlet: Issues and Responses in 1600.* Princeton, 1984.

Gardiner, Samuel Rawson. *History of England from the Accession of James I to the Outbreak of the Civil War, 1603–1642.* 10 vols. London, 1899–1901.

Goldberg, Jonathan. *James I and the Politics of Literature: Jonson, Shakespeare, Donne, and Their Contemporaries.* Baltimore, 1983.

Goodman, Godfrey. *The Court of King James the First.* 2 vols. Ed. John S. Brewer. London, 1839.

Gordon, D. J. "Academicians Build a Theater and Give a Play: The Accademia Olimpica, 1579–1585." In *The Renaissance Imagination.* Ed. Stephen Orgel. Berkeley, 1975.

Greenblatt, Stephen. "Invisible Bullets: Renaissance Authority and Its Subversion." In *Political Shakespeare: New Essays in Cultural Materialism.* Ed. Jonathan Dollimore and Alan Sinfield. Ithaca, 1985.

———. *Shakespearean Negotiations: The Circulation of Social Energy in Renaissance England.* Berkeley, 1988.

Gregorio, Laurence A. *Order in the Court History and Society in* La Princesse de Clèves. Stanford French and Italian Studies, 47. Saratoga, Calif., 1986.

Gunther, R. T. *The Architecture of Sir Roger Pratt.* Oxford, 1928.

Hall, Vernon. *Renaissance Literary Criticism: A Study of Its Social Content.* New York, 1945.

Hannay, Margaret P. *Philip's Phoenix: Mary Sidney, Countess of Pembroke.* Oxford, 1990.

Hanson, Ellis. "Sodomy and Kingcraft in *Urania* and *Antony and Cleopatra.*" In *Homosexuality in Renaissance and Enlightenment England: Literary Representations in Historical Context.* Ed. Claude Summers. New York, 1992.

Harbage, Alfred. *Shakespeare and the Rival Traditions.* New York, 1952.

———. *Shakespeare's Audience.* New York, 1941.

Harington, John. *Nugae Antiquae.* 2 vols. Selected by Henry Harington. London, 1804.

Harrison, G. B. *A Jacobean Journal: Being a Record of Those Things Most Talked of during the Years 1603–1606.* London, 1941.

———. *A Second Jacobean Journal: Being a Record of Those Things Most Talked of during the Years 1607–1610.* London, 1958.

Haskell, Francis. *Patrons and Painters: A Study in the Relations between Italian Art and Society in the Age of the Baroque.* Rev. ed. New Haven, 1980.

Hassel, R. Chris, Jr. *Renaissance Drama and the English Church Year.* Lincoln, Neb., 1979.

Hathaway, Baxter. *The Age of Criticism: The Late Renaissance in Italy.* Ithaca, 1962.

Hay, Douglas. "Property, Authority and the Criminal Law." In *Albion's Fatal Tree: Crime and Society in Eighteenth-Century England.* Ed. Douglas Hay, Peter Linebaugh, John D. Rule, E. P. Thompson, and Cal Winslow. New York, 1975.

Haynes, Alan. *Robert Cecil, Earl of Salisbury, 1563–1612.* London, 1989.

Helgerson, Richard. *Self-Crowned Laureates: Spenser, Jonson, Milton and the Literary System.* Berkeley, 1983.

Herbert, Henry. *The Dramatic Records of Sir Henry Herbert.* Ed. Joseph Q. Adams. Reprint. New York, 1964.

Hill, Christopher. *Reformation to Industrial Revolution, 1530–1780.* Harmondsworth, 1969.

Hobbes, Thomas. *Leviathan, or The Matter, Forme and Power of a Commonwealth Ecclesiastical and Civil.* Ed. Michael Oakeshott. Oxford, n.d.

Holderness, Graham, Nick Potter, and John Turner. *Shakespeare Out of Court: Dramatizations of Court Society.* London, 1990.

Hotson, Leslie. *The First Night of* Twelfth Night. New York, 1954.

Howard, Philip. *The Royal Palaces.* London, 1970.

Hunter, George K. *John Lyly: The Humanist as Courtier.* Cambridge, Mass., 1962.

Hutchinson, Lucy. *Memoirs of the Life of Colonel Hutchinson.* Ed. J. Hutchinson and Rev. C. H. Frith. London, 1848.

James I, king of England. *Basilikon Doron.* Edinburgh, 7 copies, 1599; London, 1603. In McIlwain.

———. *Demonologie.* Edinburgh, 1597; London, 1603.

———. "The Lepanto." In *His Majesties Poetical Exercise as Vacant Hours.* 1584. Ed. R. P. Gillies. Edinburgh, 1818.

———. *Letters of James VI & I.* Ed. G. P. V. Akrigg. Berkeley, 1984.

———. *A Premonition to all Most Mightie Monarchs, Kings, Free Princes and States of Christendome.* 1609. In McIlwain.

———. *Ane Schort Treatise conteining some Reulis and Cautelis to be observit and eschewit in Scottis Poesie.* 1584. In G. Gregory Smith, I.

———. *The Trew Law of Free Monarchies.* 1598. In McIlwain.

———. *The Workes of the Most High and Mightie Prince, James.* Ed. James Montagu. London, 1616.

Jardine, David. *Criminal Trials.* 6 vols. London, 1966, vol. II.

Javitch, Daniel. *Poetry and Courtliness in Renaissance England.* Princeton, 1978.

Jones, Inigo. *The Most Notable Antiquity of Great Britain, Vulgarly Called Stone-Heng on Salisbury Plain.* Ed. John Webb. London, 1655.

Jones, Marion. "The Court and the Dramatists." In *Elizabethan Theater.* Stratford-upon-Avon Studies 9. Ed. J. R. Brown and Bernard Harris. New York, 1967.

Jonson, Ben. *Ben Jonson.* 11 vols. Ed. C. H. Herford, Percy Simpson, and Evelyn Simpson. Oxford, 1925–52.

Kent, William. *Designs of Inigo Jones.* London, 1727.

Kernan, Alvin. "The Henriad: Shakespeare's Major History Plays." *Yale Review* 59 (1969): 3.

Kinney, Arthur F. "Shakespeare's *Macbeth* and the Question of Nationalism." In *Literature and Nationalism.* Ed. Vincent Newy and Ann Thompson. Liverpool, 1991.

Knox, John. *The History of the Reformation of Religion within the Realm of Scotland.* Ed. Ralph Walker. Edinburgh, 1940.

Kurland, Stuart M. "*Henry VIII* and James I: Shakespeare and Jacobean Politics." *Shakespeare Studies* 19 (1991): 203.

Lafayette, Madame de (Marie-Madeleine Pioche de la Vergne). *The Princesse de Clèves.* 1678. Trans. Nancy Mitford. London, 1984.

Larkin, James F., and Paul L. Hughes, eds. *Stuart Royal Proclamations: James I, 1603–1625*. Oxford, 1973.

Laudun, Pierre de. *L'Art poétique françois*. 1598. Ed. J. Dedieu. Toulouse, 1909.

Law, Ernest. *The History of Hampton Court Palace*. 3 vols. London, 1888.

Lee, Maurice. *Great Britain's Solomon: James VI and I in His Three Kingdoms*. Urbana, Ill., 1990.

Leinwand, Theodore B. "Conservative Fools in James's Court and Shakespeare's Plays." *Shakespeare Studies* 19 (1991): 218.

Levack, Brian P. *The Formation of the British State: England, Scotland, and the Union, 1603–1707*. Oxford, 1987.

Loades, D. M. *Politics, Censorship, and the English Reformation*. New York, 1991.

Lockyer, Roger. *The Early Stuarts: A Political History of England 1603–42*. London, 1989.

Loftie, W. J. *Whitehall: Historical and Architectural Notes*. London, 1895.

Lovejoy, A. O. *The Great Chain of Being: A Study of the History of an Idea*. Cambridge, Mass., 1936.

Machiavelli, Niccolò. *The Prince*. Trans. Luigi Ricci. Rev. trans. E. R. P. Vincent. New York, 1940.

Major, Virginia Burke. "Shakespeare's *The Tempest* and the Jacobean Court." *Clio* 12 (1983): 139.

Manningham, John. *Diary*. Ed. R. P. Sorlien. Hanover, N.H., 1976.

Marin, Louis. *Portrait of the King*. Trans. Martha Houle. Minneapolis, 1988.

Maxwell, John. *Historical Memoirs of the Reign of Mary Queen of Scots*. Ed. R. Pitcairn. Edinburgh, 1836.

McFarlane, I. D. *Buchanan*. Oxford, 1981.

McIlwain, C. H. *Political Works of James I*. Cambridge, Mass., 1918.

McKendrick, Malveena. *Theater in Spain, 1490–1700*. Cambridge, 1990.

McKeon, Michael. "Politics of Discourse and the Rise of the Aesthetic in Seventeenth-Century England." In Sharpe and Zwicker.

McNamara, Kevin R. "Golden Worlds at Court: *The Tempest* and Its Masque." *Shakespeare Studies* 19 (1991): 183.

Michel, Laurence, ed. *The Tragedy of Philotas by Samuel Daniel*. New Haven, 1949.

Minturno, Antonio. *L'arte poetica del Sig. A. M., nella quale si contengono i precetti heroici, tragici, comici, satyrici, e d'ogni altra poesia, 1559*. Venice, 1563. Reprinted as *De Poeta*. Munich, 1970.

Montrose, Louis A. "The Purpose of Playing: Reflections on a Shakespearean Anthropology." *Helios* n.s. 7 (1980): 51.

Mullaney, Steven. *The Place of the Stage: License, Play, and Power in Renaissance England*. Chicago, 1988.

Mullinger, James Bass. *The University of Cambridge*. 2 vols. Cambridge, 1873.

Munck, Levinus. "The Journal of Levinus Munck." Ed. Howard V. Jones. *English Historical Review* 68 (1953): 234.

Murray, Timothy C. "Richlieu's Theater: The Mirror of a Prince." *Renaissance Drama* 8 (1977): 275.

Nashe, Thomas. *Works.* 5 vols. Ed. F. P. Wilson. Oxford, 1958.

Neale, John E. *Essays in Elizabethan History.* London, 1958.

Nichols, John, ed. *The Progresses, Processions, and Magnificent Festivities of King James the First.* 4 vols. London, 1828.

Norbrook, David. "*Macbeth* and the Politics of Historiography." In Sharpe and Zwicker.

———. *Poetry and Politics in the English Renaissance.* London, 1984.

———. "'What Care These Roarers for the Name of King?': Language and Utopia in *The Tempest.*" In *The Politics of Tragicomedy: Shakespeare and After.* Ed. Gordon McMullen and Jonathan Hope. London, 1992.

Oglander, John. *A Royalist's Notebook: The Commonplace Book of Sir John Oglander, Kt. of Nunwell.* Ed. Francis Bamford. New York, 1971.

Ong, Walter J. *Orality and Literacy.* New York, 1982.

Orgel, Stephen. *The Illusion of Power: Political Theater in the English Renaissance.* Berkeley, 1975.

———. *The Jonsonian Masque.* Cambridge, Mass., 1965.

———. "Making Greatness Familiar." In *Pageantry in the Shakespearean Theater.* Ed. David M. Bergeron. Athens, Ga., 1985.

Orgel, Stephen, and Guy F. Lytle, eds. *Patronage in the Renaissance.* Princeton, 1981.

Orrell, John. *The Human Stage: English Theater Design, 1567–1640.* Cambridge, 1988.

———. *The Quest for Shakespeare's Globe.* Cambridge, 1983.

———. *The Theaters of Inigo Jones and John Webb.* Cambridge, 1985.

Osborne, Francis. *Historical Memoirs on the Reigns of Queen Elizabeth and King James.* 1658. In Scott, vol. I.

Osorius, Hieronimus. *The Five Bookes of the Famous, learned, and eloquent man, Hieronimus Osorius.* London, 1576.

Palme, Per. *The Triumph of Peace.* Uppsala, Sweden, 1956.

Patterson, Annabel. *Censorship and Interpretation.* Madison, Wis., 1984.

Paul, Henry N. *The Royal Play of Macbeth.* New York, 1950.

Pearson, Karl. *The Skull and Portraits of Henry Stewart, Lord Darnley, and Their Bearing on the Tragedy of Mary, Queen of Scots.* Cambridge, 1928.

Peck, Linda Levy. "Corruption at the Court of James I: The Undermining of Legitimacy." In *After the Reformation: Essays in Honor of J. H. Hexter.* Ed. Barbara C. Malament. Philadelphia, 1980.

———. *Court Patronage and Corruption in Early Stuart England.* Boston, 1990.

———. *Northampton: Patronage and Policy at the Court of James I.* London, 1982.

Peck, Linda Levy, ed. *The Mental World of the Jacobean Court.* Cambridge, 1991.

Peele, George. *The Works of George Peele.* 2 vols. Ed. A. H. Bullen. London, 1888.

Phillips, James E. "George Buchanan and the Sidney Circle." *Huntington Library Quarterly* 12 (1948–49): 23.

Puttenham, George. *The Arte of English Poesie.* In G. Gregory Smith, II.

Raleigh, Walter. *The Works of Sir Walter Raleigh.* 8 vols. Oxford, 1829.

Rees, Joan. *Samuel Daniel.* Liverpool, 1964.

Riggs, David. *Ben Jonson: A Life.* Cambridge, Mass., 1989.

Rigold, Stuart Eborall. "Appearance and Reality: A Carpenter's Viewpoint." In *The Third Globe.* Ed. C. Walter Hodges, S. Schoenbaum, and Leonard Leone. Detroit, 1981.

Ringler, William A., Jr. "Hamlet's Defense of the Players." In *Essays on Shakespeare and the Elizabethan Drama.* Ed. Richard Hosley. Columbia, Mo., 1962.

Ronsard, Pierre de. "Art poetique français." In *Oeuvres Completes.* 22 vols. Ed. Paul Laumonier. Paris, 1914—74, vol. XIV.

Ross, Josephine. *The Winter Queen: The Story of Elizabeth Stuart.* London, 1979.

Rowse, A. L. *Homosexuals in History: A Study of Ambivalence in Society, Literature and the Arts.* London, 1977.

——. *Shakespeare's Southampton, Patron of Virginia.* London, 1965.

Schmidgall, Gary. *Shakespeare and the Courtly Aesthetic.* Berkeley, 1981.

Scott, Walter, ed. *Secret History of the Court of James the First.* 2 vols. Edinburgh, 1811.

Shapiro, Michael. *Children of the Revels: The Boy Companies of Shakespeare's Time and Their Plays.* New York, 1977.

Sharpe, Kevin, and Steven N. Zwicker, eds. *The Politics of Discourse: The Literature and History of Seventeenth-Century England.* Berkeley, 1987.

Shearman, John. *Mannerism.* Harmondsworth, 1967.

Sheppard, Edgar. *The Old Royal Palace of Whitehall.* London, 1902.

Shergold, N. D. *A History of the Spanish Stage from Medieval Times until the End of the Seventeenth Century.* Oxford, 1967.

Sidney, Philip. *An Apologie for Poetry.* In G. Smith, I.

Sinfield, Alan. "*Macbeth:* History, Ideology and Intellectuals." *Critical Quarterly* 28 (1986): 63.

Skinner, Quentin. *The Foundations of Modern Political Thought.* 2 vols. Cambridge, 1978.

Smith, Bruce R. *Homosexual Desire in Shakespeare's England: A Cultural Poetics.* Chicago, 1991.

Smith, G. Gregory, ed. *Elizabethan Critical Essays.* 2 vols. Oxford, 1904.

Smuts, R. Malcolm. *Court Culture and the Origins of a Royalist Tradition in Early Stuart England.* Philadelphia, 1987.

Spenser, Edmund. *The Complete Poetical Works of Spenser.* Ed. R. E. Neill Dodge. Boston, 1936.

Spevack, Marvin. *The Harvard Concordance to Shakespeare.* Cambridge, Mass., 1973.

State Papers Relating to Scotland in the Public Record Office in London. 2 vols. Ed. John Thorpe. London, 1858.

Steele, Mary S. *Plays and Masques at Court during the Reigns of Elizabeth, James and Charles.* New Haven, 1926.

Stone, Lawrence. *The Crisis of the Aristocracy, 1588—1641.* Abridged ed. Oxford, 1967.

———. *Family and Fortune: Studies in Aristocratic Finance in the Sixteenth and Seventeenth Centuries.* Oxford, 1973.

Stow, John. *A Survey of London.* 1598. Ed. W. J. Thoms. London, 1876.

Strier, Richard. "Faithful Servants: Shakespeare's Praise of Disobedience." In *The Historical Renaissance: New Essays on Tudor and Stuart Literature and Culture.* Ed. Heather Dubrow and Richard Strier. Chicago, 1988.

Strong, Roy. *The Cult of Elizabeth: Elizabethan Portraiture and Pageantry.* London, 1987.

———. *Henry, Prince of Wales, and England's Lost Renaissance.* New York, 1986.

———. *The Renaissance Garden in England.* London, 1979.

———. *Splendor at Court: Renaissance Spectacle and the Theater of Power.* Boston, 1973.

Strong, Roy, and Stephen Orgel, eds. *Inigo Jones: The Theater of the Stuart Court.* 2 vols. Berkeley, 1973.

Sturgess, Keith. *Jacobean Private Theater.* London, 1987.

Sullivan, Mary. *Court Masques of James I: Their Influence on Shakespeare and the Public Theaters.* New York, 1913.

Sutherland, John. "Ingredients of a New Age." *Times Literary Supplement,* January 13–19, 1989, 43.

Taylor, Gary. "King Lear and Censorship." In *The Division of the Kingdoms.* Ed. Gary Taylor and Michael Warren. Oxford, 1983.

Tebbetts, Terrell L. "Talking Back to the King: *Measure for Measure* and the *Basilicon Doron.*" *College Literature* 12 (1985): 122.

Tennenhouse, Leonard. *Power on Display.* New York, 1986.

Thomas, Keith. *Religion and the Decline of Magic.* London, 1971.

Thomson, Peter. *Shakespeare's Professional Career.* Cambridge, 1992.

Thurley, Simon. *The Royal Palaces of Tudor England.* New Haven, 1993.

Trevor-Roper, H. R. "The Culture of the Baroque Courts." In his *Renaissance Essays.* London, 1985.

———. "The General Crisis of the 17th Century." *Past and Present* 16 (1959): 31.

———. "George Buchanan and the Ancient Scottish Constitution." In *English Historical Review.* Ed. J. M. Wallace-Hadrill. London, 1966, supplement 3.

Tyacke, Nicholas. *Anti-Calvinists: The Rise of English Arminianism, c. 1590–1640.* Oxford, 1987.

Ule, Louis. *A Concordance to the Works of Christopher Marlowe.* Hildesheim, 1979.

Urkowitz, Steven. *Shakespeare's Revision of* King Lear. Princeton, 1980.

Wallace, Willard M. *Sir Walter Raleigh.* Princeton, 1959.

Watson, Godfrey. *Bothwell and the Witches.* London, 1975.

Weimann, Robert. *Shakespeare and the Popular Tradition in the Theater: Studies in the Social Dimension of Dramatic Form and Function.* Baltimore, 1978.

Weldon, Anthony. *The Court and Character of King James.* 1649. In Scott, vols. I and II.

Wickham, Glynne. *Early English Stages, 1300–1600.* 3 vols. London, 1959–81.

Wiley, W. L. *The Early Public Theatre in France.* Cambridge, Mass., 1960.

Williams, Ethel C. *Anne of Denmark, Wife of James VI of Scotland, James I of England.* London, 1970.

Williams, Franklin B., Jr. *Index of Dedications and Commendatory Verses in English Books before 1641.* London, 1962.

Williams, Jay. *The World of Titian, c. 1488–1576.* New York, 1968.

Wilson, F. P., and R. F. Hill, eds. *The Dramatic Records in the Declared Accounts of the Office of Works, 1560–1640.* The Malone Society, Collections, vol. X, 1975. Oxford, 1977.

Winwood, Ralph. *Memorials of the Affairs of State in the Reigns of Queen Elizabeth and King James I.* 3 vols. Ed. Edmund Sawyer. London, 1725.

Wooton, David, ed. *Divine Right and Democracy: An Anthology of Political Writing in Stuart England.* London, 1986.

Wormald, Jenny. *"Basilikon Doron* and *The Trew Law of Free Monarchies."* In Peck, 1991.

Wotton, Henry. *The Life and Letters of Sir Henry Wotton.* 2 vols. 1907. Ed. Logan Pearsall Smith. Reprint. Oxford, 1986.

Wroth, Mary. *The Countesse of Mountgomeries Urania.* London, 1621.

Zagorin, Perez. *The Court and the Country: The Beginning of the English Revolution.* 1969. Reprint. Macmillan, 1971.

INDEX

Acte to Restraine Abuses of Players, 72
acting companies, xi, 5—6, 133; Admiral's
  (later Prince Henry's), 9; Bottom's,
  21—22, 166, 196; Lord Chamberlain's or
  Hunsdon's (later King's Men), xv,
  10—12; Children of Blackfriars, 15, 192;
  Elizabeth's, 9, 176; Prince Charles', 9,
  193; Prince Henry's, 8, 9; Queen Anne's,
  9, 207; St. John's College, 189, 191;
  Wittenberg troupe, 196—201;
  Worcester's (later Queen Anne's), 9. See
  also King's Men
actors and players, 5—16, 22, 29—30, 32,
  59—60, 62, 68, 72, 82, 120—21,
  133—34, 166, 180, 190—92, 194,
  195—97, 200—201; Alleyn, Edward
  (Ned), 8—9, 12, 133; Ariel, 161—62;
  Armin, Robert, 9, 23; Bryan, George,
  32; Burbage, Cuthbert, 68—69, 134;
  Burbage, Richard, 9, 23, 68—69,
  133—34; Condell, Henry, 23, 134;
  Heminges, John, 23, 134; Kempe, Will,
  32, 133; Phillips, Augustine, 11, 23;
  Pope, Thomas, 32; Shakespeare's view
  of, 166—67; Sly, William, 23; "stars,"
  133; Tarleton, Richard, 133
Aeschylus, 194
alexandrine line, 4
America, 157—59
American Indians, 155, 157—58
Andrewes, Lancelot, bishop of Chichester,
  7, 75
Antony and Cleopatra, xx, xxiii, 120—25,
  129—31, 182
architecture, 3, 5, 6, 20, 27—28, 38, 51—53,
  169, 186
art, 3—5, 125, 160, 162, 165, 169, 171,
  174—75, 184, 186—87; baroque, 176,
  179; "black," 83—84; decorative, 7;

king's view of, 14—15; patronage, xxiii,
  8, 79, 97, 110, 138, 170, 172, 177—81,
  187; propaganda, xii, 3, 79; Prospero's,
  162—66, 167—68; Stuart use of, 6—7, 8,
  155, 173
artist, xv, 3, 127, 158, 169—70, 186; artist-
  magician, 165; patronage, 3, 8, 79, 159,
  170, 173, 181; romantic, xv, 169, 184,
  187; self-portraits, 159, 160, 165, 181;
  status of, 159—60, 177—78. See also
  painters
As You Like It, xix, xx, xxii, 26, 30, 57, 195,
  203
audiences, 19, 21, 32, 58, 112, 132—33,
  149, 194—95; court, xi, 32, 62, 96, 112,
  159, 195; groundlings, 163, 197; public,
  xv, 132, 197; seating of, xxi, 18;
  Shakespeare's portrayal of, 195—200; in
  The Tempest, 161—66
Augustus Caesar, 121, 131

Bacon, Sir Francis, 112, 115, 116, 189
ballet, 5, 18, 61, 162, 190
Basil, Simon, 7, 209
Beaumont, Achille (French ambassador),
  45—48
Beaumont, Francis, and Fletcher, John, xvii,
  xix, 8, 155—56, 207—08; *A King and No
  King*, 156, 207, 208; *The Maid's Tragedy*,
  156, 208; *Philaster*, 156, 208
Bedford, Lucy, countess of, 27, 47, 174
Bible, 51, 67, 80, 83, 85, 90, 94, 185, 194
Bodin, Jean, 3, 90, 93, 97
Boece, Hector, 91
books and printing, 2, 15, 26, 51, 71, 83,
  90—93, 94, 138, 149, 171, 174, 193,
  194; censorship, 14—16, 49, 60, 72, 102,
  182—83, 193; copyright, 171;
  dedications, 171; James's books, 14, 32,

Renaissance, 1, 5, 28, 36, 116, 132, 148,
160, 179, 201; artists, 36, 130, 135, 159,
169–70, 177, 181, 195; princes, 34, 36,
44, 79, 90, 95, 132, 148
revenge, 34, 37, 38, 40–44, 116
Riccio, David, 37–38, 117
Richard II, 10–11, 55
Richard II, 10–11, 95, 99
Richard III, 95, 96, 112
rituals, xii, 83, 109, 142–43, 201; coronations, xi, 25, 53, 108, 118, 121, 126, 201;
executions, 52–58, 66, 83, 90, 151;
funerals, 25, 38, 117, 201; venery, 108;
weddings, 51, 109, 154–55, 157, 196
Ronsard, Pierre de, 4, 179
Rousseau, Jean Jacques: *Confessions,* 177
Rupert, prince of the Rhine, the "mad cava-
lier," 43, 155, 157
Ruthven family, earls of Gowrie, 40–41,
60

satire, 15, 27, 49, 70, 74, 102, 119, 166,
171, 173, 191, 192, 196
Scaramelli, Giovanni, 118
Scotland, ix, 37, 39–44, 76, 77–78, 81,
83–85, 91–93, 106–08, 117–18, 121;
union with England, 53, 96, 106
Scots, 16, 25, 91, 92, 107, 120, 128
Seneca, xxiii, 6, 174, 198
Serlio, Sebastiano, 6, 19, 209
sermons, 7, 38, 75, 154
sex, 51, 60, 62–63, 65–66, 81, 91, 99,
115–19, 122, 124–25, 149, 154, 173,
178, 180–81; sadomasochism, 125, 146.
See also homosexuality
Seymour, William, 150–51
Shakespeare, William: as artist, 165–67,
181; at court, xvi–xx, 3, 6, 9, 10, 140,
155, 157–58, 195–201; ideas on
history, 104, 132, 148; life, xxiii, 26, 48,
52, 71, 132–34, 150, 156, 166, 179,

182, 183, 194; view of madness, 99, 103;
and patronage, xxiii, 10, 11, 69, 75,
78–79, 87, 96, 102, 120, 121, 124, 148,
176–77, 181–82, 185; philosophy, xxii,
66, 95, 98–99, 102, 135; politics, xxii,
95–96, 98–99, 102, 135, 183–84, 185;
psychology, 87–88, 143–45, 149; and
public theater, xi, xv, 5, 133–34, 195;
social status, xvi, xxiii, 129, 132–35,
138, 194; sources, 61, 63, 67, 76, 78, 84,
96, 121, 127, 144; style, xxiv, xxvii, 21,
76, 80, 122, 145–47, 164, 179–80,
183, 194–95. *See also individual plays*
Shearman, John, 160, 181
Sheba, queen of, 38, 73
Sidney family: Mary, countess of
Pembroke, 11, 26, 75, 173–74, 198;
Penshurst, 175; Sir Philip, 26, 119,
170–72, 198–99
sin, 34, 43, 65–66, 158; original, 85, 151
skulls, 38–39, 43, 59
Society of Jesus, 54, 75, 90, 119, 190
Sonnets, Shakespeare's, 10, 135, 138, 160,
168, 177–81, 201
sovereignty, 41–42, 92, 94–95, 97,
99–100, 103, 137
Spain, xxi, 1, 2, 6, 16, 20, 29, 39, 44,
45–47, 55, 56, 59, 89, 91, 106, 121,
176, 181; Philip II, 36, 184; Philip III, 44;
Philip IV, xxiii, 6, 17, 22–23, 181
spectacle, 5, 6, 22, 45, 58, 67, 74, 129, 130,
153–54, 157, 159, 163, 167, 175
Spenser, Edmund, 3, 15, 172–73, 179; *The
Faerie Queene,* 6, 15, 172; *Mother
Hubberd's Tale,* 173; *Teares of the Muses,* 3
Stanhope, Sir John, Treasurer of the
Chamber, 14, 135
state and government, 1–3, 34, 36–37, 44,
74, 89–90, 91, 94–95, 103–04, 111,
132, 135, 138, 141, 143, 147; and art,
3–4, 6, 9, 169, 172–76, 184; and

union of England and Scotland, 77, 96, 106,
121, 140

Vasari, Giorgio, 159, 186
Venice, 93, 113; ambassadors, xviii, xxi, 15,
20–21, 26–27, 118, 135, 150, 182,
193; arts, xxiii, 5, 133, 170; Busino,
Orazio, 188; *Calendar of State Papers*, xiii,
10, 11, 15, 18, 21, 108, 113, 118, 135,
151, 188, 190, 193; Doge, 18; envoys,
xviii; government, 93; Lepanto, battle of,
61; Molin, Nicolò, xiii, 18, 108;
Scaramelli, Giovanni, 118; senate, xiii;
theater, 133; Titian, 184; Veneto, xxiii
Venus and Adonis, 10, 177
Vere, Lady Susan, 47, 68

Wake, Isaac, 210
war and warfare, 1, 2, 34, 44, 55, 59, 61,
72, 78, 90, 99, 104, 136, 142–46, 148,
152; class, 132–36, 183; ideological, 90,
184
Webb, John, 7, 53

Webster, John, 8, 115
Weldon, Anthony, 106, 109, 111, 113–15,
121, 152
Wickham, Glynne, xii, 13
Wilton, xx, 17, 26, 27, 30, 57, 174, 198
Winter's Tale, The, xix, 151, 156, 207, 208
Winwood, Ralph, 15, 26
witches and witchcraft, xviii, 6, 54, 80, 81,
83–87, 104, 108, 117, 182, 190, 194; of
Lothian, 54, 85, 86, 117; *maleficium*, 83;
Malleus Maleficarum, 83
Wither, George, 171
Wolsey, Cardinal, 2, 27, 28, 52
women, xii, 4, 25, 34, 58, 62, 73–75, 84,
103, 108, 114–17, 119, 125, 158, 178,
185, 194, 199; and acting, 17, 61–62,
151
Wordsworth, William, 165
Wriothsley, Henry, 3rd earl of
Southampton, 9–11, 69, 137, 158, 177,
179

Yelverton, Sir Henry, 119, 143